Sydney Dov

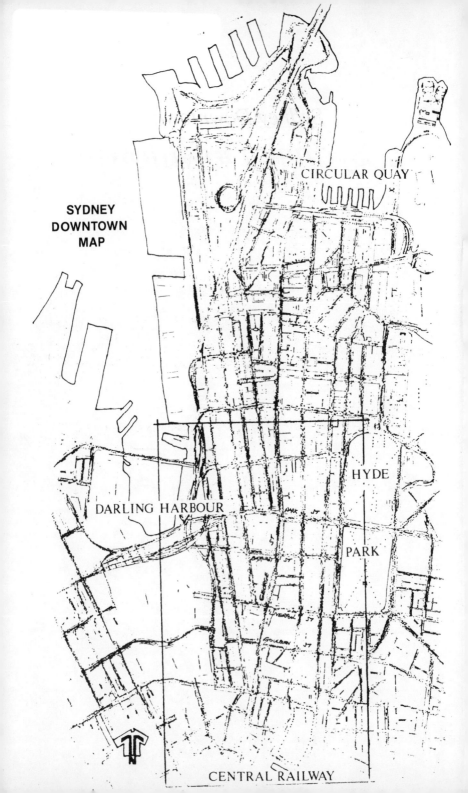

SYDNEY DOWNTOWN MAP

CIRCULAR QUAY

HYDE

DARLING HARBOUR

PARK

CENTRAL RAILWAY

Sydney Downtown

Jo Dirks

'...that life is there should be a matter of congratulations daily renewed.' *Ride On Stranger* (1943)

Kangaroo Press

Acknowledgments

I would like to express a special word of thanks to the many people who have offered me encouragement along the way. There are those who sat down with me to tell me something of their life stories: Ernie Warman, Pat Hills, Mary Shaw, Marge King, Father Austin Day, Mervyn Beck, Laurie Short and Kevin Connor. I thank those who have offered critical comments on my research and writing; Errol Lea-Scarlett, Jim Lowden, and Nigel Prescott. There are many who have offered me encouragement along the way, Mario and Marcia Majarich, Sister Margaret Press, Father Edmund Campion, Marie and Ken Davis. Fathers Frank Marriott and Hal Ranger from the National Council of Priests, Eddie and Margaret von Perger, Sister Veronica Brady, and the members of my own religious order, who have patiently allowed me to follow my project to its conclusion. I have always been given a generous welcome by the staff of the many libraries and archive offices I have consulted, among them the Mitchell Library, the City of Sydney Public Library, and St Mary's Cathedral Archives. I received valuable assistance from far too many people to be able to mention them all but I include Michael Easson, Gavan Cashman, Alan Hunt, Norm King, Jean Andersen, Vince Plummer, Dr R.M. McCredie, Brother Raphael McKenna and Father Kevin Kelly. I owe a great debt to the typists who first put my writings into print. Among them are Mary Eardley, who alas died in 1989, Jean Minard, Eileen Mason, Father Alf Rivett, Chris Tuetteman and Elizabeth Arthy. Joe Said and Vince Condon were also very helpful with tracking down current information. Along the way I learnt all about the mysteries of word processing and I owe much to Chris Spurr, Justin von Perger, and also Chris Tuetteman. Marie Davis and Mark Collins were also very generous with their help in this area. I must mention Mario Majarich again because he not only volunteered to assemble photos and maps but has supported me throughout. At a publishing level both Catherine Warne and Paul Brennan encouraged me. Finally I express my thanks to the following for permissions to quote from their works: Collins, Angus and Robertson; Jack Pollard; John Fairfax Group; Melbourne University Press; Octopus Publishing Group; Rabbi Apple; and most especially to Ruth Niland.

First published in 1993 by Kangaroo Press Pty Ltd
3 Whitehall Road (P.O. Box 75) Kenthurst NSW 2156
Typeset by G.T. Setters Pty Limited
Printed in Singapore by Fong & Sons Printers Pte Ltd

ISBN 0 86417 445 4

Contents

Source of Selected Illustrations

Introduction

The original aim of the author was modest in terms of the geographical span of his work—the Haymarket region of Sydney—but ambitious in terms of the historical sweep from Aboriginal presence and white settlement to the present day. What makes the historical coverage difficult is the enormous change that has occurred, the great complexity of the changes, and the great variety of the public and private institutions and buildings within the Haymarket region. The region takes its name from the postal district of the Haymarket. However, the original district of the Haymarket would seem to have consisted of the area bounded by George, Hay, Elizabeth and Campbell Streets. Within these boundaries were once located the old corn market, the cattle market, the weighbridge and the pound. On the pound site old St Francis' Church and School were built to look after 'the lost sheep' of the poorer or 'downtown' part of Sydney. Indeed, a secondary aim of the author is outlining the role that the churches have played within the Haymarket region.

The spirit which permeates this historical search and retrieval is a mixture of astonishment at what has been achieved, sadness at the loss of so much of the past, and humour at the many incongruities that have taken place, and still do, within the region. How many who attended the glittering city premiere of *The Man from Snowy River* in 1982 at the Hoyts Cinema complex would have realised that a short gallop down George Street a hundred years ago would have brought you to the Haymarket saleyards, with their stockades of wild horses and the occasional buckjumper trying his luck on a brumby? Who know that the Haymarket Music Hall, which opened in 1888, was built on the site now occupied by the Central Baptist Church? Furthermore, as I dug more deeply into the character of the area I began to broaden my focus to take in stories, people and events that seemed too good to omit. I soon found that I had to set limits of some sort so as to avoid being simply engulfed by the material. Therefore I set some definite, more or less, boundaries to my research. They stretch from Market Street in the north through Hyde Park, Surry Hills, Moore Park, Redfern, Chippendale, Broadway, Ultimo, Pyrmont, Darling Harbour and back to Haymarket.

1 Beginnings
(Pre-1788–1819)

POPULATION

Aboriginal Presence

The spectacular coastline around Sydney Harbour that still exists—the wilderness pockets of precipitous cliffs, creeks and gorges—suggest what the land must have been like before 1788. Larger tracts of land such as the rugged terrain around the Hawkesbury River and Ku-ring-gai Chase provide more extensive examples. Aboriginal rock carvings are still to be found in these wilderness places. The coastal Dharug people, some seven or eight bands that lived between Botany Bay and Port Jackson, referred to themselves as the Eora people. Aboriginal place names are to be found all over the Sydney metropolitan region.

Specific reference to the Aborigines as a people is found in the word *Ku-ring-gai*, the name of a tribe which inhabited the coastal district. *Maroubra* has several meanings—the name of a tribe, a place of shells and thunder. Downtown Sydney would include *Tumbulong* (Darling Harbour) and *Pirrama*, a rocking stone (Pyrmont). The *munggi* (mussels) found at low tide in Darling Harbour and the *myimbarr* (black wattle) at Wentworth Park have long since disappeared. The small number of Aboriginal place names that remain are a sad testimony to the fate of the people who once had this entire land in their sole keeping.

Native Flora

The saying 'Sydney or the Bush' only has meaning after European settlement. Even after the first 20 years of settlement, the 'bush', which covered the primeval sandstone ridges and gullies, was deemed to begin beyond the Old Burial Ground where Sydney Town Hall now stands. Prominent would have been the Sydney red gum *(Angophora costata)*, with its beautiful and smoothly textured bark, thrusting its roots through the sandstone rock. Another native tree which could grow 50 feet high was the *Banksia serrata*, which was so named by the naturalist Joseph Banks in April 1770. Many other eucalypts and wattles flourished undisturbed, none more magnificent than the crimson waratah, which originally grew no more than four feet and carried a single bloom. In Ku-ring-gai Chase to the north and at Wattamoola in the south, country too rugged for farming and development, it is still possible to obtain a sense of the original bushland of Sydney.

European Discoveries

While the Aborigines have lived on the Australian mainland at least for 40,000 years, the presence of Europeans has been comparatively recent. The Dutch landings on the western coastline of Australia in the early part of the seventeenth century led to the naming of the western half of the continent as 'New Holland'. The eastern half of Australia was unknown until Cook's voyage to the southern Pacific in 1770, principally to observe the

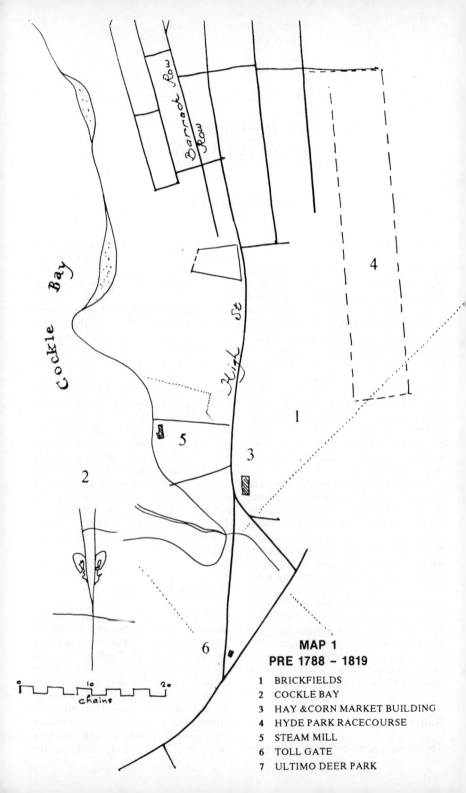

MAP 1
PRE 1788 – 1819

1 BRICKFIELDS
2 COCKLE BAY
3 HAY &CORN MARKET BUILDING
4 HYDE PARK RACECOURSE
5 STEAM MILL
6 TOLL GATE
7 ULTIMO DEER PARK

transit of the planet Venus. Cook also had instructions to search for 'Terra Australis' and after mapping New Zealand he sighted the eastern coast of Australia on 19 April 1770. After charting the entire east coast he landed north of Cape York, and on 22 August claimed eastern New Holland in the name of King George III. Later he gave it the name of New South Wales.

That Cook discovered eastern Australia has been challenged by Kenneth McIntyre. In his book *The Secret Discovery of Australia*,[1] McIntyre builds up a case on circumstantial evidence: the Dauphin maps (secretly copied or stolen from the Portuguese); the fierce rivalry between Portugal and Spain which resulted in the discovery of a 'Portuguese fort' at Eden, as well as the 'Portuguese keys' by Matthew Flinders at Corio Bay, and lastly the mysterious 'Mahogany' ship wrecked near Portland, adjudged to be part of the secret naval convoy led by the Portuguese Captain Cristovão de Mendonça. The captain is surmised to have sailed with three ships in 1523 from Timor down the eastern coastline of Australia. This move was to counterbalance Spain sending Ferdinand Magellan into the Pacific. It must be remembered that the eastern half of Australia would have come within the Spanish world hemisphere arbitrated by the Pope to avoid conflict between Spain and Portugal. Indeed, the eastern border of Western Australia is an historical legacy of the Pope's ruling. No matter how interesting McIntyre's claim may be, unless more solid evidence is forthcoming, his thesis remains a tantalising hypothesis.

When the American colonies rebelled and gained their independence in 1776, a new locale for England's convicts had to be found. Cook's voyage was remembered, especially his account of Norfolk Island as possessing a plentiful supply of pines suitable for shipping masts and flax for the making of rope and sail. Geoffrey Blainey suggests that these additional reasons led to the choice of such a faraway site as Botany Bay for the new penal colony. By way of a bonus, a naval depot in the southern Pacific would have insurance value for England's trade routes to China. The decision to establish a convict settlement at Botany Bay was made by the Secretary of the Home Office, Thomas Townshend, better known as Lord Sydney.

Australia's First Appearance on a Coin

The first appearance of Australia on a coin or medal was on a memorial thaler of Hedwig Sophia of Brandenburg (Prussia) issued in 1669. A large silver coin, it depicts the Eastern Hemisphere of the known world, at whose right extremity is clearly shown the west coast of New Holland. The thaler is located in the Mint Museum, Macquarie Street, Sydney.

Early French Presence

In 1785 the French minted a special coin to mark the scientific voyage then being undertaken by Jean-François de Galaup, better known as Comte de La Perouse, around the world in the ships *Astrolabe* and *Boussole*. In Samoa, there was a clash with the natives and 12 French were killed, 20 injured and the longboats lost. La Perouse decided to withdraw rather than retaliate and the expedition arrived at Botany Bay in January 1788 to rest and refit. During the stay of six weeks, contact was made with the First Fleet, which had already arrived and was about to move on to Sydney Cove. At the same time the expedition chaplain died from injuries received in Samoa. This was the Franciscan priest and scientist, Fr Louis le Receveur, who became one of the first Europeans to be buried in Australian soil. If Fr le Receveur did not say Mass at Botany Bay before he died on 17 February, it is reasonable to assume that his fellow chaplain, Abbé Monges, did.

The French ships set sail on 5 February and were never seen again. Forty years later the ships were discovered to have run ashore and been wrecked on Vanikoro Island in the Santa Cruz group of the New Hebrides. An altar stone was recovered by divers. Presumed to be the altar stone used by le Receveur and Monges for the celebration of Mass, it was used for the Mass to mark the two-hundredth anniversary of the death of Father le Receveur. The wooden tablet marking le Receveur's grave was removed by Aborigines. Captain Arthur Phillip had a copper plate set in its place. The inscription of the tomb at La Perouse reads: 'Hic jacet Le Receveur ex F. eminoribus galliae sacerdos physicus in circumnavigatione mundi duce d. de la perouse obiit die 17 Feb. anno 1788'.

GOVERNMENT

First European Settlement

The First Fleet of 11 sailing ships was assembled under the command of the first governor of the intended colony of New South Wales, Captain Arthur Phillip. Phillip's German father came from Frankfurt to London as a language teacher and married a widow whose previous husband had been related to Lord Pembroke of the Royal Navy. Phillip's early schooling was from his father, but at 12 he was sent to a naval school reserved for the sons of naval servicemen who had died at sea. Conventional wisdom may think Phillip's selection to lead the First Fleet was the just and fitting reward of a distinguished naval career. In truth, it seems that he was the first of our 'battlers'. From the age of 25 he was on the reserve list and on half-pay. When war broke out between Spain and Portugal, Phillip volunteered for service in the Portuguese navy. He was sent to Uruguay and he also became familiar with Rio de Janeiro harbour. These years of service in a foreign country, at the extreme limit of supply lines and with a climate and latitude similar to the proposed settlement at Botany Bay, would have helped to clinch Phillip's appointment. Phillip was also known to be able in administering his country estate and his care for less fortunate people.

Phillip was handed a one-page commission in October 1786, with the suggestion he sail in December. Phillip asked for a revision of the commission incorporating his proposals in a new commission of 14 pages. He also asked that an advance party be sent to build huts and plant crops, that free settlers be permitted to come, that he be given some information about the crimes and work capacities of the convicts, for the inclusion of skilled convict workers, that the convicts be free from venereal disease, and that the farming implements and tools be of good quality. All these requests were turned down or ignored. The fleet eventually sailed in May 1787, escorted by a naval ship for the first 300 miles.

After stopping at Teneriffe, Rio de Janeiro and Cape Town for fresh food and water and repairs, Phillip dropped anchor in Botany Bay on 18 January 1788. He immediately went ashore with some of his men, where they were confronted by a group of Aborigines brandishing spears. Phillip put down his weapons and went alone to meet them, his arms outstretched in friendship. The Aborigines put down their spears. Phillip found that there was not enough water to sustain the new arrivals, so he set off with three small boats to explore Port Jackson. In the course of his exploration he discovered more Aborigines at a cove, and called

The Arthur Phillip Statue.

them 'manly', giving rise to the suburb of Manly. Sailing further he saw what he described as 'the finest harbour in the world, in which a thousand sail of line may ride in the most perfect security'. He discovered one cove with a spring of water, suitable for building quays, and he gave this cove the name of Sydney.

So the colony was established at Sydney Cove. The settlement was laid out according to plans drawn up by Phillip's German surveyor, Augustus Theodore Henry Alt. It was the Hanoverian Baron Alt who laid out the basic grid of Sydney's streets, mapped out Paramatta and surveyed the first land grants. He had served 30 years in the British army, served another nine years until 1797, retired to Ashfield and died in 1815, aged 84. The irregularities in Sydney's streets were not the fault of Alt's plan, but the result of short cuts and of provisional buildings put up regardless of the plan.

Before long, the new settlement was having trouble feeding itself. Some grain had perished on the long sea voyage, the seed for planting had been spoiled and the botanist, Joseph Banks, had over-estimated the fertility of the soil. A voyage up the Parramatta River revealed suitable pasture at its head and a convict farmer James Ruse was given land to cultivate. Phillip had plans of his own for Albion (Sydney) and Rose Hill (Paramatta) with great tree-lined streets, comparable to Berlin and Williamsburg. When Phillip left the colony on account of ill health in December 1792, the Marine Corps built their houses in the middle of the Parramatta streets. A monument to Phillip was established in the Botanic Gardens in 1897.

'Downtown' Assumes its Unique Role

Sydney's first street was called Sergeant Major's Row (in The Rocks district), but later became George Street. The buildings of the new settlement straggled along George Street until they reached the old burial ground, where Sydney Town Hall now stands. It was not until the arrival of the colony's fifth governor, Lachlan Macquarie, in 1810, that town-planning was resumed. Macquarie began by having the streets widened and the tree stumps removed. The markets were moved away from the overcrowded Rocks area to a more spacious site, now occupied by the Queen Victoria Building, and the steep and dangerous extension of George Street down Brickfield Hill was improved. Captain Collins in his journal affirms that the road down Brickfield Hill became populated within a year or two of the foundation of the colony. By Macquarie's time there existed a little village called Brickfield which nestled in a fertile bowl bounded by hills on three sides and open on the fourth to the waters of Cockle Bay (renamed Darling Harbour in 1829). Large pits were dug in the side of Brickfield Hill for making the building bricks of the colony. Macquarie ordered a bridge to be built over the creek where George and Hay Streets intersect. This was

An early view of the Brickfields.

the second bridge built in the colony—the first being over the Tank Stream. The road westwards became the main route to the interior settlement at Parramatta and along the Hawkesbury River. It was still easier to reach these places by boat than by road.

At the town's southern exit there existed a compound for convict labourers who worked in the brickfields and were housed and fed there. When Macquarie built the Toll Bar he ordered the assigned and bonded servants who drove the produce wagons to the town market to be lodged in these buildings. The barracks stood on the site of the present Central Railway station. Item 28 of Macquarie's 'List of Public Buildings and Works' reads: 'Another barrack (commonly called the Carters' Barracks) for 200 male convicts at the 'Brick Fields', and also stables for the whole of the Government working horses and bullocks, with a garden for the use of the convicts'. There was plenty of grazing land for stock around these barracks, which James Maclehose described in 1839 in his *Stranger's Guide*:

This building is situated on a rising eminence at the extremity of the old Brickfields, and commands a picturesque view of the town. It was erected in Governor Macquarie's time, for the accommodation of convict carters, brickmakers etc. A portion of it, however has of late been converted into a Debtor's Prison. It has recently been partially destroyed by fire.

Conflict with Aborigines

Phillip had good intentions towards the Aborigines. His official instructions were to treat the native peoples with friendship and kindness. Conflicts soon occurred, but Phillip blamed the convicts rather than the Aborigines. Even after being speared in the shoulder, he refused retaliation. However, by 1791 when some 50 blacks were reported near the brickfields, orders were sent to 'a strong party to disperse them, and to make a severe example of them, if any spears were thrown'. When the soldiers arrived at the brickfields the Aborigines had disappeared.

INDUSTRY AND TRANSPORT

The Steam Mills of Cockle Bay

Windmills were constructed in The Rocks to grind corn, but the days of wind-power were numbered when the *Earl Spencer* docked in Sydney in late 1813 and the Scottish engineer John Dickson and his young protégé, Thomas Barker, disembarked along with a very special cargo—a steam engine, tools and turning lathes valued at more than £15,000. An inventive man, Dickson had taken out patents in 1798 and 1808 for valves and machinery related to pumping. The Colonial Office informed Macquarie that Dickson was a first-class engineer and millwright, and was to be given a town grant and land in the interior.

> The steam-engine was erected at the town grant on Cockle Bay on a site commanding a water conveyance of grain, timber and firewood. A portion of land at the mouth of a small stream at the head of the bay was dammed to exclude salt water and from this reservoir the engine pumped its own water. It began operations in 1815, but though intended to power saw-mills and tan-bark mills it seems to have been solely used for milling grain.[2]

Governor Macquarie himself was present to see the steam engine crush the grain at a rate of 10 bushels an hour. Under the most favourable conditions, windmills could crush only 70 bushels a week. In 1826, along with John Mackie, Dickson established a brewery and a soap and candle works near his flour mill. He sold his assets in 1833 and returned to London in the following year.

Thomas Barker, orphaned at nine, was only 14 when he arrived in Sydney, but he soon became a skilful engineer and millwright. In 1823 he married a niece of John Dickson. He built several windmills at Darlinghurst in 1826 and two years later he bought a steam flour mill which he greatly enlarged. By the 1840s he had extensive flour mills near the corner of Sussex and Bathurst Streets. The machinery was mostly manufactured on the premises. By the end of the decade Barker had also built a cloth mill. Like Dickson, Barker took up grazing and established pastures at Yass, Cowpastures and along the Murrumbidgee:

> Equally energetic in public affairs, Barker was one of the earliest promoters of railways in the colony. He and a few others paid for the survey from Sydney to Goulburn, conducted by Thomas Moore. He was a director and president of the Sydney Railway Co. and in 1855 held an honorary appointment from the government as commissioner for railways. He was a director and chairman of the Commercial Banking Co. of Sydney, a founder and director of the Royal Exchange and a trustee for nearly forty years of the Savings Bank of New South Wales.[3]

Also active in encouraging education, Barker was a trustee of both Sydney Grammar School and the Sydney Mechanics' School of Arts. He gave a gift of £1,000 for a mathematics scholarship at the University of Sydney. By 1848 he was also a member of the Denominational School Board, a founder of the Destitute Children's Asylum, and with his wife Joanna, an active member of the Sydney Female Refuge Society.

In the shadow of the Western Distributor once stood the humble Steam Mill Street, as mute witness to Australia's first steam mill.

The 'Haymarket'

Bullocky drivers and draught horse teamsters were contained by the steep slope up Brickfield Hill. All the diversion they sought was available to them in downtown George Street and the neighbouring alleyways. There were dog

The Corn Exchange.

The old Toll Gate.

fights, cock fights, boxing matches, gaming contests, brothels, dance halls and countless pubs which bore the names of the bush people who frequented them like The Fleet, The Plough, The Squatter's Arms and The Woolpack Inn. The many creeks which tumbled down the rocky heights of Surry Hills collected in a marshy swamp around Hay Street known as Dickens' Pond. Ducks, swans and other waterbirds nested there. Fish traps were built, mud-eels speared and geese caught.

The hay and wool wagons from Parramatta had to travel over a causeway which was sometimes washed away at high tide. The brokers met the wagoners at the Haymarket inns and bargained over an ale for the wool that was rapidly becoming the colony's greatest wealth.

The Toll Gate

In 1810 Governor Macquarie commissioned Francis Greenway to design and build a toll house and gate to collect money for the upkeep of the Parramatta Road. A coloured print made in 1836 by J.G. Austin shows the City Toll Gate and Benevolent Asylum in George Street South, where Railway Square is located today. Wrought-iron gates were hinged on stone pillars topped with castellated crowns. The little gatehouse building was constructed in sandstone, with long pointed Gothic windows. The present Sydney University gatehouse further along Parramatta Road gives something of the effect of the old Toll Gate. The construction of the turnpike and the imposition of the toll resulted in a clash between Governor Macquarie and Judge Jeffrey H. Bent, brother of the judge advocate Ellis Bent, who considered himself exempt from the toll (only to be paid by vehicular or mounted traffic) and refused to pay. He lost his temper and put on an angry display, vowing never to pass by that stretch of road again. One surmises that the good judge must have henceforward made a detour via the private road which ran through the adjacent estate and deer park of John Harris.

RELIGION

Early Religious Traditions

When it was decided to establish a convict settlement at Botany Bay, a request for an appointment as Catholic Chaplain was made by Father Thomas Walsh. This was turned down by Lord Sydney, who did not wish to weaken the Protestant ascendancy, and an Evangelical, the Rev. Richard Johnson, was appointed Chaplain to the First Fleet. Johnson preached his first sermon in Sydney Cove on 3 February 1788 and five weeks later, on 10 February, 14 couples were joined in matrimony. On 13 February Governor Phillip took his oaths of office, including the following declaration against transubstantiation: 'I, Arthur Phillip, do declare that I do believe that there is not any Transubstantiation in the sacrament of the Lord's Supper or in the Elements of Bread & Wine at or after the Consecration thereof by any Person whatsoever'. On 17 February Holy Communion was administered.

Not until 1803 was Mass allowed to be publicly celebrated by a convict priest, James Dixon, who had been transported after the Irish uprising of 1798. In 1804, in the aftermath of the Castle Hill rebellion, which involved Irish convicts, permission to celebrate Mass was withdrawn for another 16 years.

However, in November 1817 Fr Jeremiah O'Flynn arrived in Sydney with permission from Rome to minister in the colony, but when no written authority arrived from England he was deported by Governor Macquarie in May. O'Flynn's deportation was interpreted by Catholics of the time as religious persecution, with Macquarie cast as the villain. In fact, Macquarie is more properly seen as the efficient administrator than as a zealous bigot. It was not O'Flynn the Catholic priest who was deported, but O'Flynn 'the muddling, ignorant dangerous character', Macquarie wrote to the Colonial Office, adding that if priests were to be sent, 'I would beg to suggest they should be Englishmen of liberal Education & Sound constitutional principles'.

The fugitive priest did not have time to consume the Blessed Sacrament, and so began one of the legends of Australian Catholicism. The Blessed Sacrament was kept at the house of a Carmelite tertiary, James Dempsey, in Kent Street, near Erskine Street, and became the focal point of prayer and devotion for the Catholic and priestless people of the colony. Monsignor C. Duffy, the Cathedral archivist, corrected an earlier tradition which attributed the 'hidden house of prayer' to another early lay benefactor, William Davis. It was Polding's vicar-general, Dr Ullathorne, who started the erroneous tradition of the Davis cottage. The occasion was the laying of the foundation stone of St Patrick's, Church Hill, which was right alongside the Davis cottage.

PERSONS AND EVENTS

Some Pioneers

James Ruse, who was given one of the first land grants, grew the first crops in the colony and his farm became a success. Surgeon John Harris bought the holding at Parramatta and named it Experiment Farm. Ruse died in 1837, and his grave lies in the churchyard of St John's, Campbelltown. The tombstone bears the inscription:

My Mother Reread Me Tenderley
With Me She Took Much Paines
And When I Arrivd In This Coelney
I sewd The Forst Grain. And Now
With My Hevenly Father I Hope
  For Ever To Remain.

I can identify with the faith of the Ruse inscription. James Ruse died a convert to the Catholic faith and I belong to a religious order which places strong emphasis on the consecrated bread of the Lord's Supper.

The trader Robert Campbell, who had his own wharf at the Rocks, was one of the few citizens to support Governor Bligh during the rebellion of 1808. Campbell Street in the Haymarket is named after him. A Calcutta merchant who arrived in Sydney in 1798 in his own cargo ship, Campbell stayed on, buying leases on the west side of Sydney Cove and building the first serviceable wharf and storage sheds in the colony. His ventures prospered. He invested in land and became a wealthy man, the first merchant prince of the colony. The suburb of Ashfield perpetuates the name of his family's estate in Scotland. He built a mansion, Duntroon, on the Molongo River, near Canberra, and this site is now the Defence Force Academy.

Some Emancipists

James Meehan was 24 years old when the Irish rebellion of 1798 occurred. He was sentenced to transportation and when he arrived in Sydney in 1800 he was assigned as a servant to the acting surveyor-general, Charles Grimes. When Grimes was on leave in 1803–06, most of the departmental work was done by Meehan, who received an absolute pardon in 1806. However, Grimes was involved in the rebellion against Governor Bligh. Paradoxically, this benefited Meehan, who was appointed acting surveyor of lands with a salary of £182 10s. 0d. while Grimes was not permitted to return to New South Wales. Macquarie confirmed Meehan's appointment. In 1812, at a time when John Oxley was Surveyor-General, Meehan was appointed deputy-surveyor of lands. Two years later he became collector of quit-rents, and superintendent of roads, bridges and streets in the colony. Meehan was involved in exploration of the Hunter River, King Island, Port Phillip, the Derwent and Shoalhaven Rivers, discovered Lake Bathurst and the Goulburn Plains, drew a map of Sydney in 1807, and laid out the townships of Richmond, Castlereagh, Windsor, Pitt Town, Wilberforce, Liverpool, Bathurst and Hobart Town. He also organised the details of the land grant for the Catholic chapel, destined to become St Mary's Cathedral. Macquarie welcomed Meehan to Government House and paid him this glowing tribute in a dispatch to London:

I have ... had opportunity of witnessing his indefatigable assiduity in the fulfilment of his arduous duties. I believe that no man has suffered so much privation and fatigue in the service of this Colony as Mr Meehan has done ... His integrity has never, to my knowledge, been impeached; and I certainly consider him to be, both on account of his professional skill, and the faithful and laborious discharge of his duty, a valuable man.

Commissioner Bigge later found that Meehan's original offence was not serious.

William Redfern was another emancipated convict whose skills benefited the colony. After passing examination by the London Company of Surgeons, he joined the Royal Navy as a surgeon's mate in 1797. However, he was soon after involved in a naval mutiny and sentenced to death. On account of his youth he was transported after four years in prison and arrived in Sydney at the end of 1801, where he was employed as a surgeon's assistant. After being given a conditional pardon, he received a full pardon from Governor King in 1803. He returned to Sydney from Norfolk Island in 1808, studied medicine after his arrival and went on to become one of the greatest medical practitioners of the colony. He was both the first to receive an Australian medical qualification and to teach Australian medical students.

In 1818, when D'Arcy Wentworth resigned as principal surgeon, Redfern was expected to take the position. Although Macquarie strongly backed Redfern, Bathurst, who did not like to employ pardoned convicts, appointed a former naval surgeon James Bowman instead. Macquarie consoled Redfern by appointing him magistrate. This only added fuel to the fire of controversy, as Commissioner Bigge had expressly warned Macquarie against 'nominations of Convicts to the Magistracy'. A London judicial ruling in 1817 had undermined the status of emancipists in the colony to personal legal rights and property rights by stating that the governor's pardon was insufficient to establish these rights. Judge Barron Field enforced this position in Sydney in 1820. Redfern and Edward Eagar were elected at a protest meeting in Sydney in 1821 to present a petition to the King himself. Redfern did not return until 1824, but the appeal was successful and the law was amended. Redfern had great force of character and indeed Commissioner Bigge had complained that Redfern had been the only one in the colony to resist his authority.

Edward Eagar was convicted of forgery as a solicitor aged 22 and condemned to death in Cork court. It is unclear whether family influence or death-cell conversion resulted in reprieve and transportation. He was assigned to teach a clergyman's children and organised Bible classes around Windsor. After being conditionally pardoned by Governor Macquarie, Eagar set himself up as an attorney, but was ruled ineligible by Judge Ellis Bent. Given a full pardon by Macquarie in 1818, he found he still could not practise and became devoted to the emancipists' cause. After taking a petition with Redfern to England, Eagar did not return to the colony. He left behind his wife and four children. With Ellen Gorman, whom he met after his arrival in London, he had 10 more children. One of the early Methodists, Eagar's name is perpetuated in the multi-storey shelter for homeless men built by the Uniting Church near St Margaret's Hospital and opened in the 1970s.

Ultimo Estate

One of the first mansions in the colony was that of Dr John Harris, surgeon to the New South Wales Corps, commonly known as the Rum Corps. Harris arrived in the colony with the Second Fleet in 1790. In the Mourot Map of 1822, Harris' country estate occupied all the land between Cockle Bay (Darling Harbour) and Blackwattle Bay bounded by Parramatta Road, George Street and Hay Street. Harris' private road to his manor forked off George Street at Hay Street, thus neatly bypassing Macquarie's Toll Gate and rejoining the Parramatta Road in the vicinity of Jones Street. The house itself was reputedly one of the largest in the colony during the Macquarie era, being a two-storey manor house with columns and battlements, all in stone. Spotted deer, originally imported from India and now 400 in number, ranged in the vast park around the mansion.

Harris was the first police chief in the colony. When Governor King ordered from June 1801 a weekly inspection of all police stationed in Sydney and nearby, these units were still under military control and supervised by John Harris in his dual role as surgeon of New South Wales Corps and Sydney police magistrate. Governor King reported that Harris was performing his duties 'to the evident public benefit, and conspicuous good of His Majesty's Service, without neglecting an hour's duty as surgeon of the Corps'. Harris gave Governor King total support in his endeavours to suppress illegal trading in liquor, which made Harris very unpopular. Discharged from his post as police chief in 1802, he was restored to it in 1804, dismissed by Governor Bligh in 1807, and again restored to it in 1809. Harris' neighbour was John Macarthur, who had a town residence at Pyrmont peninsula, down to Union Street, which provided access to the Pyrmont Bridge.

Harris' manor house stood in a park of 232 acres and was called by him Ultimo House to commemorate the outcome of a court martial. The Rum Corps officers used Harris as a scapegoat to strike back at Governor King for making the surgeon deputy judge advocate. A military court had summoned Harris 'on the 12th ultimo', a slip for 'instant' which the classically educated Harris seized upon with glee. The suburb of Ultimo thus obtained its name. The Harris manor featured again in the prelude to the Rum Rebellion. Major Johnston rose from his sick bed at Annandale, dined with Harris at Ultimo House and then arrived in the evening at Wynyard Barracks to release Macarthur from prison. This was to precipitate the arrest and deposition of Governor Bligh by the officers of the Rum Rebellion. Sydney Technical College now stands on the site of Ultimo House.

A Wild and Woolly Saga

Was he an arrogant troublemaker or the venerable father of Australia's wool industry, a fighter of duels or the innovative pastoralist, an aristocratic officer or the banished son of noble

concealed birth? Whatever the case, John Macarthur was by far the most colourful character of the early days of the colony, a man about whom the truth seems stranger than any fiction. Was he the son of a fugitive Jacobite Scot and the second of 12 children of a humble tailor and mercer, or the illegitimate son of George III, as has also been claimed?

Lieutenant Macarthur, aged 23, was a member of the New South Wales Corps which was to replace the marines in Sydney. With him for the voyage were also his wife Elizabeth, aged 21, the daughter of a minor Devonshire squire, and his young son Edward. The hot-headed Macarthur fought his first duel before the Second Fleet sailed in 1790 with the master of the ship that was to take him to Australia. The cause was the cabin, which Macarthur claimed stank and was too near the convict women's quarters. The duel was fought with pistols but neither Macarthur nor John Gilbert was hurt.

When Phillip returned to England on account of ill health, the young Macarthur did well in the land grab that followed. Unlike Phillip, who restricted grants to men who could work them, Lieutenant-Governor Grose doled out land to his cronies. Convicts, fed and clothed by the government, went with the deal. Macarthur acquired 250 acres of prime land at Parramatta. He bought 55 acres of Jones' Farm on the end of the Pyrmont peninsula in 1799 for £10 worth of rum. His first serious visit was probably during Bligh's time.

On Thursday, 18th inst., a select party of ladies and gentlemen, twenty-one in all, made an aquatic excursion from Parramatta to Captain Macarthur's estate at Cockle Bay. After examining, with inexpressible satisfaction the picturesque beaches which that romantic scene afforded, a handsome collation ushered in the evening festivity beneath the shelter of a spreading fig tree.

To this enviable retirement one of the young ladies was pleased to give the name of Pyrmont, from its pure and uncontaminated spring, joined to the native beauties of the place of which the company took leave at five . . . Pyrmont, near Hanover, Germany, has medicinal springs.[4]

There is no record of Macarthur visiting the place again, or making any improvements, and his son Edward later divided the estate and sold it off in 59 lots. Edward Macarthur spent most of his time in England, an absentee landlord. He was to be one of the many who made handsome profits from the working people of the colony who sought homes to live in.

Macarthur's second duel was fought at Parramatta against his commander, Lieutenant-Governor William Patterson. Macarthur shot Patterson in the right shoulder. In due course Governor King arranged in 1802 to send Macarthur to England for court-martial. King thought he was quit of the 'perturbator who had come to Sydney 10 years earlier £500 in debt, according to some, and was now worth at least £20,000'. But by 1805 Macarthur was back to wave an order from Lord Camden in front of poor King, ordering him to give Macarthur 10,000 acres of the lush Cow Pastures with 4,000 healthy wild cattle on it as a bonus.

The next governor, William Bligh, did Macarthur the honour of calling him 'venomous serpent' and 'arch fiend'. Macarthur in turn called Bligh a tyrant and found himself under arrest for sedition. On Australia Day, 1808, officers of the Rum Corps rallied to him, freed him from prison, marched on Government House and placed Bligh under house arrest in the infamous Rum Rebellion. A notice dated 15 February 1808 announced that Macarthur was now secretary to the colony and magistrate. However, a group of settlers wrote to Major Johnston protesting against the appointment as Macarthur was 'the scourge of this colony'. Finally Macarthur's old enemy Lieutenant-Governor Patterson arrived from Van Diemen's Land on New Year's Day 1809. He decided the best way of cleaning up

the mess was to have Bligh, Johnston and Macarthur do their explaining back in England. Johnston and Macarthur were willing, but Bligh was not. Even when Macquarie came as the new governor, Bligh was thirsting to bring his enemies to trial. Bligh left Sydney on 10 May 1810. The mainly military court found Johnston guilty of mutiny, but only sentenced him to be cashiered.

Afraid to return to the colony for fear of being put on trial, Macarthur spent eight years of self-imposed exile in England, asking his wife to sell out and join him. But Elizabeth refused to abandon the heritage she had built up for their children. Governor Macquarie had been supportive of Mrs Macarthur while her husband was away and Lord Bathurst eventually permitted Macarthur to return to the colony, provided he stayed out of public affairs. When Commissioner Bigge came out to investigate the colony, Macarthur switched his allegiance to him and away from Macquarie. Macarthur fought against the Wentworth party which was campaigning for trial by jury and self-government. He quarrelled with Governor Darling, boasting that he had 'never yet failed in ruining a man who had become obnoxious to him'. In 1832 he was removed from the reformed Legislative Council by Governor Bourke, who reported to the Colonial Office that Macarthur had been pronounced insane. Macarthur died on 11 April 1834 and was buried at Camden. His wife Elizabeth who had managed the farming interests died, aged 80, in 1850.

When Macarthur imported four merino ewes and two rams from Cape Town in 1796 he was not to know that the experiment would result in quality fleece and herald the birth of Australia's wool industry. Stores and auction rooms were first located around Circular Quay, but by the 1880s the industry had expanded to such an extent that it needed to be relocated. Pyrmont and Ultimo had natural advantages with deep water-frontage and railway access. So the wool trade came, but not for any historical or sentimental reasons, to the Pyrmont land once owned by Macarthur. In 1883 Goldsborough, Mort & Company built the first of multi-storey woolstores in Pyrmont–Ultimo. Nineteen other massive woolstores were later built by various companies such as Dalgety and Elders. The woolstores were fitted with hydraulic lifts activated by water pumped in underground pipes from the Pier Street pumping station. By 1910 most of the 1.7 million bales of wool exported from Sydney came from the Ultimo stores, some of which were eight storeys high. Fires in 1935 and 1947, plus inner-city freeway planning, spelt the end of the Ultimo wool trade. In the 1960s another relocation took place to the western suburb of Yennora. So ended an era which lasted 80 years and saw as much as one-third of Australia's wool clip pass through Ultimo.

Cleaveland House

Captain Thomas Sadlier Cleaveland arrived with Macquarie's regiment in 1809. The gardens of the estate behind the Sandhills were named after Cleaveland, who left Sydney in 1811 and died the following year. The manor house of the Cleaveland estate has a most interesting history and deserves to be fully documented.

1810	former convict, Charles Smith (market gardens)
1825	Daniel Cooper, merchant Joseph Wallen (George Waller?)
1834	Mr and Mrs de Metz (school)
1840s	John Tooth Wooley's (ladies school)
1845?	Rectory of Christ Church James Keane (school)
1890s	Labour bureau
1901	Sisters of the Good Samaritan (refuge)
1940s	Franciscan Missionaries of Mary (aged persons)
1960	New South Wales Society for Crippled Children

It seems that Daniel Cooper may have had the two-storey sandstone residence constructed, and there is some evidence that it was to a Francis Greenway design.[5] The location of the house is not stated. Cleaveland House still stands and its history reveals a fascinating mixture of convicts, merchants, brewers, schoolteachers, parsons and nuns.

ENTERTAINMENT

The First Race Meeting

To soothe the colony after the turbulent Bligh years, Macquarie decided on a grand gesture of reconciliation, a race meeting to be held over three days. But first a racetrack had to be found. The temptation was to commandeer 'the Common', a large open space reserved by the wisdom of Governor Phillip in 1792 with the proviso, 'never to be granted or let on lease'. The *Sydney Gazette* of 13 October 1810 published a decree of Governor Macquarie:

The whole of the open ground yet unoccupied in the vicinity of the Town of Sydney, hitherto known and alternately called by the names of 'The Common', 'Exercising Ground', the 'Cricket Ground', and 'Racecourse'; bounded by the Government Domain on the north; the Town of Sydney on the west; the Brickfields on the south; and Mr Palmer's premises on the east, being intended in future for the Recreation and Amusement of the inhabitants of the Town, and as a field of exercise for the Troops; the Governor has thought proper to name the ground thus described 'Hyde Park'; by which name it is henceforth to be called and denominated.

Angry goat and cow owners had to be pacified when the people's common, now renamed as Hyde Park, was appropriated. Macquarie gave the herdsmen new pastures so distant and marshy that the common (Centennial Park) was known as Lachlan's Swamps. In the meantime the officers eagerly sent soldiers to grub out tree stumps along the course, 10 furlongs in length. Macquarie brought in a law that any brickmaker caught digging clay out of the new racecourse which was next to Brickfield Hill would lose his brickmaking licence. The new clerk of the course, John Reddington, warned the citizens against using the course and that any stray dogs would be shot. On Monday 15 October the three-day carnival began. Perhaps it was the first real coming together of the 11,500 people of the colony. There were races aplenty and betting went on, despite the governor's ban. Currency used was in ducats, rupees, Spanish dollars, guilders and shillings. There were cock fights, jigs, Punch and Judy shows, a corroboree and boomerang throwing. The first cricket matches in Australia were also played here in a simple bush clearing, without benefit of turf or grandstand.

One year later Macquarie published a similar order outlining an area known as Sydney Common that included what is now Moore Park and most of Centennial Park.[6]

CRIME

A Grisly Murder

In a penal colony marked by the presence of chains, irons, the lash, the treadmill and the gallows, there was no absence of lawless activities. Apart from thieving, drinking, fighting and prostitution, a grim tale centres on a house now occupied by a hotel on the corner of George and Goulburn Streets. In 1798 the house belonged to a Private Jones and his wife. An English missionary had kindly lent them money, but when he innocently asked for its return, they took to him with an axe. After the grisly deed, the couple had a night on the town along with an accomplice, Elbray. After their arrest, Governor Hunter, not prone to do things by halves, sent troopers to burn down their bark shanty. Amid the ashes a higher gallows than usual was erected and all three met their ending. The remains of Jones and Elbray were left there to rot in nets of chains, but Mrs Jones was handed over to the surgeons for dissection.

ARTS

Brickfield Hill Clay and Potteries

In a letter dated 16 November 1788, Governor Phillip wrote to Sir Joseph Banks that he was sending the first shipment of 'the white clay with which the Natives mark themselves. You mention it in your *Voyage* and l'Abbé Mongez, a very sensible man, and I believe a good naturalist, told me that it would make very good china.' Banks gave the white clay to Josiah Wedgwood, who fashioned the Sydney Cove Medallions from it. The medallion depicts four figures representing Hope, Peace, Art and Labour. Wedgwood's factory, Etruria, is embossed, as is the year 1789. The medallion is currently worth $30,000.

Although Governor Phillip recognised the suitability of Sydney clays for pottery production, such an immediate development would have meant fewer workers for agriculture. However, pottery was being produced at Brickfield Hill by 1800. The clay was first used in brickmaking, but later tiles, pipes and domestic pottery were made. In 1791 a convict, Elijah Leeke, was producing basins, plates, jars and clay pipes. Later Samuel Skinner followed his transported wife to the colony. Skinner was a skilled potter and established a successful pottery at Brickfield Hill which included domestic ware such as cups, saucers and teapots.

2 Towards the End of Transportation (1820–49)

POPULATION

Convict Settlements

The basic policy of convict transportation to the new colony continued. Other settlements had been established. Penal bases like Norfolk Island, Port Arthur, Macquarie Harbour, Moreton Bay only served to highlight the importance of Sydney and its natural harbour facilities. The stream of immigrants from the United Kingdom resulted in the growth of trade and commerce and the importance of Sydney as a trading post. The town of Sydney continued to grow. The burial ground (site of the present Town Hall) was now full up and a new cemetery was needed. This was located in the Sandhills area, where Devonshire Street now runs into Central Railway.

GOVERNMENT

Brickfield Hill Gallows

The old race ground which was to become Hyde Park possessed a gallows from 1802, though many hangings still took place at the old gaol near George and Essex Streets.

One of the most hated governors of the early colony was Sir Ralph Darling. On 12 March 1827 a squad of redcoat soldiers, muskets at the ready, escorted five convicts to the gallows at Brickfield Hill. Hanging was a public spectacle. Usually the crowd was quiet, but this time there was angry murmuring. Governor Darling had wanted to hang all the convicts who had seized command of the brig *Wellington*. Sixty convicts led by John Walton, a former army officer convicted of receiving stolen goods, overpowered 12 soldiers and a crew of 25. The plan was to take on food and water in New Zealand and sail to freedom in South America. However, the presence of two sealer ships from Sydney in the Bay of Islands proved the undoing of the mutiny. Walton had used minimal force and there had been no deaths during the seizure of the *Wellington*, and he was loathe to use violence in order to escape. He surrendered, and 23 convicts were taken back to Sydney for trial. Darling's Executive Council restrained the governor from his intention of hanging every one

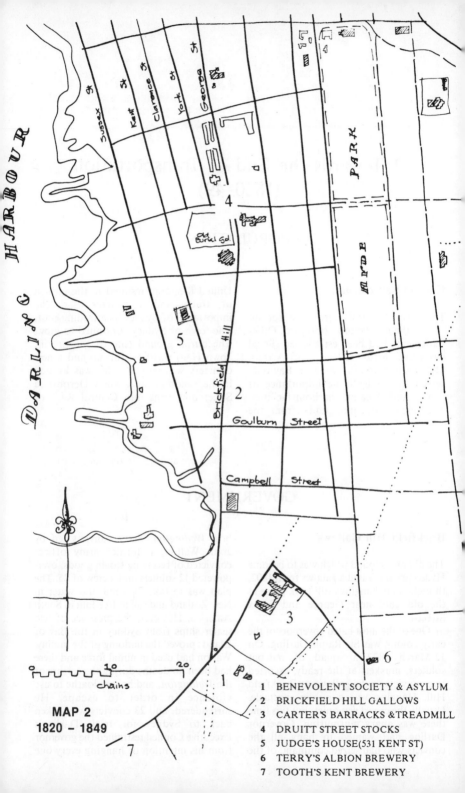

HARBOUR

DARLING

Sussex St

Kent St

Clarence St

York St

George St

PARK

HYDE

Old Burial Gd.

Brickfield Hill

4

5

2

Goulburn Street

Campbell Street

3

6

1

0   10   20
chains

MAP 2
1820 – 1849

1 BENEVOLENT SOCIETY & ASYLUM
2 BRICKFIELD HILL GALLOWS
3 CARTER'S BARRACKS & TREADMILL
4 DRUITT STREET STOCKS
5 JUDGE'S HOUSE (531 KENT ST)
6 TERRY'S ALBION BREWERY
7 TOOTH'S KENT BREWERY

of the convicts and after a two-day trial five of the convicts were condemned to hang, the remainder being sentenced to life imprisonment on Norfolk Island. What was the fate of the ringleader John Walton? Four days before the executions HMS *Amity* had set off for Norfolk Island with the rest of the mutineers, among them John Walton. The entry from the 1828 Census of New South Wales makes the issue clear. Under the section, Employer's Remarks, are the words: 'Life in chains'.

Convict Work Gangs and Public Stocks

A walk down George Street in 1829 by an anonymous journalist provides the following eyewitness description of convicts. The initials refer either to the Carters' Barracks or the Park Barracks:

> What company is this, with straw hats on and kangaroo caps, some with shoes and some without, clad in jacket and trowsers? On the latter appendage there is the imprint of a javelin and the initial characters P.B., P.B. and C.B. They step in rank and file, with a deliberation of movement, unknown to more giddy mortals ... Some have an obdurate scowl about their eyes, and others an innocent twinkling; and others, have a settled expression of either apathy, despair, or resignation. Yet wretches at home think, that loss of freedom is nothing here, that slavery is not slavery![1]

The character of the town which greeted Bishop Polding on his arrival in the colony in 1835 is best summed up in the notice:

> Stocks with comfortable accommodation for 5 couples of ladies and gentlemen who cannot pay the usual fines for indulging at the Shrine of Bacchus have been erected at the corner of Bathurst Street. They are accompanied by a whipping post and have a fine appearance. They are quite an addition to the Scots Church which is nearly completed.[2]

Another visitor to Sydney was the American naval commander, Captain Charles Wilkes, who recorded his impressions as follows:

> Sydney contains about 24,000 inhabitants, which is about one-fifth part of the whole population (120,000) of the colony; and about one-fourth of this number are convicts. In truth, the fact

The Carters barracks.

that it is a convict settlement may be at once inferred from the number of the police officers and soldiers that are everywhere seen, and is rendered certain by the appearance of 'chain-gangs'. The latter reminded us, except in the colour of those composed of them, of the coffee-carrying slaves at Rio; but the want of the cheerful song, and the apparent merriment which the Brazilian slaves exhibit in the execution of their tasks, was apparent.[3]

Benevolent Society

The Benevolent Society of New South Wales was established to provide shelter and care for the poor, many of whom were former convicts. It was the first voluntary charitable organisation founded in Australia. Under the leadership of E.S. Hall in 1813, the title was to be 'The New South Wales Society for promoting Christian Knowledge and Benevolence in these Territories and the Neighbouring Islands' and its basic aim that of 'relieving the distressed and enforcing the sacred duties of Religion and Virtue in N.S.W.' After reorganisation in 1818 the Benevolent Society came into being. With strong support from the patron, Governor Macquarie, a building was erected near the Turnpike House, at the southernmost end of Pitt Street, near the Carters' Barracks. Item 29 of Macquarie's 'List of Public Buildings and Works' reads: 'Another barrack for 100 convict boys, contiguous to the aforementioned barrack at the Brick Fields, but separated by a high party wall, with workshops for the boys ... the whole range of these buildings being enclosed with a strong brick wall twelve feet high'. Governor Macquarie opened up an asylum for the 'Poor Blind, Aged and Infirm' in 1820.

The Benevolent Asylum was able to house 60 persons. An annual grant was provided by the government. Noting the changes in the colonial society, the secretary of state in London gave notice in 1842 that the grant would be tapered off and that private charity would have to take over. On 30 June 1843 the Benevolent Asylum housed 370 (273 men), of whom 262 had once been convicts. More than 220 were over 50 years of age. Among them were 39 blind and 32 paralytics. The Society's *Report* for 1843 noted:

> It is indeed a refuge for the distressed, an hospital for the diseased, an asylum for the aged poor, and a home for the wretched wanderer...
>
> To meet such cases there is no Government or Municipal provision. The Benevolent Asylum is the only sure and ready shelter for the wretched in this part of the colony: it alone stands between us and all the extortions and abuses, and waste of a poor-rate. The blessings which it dispenses, are dispensed freely and generously, and to all: its gates are open night and day; and without difficulty, and without delay, those who really need its aid are freely admitted.

Poor women would have their confinement at the asylum and in 1862 a new wing was added, called the Lying-in-Hospital of New South Wales. In 1868 the Florence Nightingale-trained Lucy Osborn took charge of nursing at Sydney Hospital. One of the five nurses who came with her was Eliza Blundell, who went on to become matron at the Benevolent Asylum for 24 years. By 1878 the Benevolent Asylum was a training school for nurses and midwives and by 1886 it was recognised also for university students. In 1901 the whole site was resumed by the government and from the compensation received the Royal Hospital for Women was established in Paddington in 1906. The original foundation stone is now located there. The society itself has diversified into caring for senior citizens and has established many hostels and nursing homes, child-care and other welfare services.

INDUSTRY AND TRANSPORT

The Haymarket

Governor Darling had a cattle market and a corn market opened in 1829 in the entire area bounded by George, Hay, Castlereagh and Campbell Streets. The George Street frontage was used as a cattle market until 1834. This occurred after an edict prohibiting the droving of stock through the uptown streets. A brick building was erected, known as the Hay and Corn Market. This building was demolished in 1875. The Haymarket Post Office began its operation on this site in 1909 and moved to its present location across the road in 1923.

Terry's Albion Brewery

Samuel Terry was convicted of stealing stockings and sentenced to transportation for seven years. Three years after his sentence expired he was in Sydney and granted one of 20 liquor licences issued by Macquarie. Established as an inn-keeper, he married a rich widow and steadily built up a fortune so great that he became known as the 'Botany Bay Rothschild' and was a millionaire by the time of his death in 1838. In 1827 Terry established the Albion Brewery, the site of which was determined by a freshwater creek from Surry Hills. In 1873 Tooheys Brewery was moved from Darling Harbour to the old Albion Brewery site. The new proprietors were the Toohey brothers. Their new Standard Brewery prospered. Both were popular in the sporting world. John Thomas Toohey played a major role in the construction of the 'Heroes of 1898' memorial at Waverley cemetery. The advertising symbol for the brewery was a blacksmith in a leather apron holding up a foaming tankard and saying 'Here's to 'ee', and dates back to 1894. The site has been redeveloped but Tooheys Ltd still trades from premises at Lidcombe. So the chant 'I feel like a Toohey's' goes on.

Tooth's Kent Brewery

The beautiful fresh water that flowed from the government paddocks into Blackwattle Bay led to the siting of the brewery in 1834. John Tooth wrote to his relatives in Kent for an experienced brewer, and Charles Newnham arrived in the following year. A well, 13 feet in diameter and 60 feet deep, was established. Before long ale was available at the following prices: X ale at 1s. per gallon; XX ale at 1s. 6d. per gallon; and XXX ale at 2s. 6d. per gallon.

The business expanded at a tremendous rate during the gold-rush boom of the 1850s and the Tooth family became prominent in politics and farming, Kameruka cheese-making, sugar-refining, fruit canning and frozen meat. In 1929 Tooth's took over Resch's Brewery in Redfern. The Great Southern Hotel in George Street was one of the Tooth hotels. In 1983 Tooth & Co. sold their modernised Kent Brewery to Carlton and United Brewery. The Waverley Brewery in Dowling Street was subsequently demolished and the site has been redeveloped for housing.

Early Chippendale

The area upstream of Blackwattle Swamp was low-lying and damp, but the land was cheap and its proximity to the town and the abundant water supply attracted business and light industry. These included Tooth's Brewery, the Brisbane Distillery, a cooperage, timber yards, corn chandlers, storehouses and a slaughterhouse.

The major land route out of Sydney to the west and south passed through the region. In the beginning it was known as the road to Parramatta, then as Parramatta Road, as George Street West and finally as Broadway. In 1858, when W. Stanley Jevons set out to describe the social conditions of Sydney, he divided the townsfolk into three groups based on their residences. In the first group were the merchants and professional men, in the second were the shopkeepers and tradesmen and in the third were the 'labourers and indefinable lower orders': 'Third class residences collect about a few distinct centres, or form a part of the town peculiar to themselves generally in the lowest and least desirable localities—the north part of Chippendale and Marketland are the chief and worst third class quarters'.[4] Even today the narrow streets of Chippendale and their cramped houses with their narrow frontages bear testimony to the hardships of a bygone age.

Market Gardens

A battered and worn sandstone fountain in Hyde Park bears the inscription of John Baptist, a market gardener who farmed in Surry Hills—along Bourke Street to be more precise. John Baptist also had a market shed in the city where his produce would be sold. *Ford's Sydney* directory shows a listing for John Baptist up to 31 December 1850.

RELIGION

A Turbulent Priest

Fr O'Flynn's deportation caused such a rumpus back in England that provision was made for the appointment of two Catholic chaplains with salaries of £100 per annum each. The first two Catholic chaplains arrived in Sydney in May 1820, more than 30 years after the first Catholic convicts. However, Fathers John Joseph Therry and Phillip Connolly soon quarrelled and parted company, with Connolly going to Tasmania. Therry soon organised a meeting to raise subscriptions for a Catholic chapel, and land was granted on the site where St Mary's Cathedral now stands. This decision displeased Therry, who had asked for a central site on Church Hill, but on 29 October 1821 Governor Macquarie laid the foundation stone of St Mary's.

The full story of Therry's work is beyond the scope of this study. Nonetheless, a key incident, one which caused his dismissal as chaplain, is pertinent. It would seem that Fr Therry was based, albeit temporarily, at the Haymarket. He gave his address as 'Priest's Lodging, Campbell Street, Brickfields' in an advertisement in the Sydney newspaper, *The Australian*, in 1825. The occasion was his protest at the exclusive rights about to be given to the Anglican Church in the matter of orphan education. Therry spoke of his 'unqualified respect' for the Protestant clergy, but a printer's error altered it to read 'qualified respect'. Despite correction and apology by the *Sydney Gazette*, Therry lost his position as chaplain and with it his salary. Therry was not reinstated until 1837.

Father Therry and the Druitts

In his diary Fr Therry mentions saying Mass in Sydney at Major Druitt's house. It was Saturday, 8 February 1833, and he received £1 for the Mass. Major Druitt was not himself a Catholic, but his wife was. She was formerly Peggy Lynch. The couple first met on board ship when Druitt was *en route* from Cork to Sydney with his 48th Regiment. After two days at sea, a beautiful young stowaway was discovered in the soldiers' quarters. Peggy had been swept off her feet by a Private Terence Burns. Rather than turn the ship back, the solution adopted was that Burns should marry the lady forthwith. The ship's captain married the couple, with Druitt acting as clerk of the ceremony, but before the end of the long voyage Peggy had abandoned her new husband for the gentleman officer. When the ship docked in August 1817, she lived with Druitt in a fine seven-room house in Bent Street. They married in 1825. Burns registered no complaint and returned to Ireland in 1818.

Druitt became Macquarie's acting engineer and Inspector of Public Works. He was officially in charge of Francis Greenway's work and supervised construction of Fort Macquarie, the government stables, St James' Church, the convict barracks, and many roads and bridges. When Macquarie left the colony, Druitt resigned his posts and settled down with Peggy on his 1,000-acre grant near St Mary's, where he built an Etruscan villa and became a wealthy landowner and a magistrate. Peggy presented him with four children after their wedding, in addition to the two they already had. She died in 1842. Druitt died three months later but not before the newly constituted City of Sydney named a street after him adjacent to the old burial ground which it was hoped would be the site of the future Town Hall. This was quite a step upwards for the new Druitt Street, as the stocks were located there in front of Greenway's police station and municipal markets. On market days there was plenty of ammunition in the form of rotten eggs and vegetables to hurl at the unfortunate offenders in the stocks.

From Archpriest to Archbishop

With Fr Therry out of government favour, Fr Daniel Power was the official Catholic chaplain from 1826 until his death in 1830. Fr Christopher Dowling arrived in 1831 to take over. Each of them had difficulties with the aggrieved Therry, who had a strong lay following. The lay base of the Church was considerably strengthened with the arrival of two prominent Catholic laymen: Roger Therry, who was commissioner of the court of requests, and John Hubert Plunkett, the solicitor-general. These appointments followed upon the Emancipation Act of 1829 in England, which allowed Catholics to serve in government positions. Before Plunkett left for Australia he obtained permission for another Catholic chaplain, Fr John McEncroe, an experienced priest who had worked as vicar-general in America. The arrival of Governor Bourke in 1831 marked a turnaround in the attitude of the Colonial Office towards Catholics. The colonial government wanted a church authority it could negotiate with, but the truculent Therry did not fit this bill. William Morris, successor of Bishop Slater in Mauritius, appointed William Ullathorne, a young English Benedictine and former student of Dr Polding, as his vicar-general in Australia. Ullathorne quickly summed up the situation and urged the appointment of a local bishop as a church authority based in Mauritius was totally unsatisfactory for Australia.

Ministry of Polding

John Bede Polding was the colony's first Catholic bishop. He was consecrated bishop in London in 1834 and his episcopate lasted until 1877. In 1844 he set up an Australian hierarchy. Polding was the first prelate to achieve this remarkable feat in a Protestant-ruled country; even Britain at this stage did not have a Catholic hierarchy. Polding's own appointment to the Australian mission came in the wake of the failure of his Benedictine colleagues, Slater and Morris, to administer Mauritius efficiently and equitably. Orphaned at the age of eight by the death of his mother and German father (Polten), the young Polding was brought up in a monastic school by his uncle Bede Brewer, who became President of the English Benedictine Congregation. Polding entered the Order at 16 and was ordained when 25. The following year he became novice-master and sub-prior. He was 40 when he received his brief of appointment to New South Wales on 17 May 1834.

When Polding arrived in 1835 there were three priests, three churches being constructed, 10 schools and 200 communicants. Six years later, there were a bishop and 24 priests, nine completed churches, six being constructed, and 31 schools. Polding's spiritual impact had been similarly enormous, with the number of communicants now 23,000. Polding's greatest problem in obtaining sufficient priests for his mission was never resolved. The Benedictine Order in England, of which Polding was a member, refused his requests. The priest to people ratio was considerably worsened by the gold rush. This imbalance created an emergency situation, not fully realised at the time and not rectified until the 1870s.

Abbott Henry Gregory was appointed vicar-general in 1844. It was a most unfortunate choice. Autocratic and inflexible, though very loyal to Polding, Gregory was made a scapegoat to restore peace and recalled by the English Benedictines in 1860 at the explicit order of the Holy See. However, Gregory was not entirely the villain he is made out to be. A public meeting was held in Sydney on 31 August 1846 to organise famine relief for Ireland in the wake of the failure of the potato crop. There was no trace of the usual sectarian rivalry in the speeches and F. Merewether, Esq., was elected secretary and the Very Rev. Dr Gregory treasurer of the fund. This is the first time in the colony that financial aid flowed back to Europe.

Polding's desire to establish a monastic community at St Mary's slowed the growth of parish structures in the inner city. Resident parish priests at St Benedict's, George Street West and Darlinghurst were not established until 1856. Haymarket parish came even later. Instead, Polding was keen to foster tertiary studies and establish a seminary. In 1852 he secured the Lyndhurst estate of Dr James Bowman, overlooking Black-wattle Bay. This venture was deemed elitist by the Catholic population and Lyndhurst eventually closed in the 1870s.

Forty Hours Devotion

Archbishop Polding himself inaugurated the Forty Hours Devotion of the Blessed Sacrament. The immediate occasion would seem to have been the desire to make reparation for the scandalous relationship one of his own Benedictine monks enjoyed with an unnamed woman. The monk in question was the French sculptor, Jean Gourbeillon, who sought refuge with his French compatriots, the Marists at Church Hill, before returning to his native France. The Forty Hours Devotion consists in the exposition of the consecrated host in a special sacred vessel, the monstrance, on or above the altar, for the people's veneration. The devotion encourages prolonged periods of prayer before the exposed Sacrament. Adoration and reparation were favoured themes. Voluntary rosters for hourly periods of prayer were common.

PERSONS AND EVENTS

The Judge's House

Only Cadman's Cottage near Circular Quay is an older dwelling in the City of Sydney than the Judge's House, which stands at 531 Kent Street. An early description is given as follows: 'The elegant cottage belonging to Mr Harper, which commands a fascinating prospect of Darling Harbour, has been let to Judge Dowling. A finer residence could not have been chosen in Sydney.'[5] William Harper was a well-to-do young surveyor who arrived as a free settler in 1821. Governor Macquarie appointed him assistant surveyor and commissioned him to survey

The Judge's House has been restored.

the township of Sydney. His work was much used in subsequent maps of Sydney. Harper built a cottage for his wife and four children in Kent Street, which was a cul-de-sac at the time. French doors and internal folding shutters are noteworthy. The architecture is Georgian style, set off by a stone flagged verandah, and the French doors and internal folding shutters are noteworthy.

The judge, to whom the house owes its popular name, lived there only from 1828 to 1831, when he moved to a house built for him in Darlinghurst. Other tenants included a vinegar maker, a master mariner, a surgeon and a butcher, until the house was leased by the Sydney Night Refuge and Soup Kitchen in 1868. The following year the Refuge Committee bought the site and erected a three-storey building for homeless men on the northern side. This building was opened by Lord Carrington in 1887. Ten years later another building was added on as a women's and children's shelter. In 1945 the Sydney City Mission took over the refuge. In 1973, the site was sold to Grosvenor International and the refuge was reestablished in modern premises in Campbell Street, Surry Hills. Grosvenor International demolished the old refuge but restored the cottage to its original condition.

Frederick Goulburn

Frederick Goulburn had an elder brother, Henry, who was under-secretary for the colonies from 1812 to 1821. After the battle of Waterloo, Goulburn was promoted to major and placed on half-pay in 1816. Born in 1788, Goulburn was still only 28 in 1820 when he was appointed secretary and registrar of the records of New South Wales. He took over from J.T. Campbell, but he was the first official colonial secretary of New South Wales, as his predecessors had been merely private secretaries to the governor. Goulburn was the first to act in both capacities. He earned the enmity of the gentry, including John Macarthur, who called him 'a worthy successor to Governor Bligh in despotic behaviour'. Goulburn has a street named after him which is an important traffic route in the southern half of the city.

William Charles Wentworth

In 1826 some 100 guests of the emancipists gathered at Mrs Hills' Hyde Park Tavern to celebrate the foundation of the colony. As might have been expected W.C. Wentworth presided, assisted by William Redfern. Phillip and

Macquarie were toasted, as were trial by jury, the House of Assembly and all those who had regained their freedom. William Charles Wentworth was the Australian-born son of D'Arcy Wentworth, assistant surgeon in the Second Fleet. At 17, Wentworth won one of the horse races at the Hyde Park meeting in 1810. Three years later he used his riding skills to good advantage in the epic first crossing of the Blue Mountains with Gregory Blaxland and William Lawson. He went to England and studied law at Cambridge, where he also won second prize in the chancellor's poetic competition for the patriotic *Australasia*. On his return to the colony he took up the cause of self-government. As a qualified barrister he figured prominently in Australia's first breach-of-promise case. In May 1825 he championed the beautiful 18-year-old Sarah Cox's recourse to legal justice, and persuaded the jury to such an extent that £100 damages were awarded to her. Four years later Wentworth, aged 39, took her to wife and settled her in at his Vaucluse House. Wentworth was newspaper owner, patriot, parliamentarian when appointed a Member of the Legislative Council in 1843, and also proponent of the infamous 'bunyip aristocracy'. He was the prime mover in the establishment of Australia's first university. The Act to incorporate the University of Sydney was passed in 1850 and Wentworth was a foundation member of the Senate, serving in that capacity until his death in 1872. The street running south of Hyde Park that enshrines Wentworth's name was formerly Wexford Street, a notorious slum where Jack Lang spent some of his childhood years.

ENTERTAINMENT

Sydney Cricket Club

Club cricket in Sydney began in 1826, when enthusiasts from the military formed the Military Cricket Club. The Australian Club, exclusive to native-born players, was also formed. According to Jack Pollard:

> The Sydney Club began in 1829 in a government paddock 'on the site of the turnpike', which was in the area of the present-day Central Station. The players were keen to get away from pitches dominated by soldiers or the aloof members of the Australian Club, but they were soon ejected from their ground and the club disbanded.[6]

First Boxing Gloves

The first boxing gloves in Australia were used at an exhibition bout at the Dolphin Inn, Elizabeth Street, on 8 November 1834. Bare-knuckle fights had previously been the order of the day. It was another 15 years before the first recorded fight with gloves took place at the Tennis Court Inn in Sussex Street. William Thompson, the colony's athletics champion, knocked out Bill Sparkes in five rounds on 25 July 1849.[7]

Snowy Sydney

A most remarkable event occurred in Sydney Town on Tuesday, 28 June 1836. It snowed! The report in the *Sydney Morning Herald* on Thursday, 30 June, is full of droll comparisons with the old country. Evidently snow fell at 7 a.m., resulting in drifts up to an inch deep. The 'natives' stared at the unexpected visitor. However, any fears that 'Messrs Frost and Snow' were going to emigrate proved to be unfounded.

CRIME

The Treadmill

Adjoining the old Carters' Barracks was the treadmill, blithely described by James Maclehose in his *Stranger's Guide* of 1839 as 'a very useful piece of machinery for the purpose of correcting the tarnished morals of Botany Bay'. This treadmill had been set up in 1823 in a building euphemistically called the house of correction. The devilish device, imported from Britain, was operated by 8 to 10 convicts who were chained by the wrist. The *Sydney Gazette* of December 1825 gave a graphic description of the treadmill. It was likened to a never-ending moving staircase up which one climbs. The treadmill began operation at dawn and stopped at sunset. There was a break of one hour for lunch. The committee of management at the time recommended that other prisons install the treadmill, as it proved more effective punishment than flogging. The *Sydney Morning Herald* of 1 June 1840 reports that 149 men were then operating the treadmill, which was producing half a ton of flour per day. In 1846 the treadmill was closed down and removed to Darlinghurst gaol.

The Houdini of the Gallows

Joseph Samuels was transported to the colony for an offence committed at the age of 14, as a 'lookout' during a petty burglary. When Samuels arrived in 1801 there were a few dozen Jewish convicts already present. In 1803 Constable Luker was found murdered after the robbery of a wealthy prostitute and suspicion fell on Samuels and on the tough Isaac Simmons, employed as a convict watchman, who had been transported for highway robbery. After damning circumstantial evidence, Samuels confessed to being an accomplice in the robbery but not in the murder. The magistrate, Surgeon John Harris, and the military court sentenced Samuels and James Hardwicke to death, for theft. The cart with two coffins stopped at the Brickfield Hill gallows. The Rev. Samuel Marsden asked the condemned to make a full confession. Samuels declared that Simmons had made him swear a Jewish oath not to reveal that he had killed Luker after having been surprised by him. Meanwhile, a last-minute pardon arrived for Hardwicke. But as Samuels swung, the rope snapped. Another rope was found, and this time it slipped until the condemned man's legs touched the ground. A third time the rope was placed around Samuel's neck, and this time the rope snapped close to the neck. The crowd shouted in amazement. A reprieve was obtained from Governor King, who commented that there had been 'Divine intervention' for the now half-conscious Samuels. The broken ropes were tested and were found capable of supporting 392 pounds without breaking. Samuels seems to have perished at sea in a later escape attempt. Simmons survived to old age and was buried in the Jewish section of the old Devonshire Street cemetery.[8]

3 The Gold Rush Quickens the Pace (1850–79)

POPULATION

Gold Rush

The service role of the Haymarket was first summed up in the Carters' Barracks, and then followed up by the inns and hotels which housed the growers, producers, farmers and team drivers when they came to town for business. But the shepherds of New South Wales, who had served their wealthy masters like the Macarthurs, were about to be joined by men who would be their own masters, the diggers. When Edward Hargraves found gold near Bathurst in 1851 he came to Sydney to claim a reward from the Colonial Secretary and a great fortune-seeking madness began. The local press had already been critical of the social upheaval caused by the discovery of gold in California and reaction to the local discovery was also negative. The *Sydney Herald* reported on 16 May, 'it appears that this colony is to be cursed with a gold-digging mania', and by 23 May: 'Many persons are going to dig for gold who are wholly unfit for such work; men who would hesitate to walk the length of George Street in a shower of rain ... What can be the result of such reckless conduct but that which happened in California—ruin, misery, disease, death.'

Signs bearing gold shovels in the shop fronts of George Street reflected the times. In an attempt to slow the crazy exodus to the goldfields, Governor Fitzroy proclaimed a digger's licence at £1 10s. 0d. per month. Moral improvers warned men not to surrender to the 'unholy hunger' for gold. Archbishop Polding in Sydney warned the members of his church that any Roman Catholic found selling sly grog on the diggings would be denounced from the altar. Men walked off jobs, sailors jumped ship and teachers abandoned their classes as the mad fever took hold of them. According to one contemporary:

> Sydney assumed an entirely new aspect. The shop fronts put on quite new faces. Wares suited to the wants and tastes of general purchasers were thrust ignominiously out of sight, and articles of outfit for goldmining only were displayed. Blue and red serge shirts, Californian hats, leathern belts, 'real gold-digging gloves', mining boots, blankets white and scarlet, became show-goods in the fashionable streets. The pavements were lumbered with picks, pans and pots; and the gold-washing machine or Virginian 'cradle', hitherto a stranger to our eyes, became in two days a familiar household utensil, for scores of them were paraded for purchase, 'from 25s. to 40s.'[1]

The discovery of gold had important consequences for the colony. It coincided with the closure of the era of convict transportation from England. It resulted in a wave of new immigrants. For Sydney Town, it led to new opportunities for commerce and retail. During this time the progenitors of great retail stores began to trade. Their origins, however, were humble. Anthony Hordern arrived from England in 1824, David Jones in 1834 and Joseph Farmer in 1839. Some of the tales of these and subsequent store-founders,

MAP 3
1850 – 1879

1 HAYMARKET
2 KENT ST NIGHT REFUGE
3 PRINCE ALFRED PAVILION
4 ST ANDREW'S CATHEDRAL
5 SYDNEY FUNERAL STATION
6 SYDNEY TOWN HALL
7 ST BENEDICT'S

Sailing ships in Darling Harbour

including the Grace brothers and the Australian-born Mark Foy, will be found in later sections of this book.

Immigration and Caroline Chisholm

Caroline Chisholm was 28 when she first came to Sydney, and 50 when she returned there, for the sake of her health, from the Victorian goldfields. She was then the mother of six children, two sons having been born in India, another son in Sydney, one four months out of Sydney at sea and appropriately named Sydney Lawrence, and two daughters in England.

Born Caroline Jones into a philanthropic farming family in England in 1808, at the age of 22 she agreed to marry Captain Archibald Chisholm provided she could continue her philanthropic work. Chisholm was a Catholic and Caroline became a convert. When she was 24 her husband was posted with his regiment to Madras to provide military back-up to the East India Company, and while there Caroline founded the Female School of Industry for the Daughters of European Soldiers.

The Chisholms decided to spend leave from India in Australia and arrived in Sydney in 1838. They settled at Windsor. Their third son Henry was born and baptised in August 1839 at St Mary's Cathedral. Captain Chisholm was obliged to leave Sydney in 1840 and return to his regiment, but it had been agreed that Caroline and her three sons would stay behind until his return. So began her work for female immigration. She succeeded in obtaining the vacant barracks on the corner of Phillip and Bent Streets as temporary accommodation for newly arrived girls. The barracks could shelter up to 96 women, and also housed the only free employment register in Sydney. She made many journeys into the bush, riding her white horse, Captain, and personally settled 11,000 people on the land. In 1842 she published *Female Immigration, considered in a Brief Account of the Sydney Immigrants Home*. This work seems to be the first women's publication in Australia geared to the general population.

Her efforts to disperse immigrants to the interior were so successful that the home was able to be closed. In 1846 Caroline Chisholm and her husband, now retired, left for England. There she continued her immigration campaign, which led to the formation in 1848 of the Family Colonisation Loan Society, to assist the poor to emigrate as families. The society built a ship, the *Caroline Chisholm*, and in 1853 it brought 153 immigrants to Melbourne.

In 1851 Archibald Chisholm sailed for

Caroline Chisholm.

Australia to make preparations for a permanent home. Meanwhile Caroline was working hard to ensure improved passenger conditions. The *Passenger Act* of 1852 was passed, which provided for minimum standards of accommodation. *The Times* noted on 8 August 1853:

> Strange as it may sound, it was reserved for her to enforce on board emigrant ships the most ordinary rules of decency and propriety. It was Mrs Chisholm who broke down the demoralising and disgusting system by which all sexes and all ages were huddled into the same cabin, and compelled to sleep, dress, and undress, in the presence of each other.

In 1852 Caroline toured Germany, France and Italy. While in Rome she was presented a gold medal by the Pope and several other gifts. In 1854 she sailed with her younger children to Melbourne in the *Ballarat*. After touring the goldfields she proposed at meetings that shelters be set up along the routes to the diggings.

After she developed a kidney disease, the family moved to Kyneton, where Archibald Chisholm was appointed magistrate. Advised by her doctor to go to Sydney as her only chance of recovery, Caroline set out overland for Sydney in 1858. She was forced to write to her old friend, Fr Therry, for a loan of £20. Fr Therry answered immediately and a small

cottage in Albert Street, Redfern, was rented at a cheap rate. A school friend of the Chisholm children remembered that 'The family lived in a house on the east side of the old Toll Bar back from the road, and were in very poor circumstances'. About this time she received the news that her second eldest son had died suddenly in Melbourne. When J.K. Heydon, publisher of the *Freeman's Journal*, called around to write an obituary for William, he was greatly shocked to find Mrs Chisholm 'in deepest distress from poverty and sickness', as he wrote to Fr Therry, and asked him to visit. Caroline's health improved slowly and Heydon noted that she was able to supplement the family income by giving 'lessons in English, to China Men at 1s 6d per lesson'.

Caroline Chisholm came out of retirement to join in the land reform battle by giving a public lecture, on 10 December 1860, on 'Free Selection before Survey' at the Temperance Hall, Pitt Street. The *Sydney Morning Herald* reported the next day:

> She saw crowds of unemployed in Sydney and millions of acres lying idle ... She saw that the secret of the whole thing lay in the land and she perceived, with regret, that Dr Lang (of all the other ministers of religion) was the only man who was working to obtain that for the use and the support of the people (Cheers).

In 1861 Caroline gave a lecture to the Young Men's Society at St Benedict's Church. Archy, her eldest son, was the president. The hall in Abercrombie Street was full to overflowing. She spoke in a humorous vein to the young men desirous of obtaining the affections of young women, and more seriously against late trading hours as being harmful to employees and domestic servants. Financial hardship compelled her to open a girls' school at Newtown in 1862. It was later moved to Tempe. Her last years in Australia were spent in obscurity, as she had scorned material gain and fame. In 1866 the Chisholms returned to England. They lived in small lodgings in London

View over Brickfield Hill.

and were granted a pension of £100. Caroline Chisholm died of bronchitis on 25 March 1877, aged 68. She was commemorated until 1992 on the Australian five-dollar note, which honoured her and the Family Colonisation Loan Society. The inscription on her grave at Northampton calls her 'The Emigrants' Friend'.

GOVERNMENT

Sydney Town Hall

After its incorporation in 1842, the City Council had no suitable venue. First meetings were held in the Market House (Police Court) and later the Royal Hotel and the Pultney Hotel in York Street. The Sydney Town Hall was built on the site of the burial ground that had served the needs of the colony from 1788 until 1818, when the Devonshire Street cemetery was opened. The foundation stone of Sydney Town Hall was laid in 1868 by H.R.H. Alfred, the Duke of Edinburgh. In 1869 the City Engineer and Surveyor Edward Bell prepared a plan on the designs of J.H. Wilson, but it was Thomas Sapsford,

appointed city architect in 1879, who completed the plans. Construction was delayed when Alderman John McElhone discovered faults. The supervising architect resigned before he could be dismissed. The foundation stone of the main hall was re-laid by the Lady Mayoress, Mrs John Harris, in 1883. The Centennial Hall, as it was known, was not completed till 1895.

The coat of arms for the city of Sydney was granted on 30 July 1908. The shield contains the arms of Thomas Townshend, Viscount Sydney, who was principal under-secretary of state in 1788 (top left); then the naval or St George's flag plus the Globe and two stars in honour of Captain

Cook (top centre); the arms of the first Lord Mayor of Sydney, the Hon. Thomas Hughes, MLC (top right); and a three-masted sailing ship on a field of blue and gold, depicting a shipping port of the Golden South (bottom centre). The shield is flanked by two supporters, an Aborigine with a harpoon and a Colonial with a whaling lance. The helmet is mounted by an anchor with a star and crown. The motto reads: 'I take but I surrender'.

In 1973 the Lord Mayor of Sydney, Sir David Griffin, CBE, unveiled a ten-foot high foundation cairn for the 24-storey Town Hall House to supply the new council offices. The building was opened in 1977. The Town Hall itself has served as meeting place for civic, political, social and musical functions. The main hall boasts one of the largest pipe organs in the world. There are 8,756 pipes, some of them 135 centimetres in diameter. The organ, and the hall, were restored in 1992.

Sydney Town Hall.

Beginnings of the Labour Movement

Stonemasons working on two Sydney churches in 1855 were the first to win an eight-hour day. Not until 1871 was a confederation of organised labour formed, when a small group drawn from six unions formed the Trades and Labour Council of New South Wales. There had been activities by groups of workers before this, but it took time for permanent structures to arise. It was commonly held in the mid-nineteenth century that trade unions were a conspiracy in constraint of free trade, and that any restraint to free trade was illegal. By 1874, of the 41 unions in the colony, 25 were members of the Trades and Labour Council. A key figure was Francis Dixon, secretary of the Trades and Labour Council, who was influential in having all the unions seek the eight-hour day. Dixon also presided over the first Inter-Colonial Trades Union Congress in 1879, held in the Lecture Hall of the Mechanics School of Arts. Topics debated included: extension of consolidation of the

Eight-hour-day poster.

eight-hour system, legislation of trade unions, encouragement of native industries, education and workers' compensation. Discussion on the exclusion of the Chinese who had remained after the gold rush raised strong passions. Not long before the conference, the Seamen's Union of New South Wales had gone on strike over the introduction of Chinese seamen by the Australasian Steam Navigation Company.

The Labour Council was preoccupied as to how it could influence government. Its first secretary, Angus Cameron, won a seat for the electorate of West Sydney in 1874. Other members of the union movement also went into parliament. Eddie O'Sullivan, president of the Trades and Labour Council in 1883, was elected to the Legislative Assembly in 1885.

First Palace School

The imperial style of architecture reinforced the pride and new wealth of the colony. Signs of this architectural grandeur in downtown Sydney were the new Sydney Town Hall, the Prince Alfred Pavilion and, further down Chalmers Street, Cleveland Street Public School. This last-named expensive new building was constructed by G.A. Mansfield for 700 pupils. It was the first of the 'Palace' schools, as critics of the Council of Education dubbed them. Henry Parkes was president and W. Wilkins secretary of the council. Nearby, on the other side of the new railway line, was the Chippendale Wesleyan School. In 1870 it had over 200 pupils. Closer to the city, Christ Church Anglican School in Pitt Street had nearly 500 pupils.

Dixon Street Soup Kitchen

At a meeting in the office of one C.W. Weekes, on 5 July 1867, a decision was taken to open up a soup kitchen in a central part of the town. Premises were found and fitted out in Dixon Street, and service began on 22 July 1867. Four people presented tickets on the first day and more than 30,000 meals were given out during the year ending 1 July 1868. Mr Weekes was chairman, Mr A. Allen, secretary, and Mr H.B. Lee, treasurer, of this charity.

Kent Street Night Refuge

In May 1868 H.B. Lee was present at a meeting which took place at the Central Police station with the Mayor of Sydney, C. Moore, in the chair. Captain Scott proposed the setting up of a night refuge. The meeting was adjourned to 4 June to consider the desirability of amalgamating with the existing soup kitchen. Captain Scott was elected chairman, Mr W. Day secretary, Mr W.A. Cook treasurer and Mr H.B. Lee manager of the duly extended work. In 1868–69, the first year of operation, 65,000 meals were served and 12,000 separate nights of shelter were provided. In the second year of operation, 70,000 meals and 14,000 beds were provided.

INDUSTRY AND TRANSPORT

City Abattoirs

The paddocks and saleyards around the Carters' Barracks region made the nearby location of abattoirs a practical necessity. Sutton Forest Butchery had premises in George Street on the corner of Valentine Street. The company T.A. Field Pty Ltd is still in the wholesale meat trade from fine old buildings in Thomas Street. T.S. Mort invested a small fortune in experimenting with freezing works so that frozen meat could be exported to Europe. The steamer *Strathleven* left Darling Harbour to test out Mort's frozen meat—some 70 bullocks and 500 sheep and two tons of butter—in a voyage through the tropics, the Red Sea and the

Suez Canal. On 26 March 1880 the London *Times* reported that the produce was in excellent condition, of superior quality and low in production cost. The foundation of an export industry was secure. The abattoirs were located at Glebe Island until they were moved to Homebush in 1916.

Railway Gets up Steam

When Sydney's railway was opened in the Cleveland Paddocks on 26 September 1855, it was honoured in a unique way, with the minting of the only Australian coin to commemorate a local event. As well, a piece of commemorative music was also composed by the Dutchman, William Henry Paling, who had arrived in Sydney two years earlier. The son of a piano-maker and a professional musician, Paling taught violin and piano, sold musical instruments and sheet music, gave concerts, conducted orchestras and composed the 'Sydney Railway Waltz'.

The first railway line in New South Wales included two terminal stations, four intermediate stations, a tunnel at Redfern, a viaduct at Long Cove Creek, 27 bridges and 50 culverts.

> Four locomotives were purchased from Robert Stephenson & Co., Newcastle on Tyne, and landed in Sydney at cost of £12,301.15s. Carriages were built by Wright & Co., Birmingham. There were eight first class, twelve second class and twelve third class with two carriage trucks and a horsebox at a total cost of £11,809.11.6d.[2]

Fares were 4*s*. first class, 3*s*. second class and 2*s*. third class. The trains carried 4,000 passengers on the opening day. Train driver William Sixsmith was suitably dressed for the occasion in frock coat and a top hat which must have rivalled the long smokestack of his 33-ton locomotive which had to pull 11 carriages of enthusiasts. A 19-gun salute was fired as Governor Sir William Denison and his family arrived for the grand opening which had been declared a public holiday.

As the train pulled out of the station, cannons manned by volunteer artillerymen boomed out an even longer salute—21 guns. The 14-mile journey to Parramatta took 40 minutes, which compares favourably with today, though it was without stops at the intermediate stations of Newtown, Ashfield, Burwood and Homebush.

Management was hesitant and railway-building was slow. But things changed when a tough and experienced engineer from Yorkshire, John Whitton, was put in charge. Before long he clashed with the governor who declared building a line over the Blue Mountains was impossible and that horse tramways ought to be built along existing roads. A select committee actually recommended horse-drawn tramways for the outback. Whitton worked and planned and stuck to his task. Goulburn was reached by rail in 1869. In 1870 the first locally built locomotive, No. 10, steamed out of the Railway Workshops. The line west from Parramatta across the Blue Mountains posed some problems but was completed in 1876. The gold-rush days had subsided by then, but the diggers who stayed on as farmers were grateful for the rail transport link back to the seaboard port. The southern line reached Albury in 1881. That same year, workers' trains, the ones used by the young Henry Lawson, were introduced into the suburban area of Sydney. In 1882 electricity, generated in a railway power station near Regent Street, was used to light up the terminal station. Work on the construction of the Hawkesbury River Bridge on the northern line was begun in December 1886 and completed in May 1889. There were seven spans on the bridge and the piers had been sunk up to 49.3 metres below the high-water mark. John Whitton was feeling a bit weary by now. After all, when he arrived in 1856 there were only 23 miles of track, 4 locomotives, 12 carriages and 40 goods trucks; when he retired, aged 70, in 1890, there were 2,182 miles of track, 439 locomotives, 1,277 carriages and 9,304 goods trucks.

Steam tram, Powerhouse Museum.

Sydney Gets Trams

Sydney's trams have had a chequered career. The first trams were horse-drawn and ran on rails in Pitt Street. The service linked Redfern Terminal Station with Circular Quay, but it met with fierce competition and opposition from the horse cabs and retailers along the route who claimed that the rails were dangerous. The rails, which had been laid above the road surface, were soon removed. The next experiment was with steam trams that came into service to connect the Terminal Station with the newly built Garden Palace near the Domain. The service actually began with horse power, as the steam engines were late in arriving from America. Double-decker carriages were introduced to service the route which ran along Elizabeth Street. The double-deckers did not last very long, but other tramway routes were opened. The steam trams were housed in the Ultimo Tram Powerhouse. Built to generate electricity for the electrification of the tram system, it is now the site of the Powerhouse Museum.

The Sydney tramway network grew into one of the largest in the world. Cable trams were used on steep inclines. One of the many tram depots was situated at Bennelong Point. When the trams were finally phased out in 1962, a magnificent venue became available for the projected Sydney Opera House. Central Sydney's unsuitability for trams was a legacy of the Rum Corps' ignoring the town planning that had been set out at the first settlement of the colony.

Will the trams ever come back? In the early 1970s the Liberal Minister for Transport, Milton Morris, was ridiculed when he produced plans for a tram loop via Pitt and Castlereagh Streets to connect Circular Quay with Central Railway Station. In the early '80s Dr John Gerofi proposed a tram network running along disused city tunnels under Hyde Park, via the Entertainment Centre, to Balmain along the Darling Harbour goods line. A further branch line was proposed for the Sydney Cricket Ground, the University of New South Wales and out to La Perouse along the median strip from Kingsford. The Baulkham Hills, Prospect and Green Valley regions are more favoured to secure light rail transport, with a new generation of sleek high-speed trams. All this is a far cry from the sad ending of Isaac Nathan, father of music in Australia, who established choirs at St James', St Mary's Cathedral and in his own synagogue. On 15 January 1864 he fell under the wheels of a horse-drawn tram at the corner of Pitt and Goulburn Streets.

In the meantime, tram lovers will have to console themselves by visiting the Powerhouse Museum where a restored cable tram is displayed as a prize exhibit.

Gas Lighting

A gas lamp had been used in a Pitt Street shop as early as 1826. But Sydney and Australia were first lit by gas on 24 May 1841, Queen Victoria's twenty-second birthday, when 200 premises were supplied gas free of charge as a goodwill gesture by the Australian Gas Light Company. A gas-filled balloon 15 feet high was launched from a happier kind of scaffold on Church Hill. The Australian Gas Light Company was established in 1836 and its 1841 lighting project covered the central spine of George Street from the wharves to the cattle markets and Toll House. The gas works were initially located in the western Rocks area. A handsome sandstone office building and gas facilities were opened by the AGL in Pitt Street South in 1869.

Mortuary Station and Sydney Terminal Station

The necropolis receiving station in Regent Street was designed by the colonial architect James Barnet. The building is a fine sandstone structure, Gothic in style, with stone carvings of leaves, angels and stars. The station was a rare example of a successful marriage of State and Church functions. From 1869 until 1948 trains travelled from there to the Rookwood Cemetery station, which had been in use from at least 1865. Funeral trains also ran from Regent Street to Woronora cemetery until 1947. The beginning of the end for funeral trains came in 1938, when motor hearses were introduced. The Rookwood Cemetery station was bought by the Anglican Church and reconstructed at Ainslie in Canberra.

A magnificent oil painting of the Australian impressionist Arthur Streeton depicts the Sydney Terminal Station in 1893. The romance of horse-drawn carriages and steam trains on a rainy day is well captured on canvas. But the station was overcrowded and a larger station was planned a short distance closer to the city.

The Mortuary Station.

This entailed land resumptions. On the night of 4-5 August 1906 new tracks were laid and in the morning the Western Mail steamed into new Central Station for the first time. The prominent Clock Tower was not completed until 1921. The first stages of the City Loop, the Museum and St James' stations, were opened in 1926. Wynyard was opened in 1932. When Circular Quay station was completed in 1956 the loop became a reality. The Eastern Suburbs Railway was first proposed in 1915 by the great engineer and builder of the Harbour Bridge, Dr John C. Bradfield, but it was not completed until 1979. I celebrated my thirty-eighth birthday on the day the Eastern Suburbs Railway was opened, 23 June, with a free ride from Town Hall to Bondi Junction and return. All seven stations of this line are underground, including the platforms at Redfern and Central.

Sydney Hospital Dispensary

The spread of Sydney westwards, plus the increasing importance of the new Terminal Station, led to the establishment of an outpatients' clinic of Sydney

The old dispensary, Regent Street.

Hospital at Regent Street. This site was opposite the station, much more accessible than Macquarie Street, and by 1911:

> The attendance at the outpatient department had progressively increased and to relieve the congestion at the Hospital, and for the convenience of the patients, who in many cases had to travel long distances from the western suburbs, a branch dispensary was opened in 1871

at Regent Street. This was carried out in rented premises and was the first time that any of the Infirmary administration was removed from the Infirmary buildings.[3]

The clinic, located on the northern corner of Regent and Lee Streets, was named John Storey Memorial Dispensary. The building is single-storey, of Gothic-styled sandstone.

RELIGION

St Andrew's Cathedral

In the early days of the colony a feeble recluse called Tom Dick grazed his cows on the future site of St Andrew's Cathedral. When poor Tom's murdered corpse was fished out of Darling Harbour near Bathurst Street, no-one claimed either his body or his land, so the former went into a pauper's grave and the latter reverted to the government. The original foundation stone of a church on the site was laid by Governor Macquarie on 1 September 1819 and relaid in its present position by Governor Bourke on 16 May

1837. Bishop Barker blessed the cathedral at its completion in 1868.

The original cathedral site stretched westward from what is now the middle of George Street to Kent Street, and was bounded on the south by Bathurst Street and on the north, including the burial ground, by Druitt Street. During Governor Bourke's term, the lands west of the cathedral spires were given as leases. A Baptist church and a Scots church were later erected on these leases. In 1858 an act of parliament led to the burial ground being set aside for the intended Town Hall, built by 1888 and known as the

Centennial Hall. In 1924 the City Council wished to reserve the entire site bounded by George, Bathurst, Kent and Druitt Streets. The old St Phillip's site in Grosvenor Street was unofficially suggested, plus compensation of £400,000 to the Anglican Church. The Lang Government renewed the offer two years later, along with £500,000 compensation. The Anglican Synod debated the issue and the final voting on a number of possible sites was as follows: Mint and District Court site 215, St Phillip's site 31, Supreme Court site 15, Victoria Barracks site 2, informal 5. State Cabinet approved of the Mint site but the incoming Bavin Government cancelled the agreement. Finally in 1935, the Stevens government returned the Kent Street frontage in return for resumptions of George Street for street-widening. This was by no means the end of the matter, as from 1932 to 1972 there were no fewer than 12 cathedral site development proposals.

St Benedict's Bells

Not long after his arrival in Sydney, Bishop Polding obtained permission from the Colonial Secretary for a new church at the corner of Parramatta Road and Botany Bay Road and for a school at Abercrombie Place. Had this option been taken a Catholic Church would have stood in what was to become Railway Square. It was decided by Polding and his trustees to build the church on the Abercrombie site.

On a visit to England, Polding was impressed with the architectural work of A.W. Pugin, a Catholic convert who made considerable contributions to the Gothic revival in English architecture. Polding returned with a Pugin design for the new church of Saint Benedict in 1850. In 1860, five years after the laying of the foundation stone, the church was fitted with six bells, the first set in any Christian church on mainland Australia. Polding was assisted at the ceremonies by Austin Sheehy as deacon and John Felix Sheridan as sub-deacon. In 1862 Fr Therry preached the sermon at the consecration of St Benedict's, making it the first Catholic church in Australia to be consecrated, even before St Mary's Cathedral.

Father Corish, one of the early great pastors of St Benedict's, when he was expecting Archbishop Polding's return from the country, would send boys on to the roof of the church. It was their job to keep an eye on University Hill and let Father Corish know when they saw the cloud of dust from the Archbishop's

St Andrew's Cathedral.

St Benedict's

entourage. About the year 1854, Father Corish got the news and began to ring the bells himself although not an accomplished bell ringer. As Polding passed by St Benedict's one of the ropes snaked around Father Corish, lifting him high, dashed him down, and he was laid up for over four months with leg injuries. This is the same Father Corish who threatened the boys with punishment if they wagged school to attend the public executions in Sydney.[4]

Sisters in the Haymarket

The Sisters of Charity had been invited to come from Dublin and arrived in the colony in 1838. They had a remarkable effect on the female prison at Parramatta. As well, they established St Vincent's Hospital at Darlinghurst. At a time when there was some controversy about the administration of St Vincent's, Fr Farrelly encouraged Sister de Lacy to set up 'a House of Refuge for fallen women'. Accordingly, a house was taken for this purpose in Campbell Street in 1846. A charitable lady, Mrs Blake, devoted her means and services to this work until the end of her life.[5] Soon this residence, known as the House of the Good Shepherd, was in need of more room.

Sister de Lacy asked the government for the use of the Carters' Barracks (old Treadmill) in Pitt Street. Permission was granted in 1848, alterations were made and the non-denominational Sydney Female Refuge took in its first residents. Social conditions of the time were appalling. The Parliamentary Committee Report on Poverty in 1859 found that one-third of the prostitutes in Sydney were young children and that there were 2,000 neglected children in the city who lived as they could. About this time, an old man, James Moore, was charged with maintaining eight brothels in Goulburn Street. These properties were found to be owned by the Hon. Edward Hunt, MLC. Moore was sentenced to 12 months imprisonment, but Hunt was not brought to trial.

A convent was built for the sisters working at the new women's refuge. Sr Scholastica Gibbons became the superior of the convent located at Pitt Street South. She formed the nucleus of a group of ladies who, at Dr Polding's bidding, adopted the Benedictine Rule and became the Sisters of the Good Samaritan. At this time the Sisters of Charity were completely caught up with the foundation of St Vincent's Hospital at a manor house called Tarmons at Potts Point. The hospital was later re-established at Darlinghurst on its present site. The Sisters did not have enough religious to spare for the women's refuge.

Furthermore, difficulties had arisen between Dr Polding and some of the sisters. The incident that triggered the conflict was the removal of some Protestant Bibles from patients at the new hospital by the local curate, Fr Kenyon. A bitter conflict eventuated, involving Dr Polding, the Protestant surgeon Dr Robertson, the leading Catholic layman J.H. Plunkett, and Sr de Lacy, who was in charge of both the hospital and the religious community. The matter was resolved when Sr de Lacy stormily and voluntarily returned to Ireland. Polding had paid for her training in Ireland specifically for his Australian mission. A postulant sister left the convent and became a Protestant. The incident is highlighted by the historian T.L. Suttor to illustrate his thesis of the clash between legitimate ecclesiastical authority and the new 'radical religious liberalism'. A fuller reading of Suttor's thesis reveals three visions struggling for supremacy in mid-nineteenth century Catholic Sydney: Polding's vision of an apostolic community, W.A. Duncan's liberal utopia, and Archdeacon McEncroe's 'Irish way'.

Marist Fathers

In 1868 the parish priest of Church Hill, Archdeacon McEncroe, on his deathbed pleaded with Dr Polding that the Marist

Fathers be given charge of St Patrick's Church. This gave the Marist Fathers a central site in Sydney, where they had established a supply base for their Pacific missions. The first Marists visited Sydney with Bishop Pompallier on 9 December 1837. Fr Colin, superior general of the Marists, did not establish a foundation in Sydney until 1844 when Fathers Debreul and Rocher were appointed. These two priests bore the brunt of a financial dispute between Father Colin and Bishop Pompallier. Rome intervened by restricting Pompallier's jurisdiction to New Zealand. Polding would certainly have sympathised with Pompallier. In 1845 Debreul wrote to Fr Colin: 'Mgr Polding is afraid of our influence in Sydney, he does not want two communities'. However, the Marists did become the second religious community of priests when they were given permission to purchase a property at Hunters Hill.

Catholic Schools in 1867

The inner region of Sydney had 3,312 Catholic students in Catholic schools in 1867. Nearly half that number were in the Downtown Catholic schools.

School	Total enrolment	Non-Catholics
Church Hill, St Patrick's	420	
Haymarket, St Francis'	196	
Kent Street North	250	18
Kent Street South	246	
Parramatta Street, St		
Benedict's	560	3
Pitt Street	434	5
St Mary's	637	
Surry Hills, Sacred Heart	345	
Waterloo, Mount Carmel	224	7
	3,312	33

The entries in italics are specifically within the downtown catchment area.

The first Catholic secondary school was opened in Sydney at Lyndhurst in 1853.

Origins of the Catholic Press

The best introduction to the role of the Christian press may well come from a Presbyterian minister of the 1840s, John McGarvie, who stated:

> Times are widely different from the Last Century. Then the Church and pulpit were the vehicles of knowledge, now it is the daily Press. Men are less evangelic for Religion. They hear a Sermon, but read Six newspapers weekly, the Bible never. The voice of the people was echoed by the Minister, now the Editor is the organ of politics and liberty!

In 1850 the *Freeman's Journal* appeared for the first time. It was not the official Catholic paper of the archdiocese, but many leading Catholics were concerned with its production. The paper's founder was Archdeacon John McEncroe and it was printed in the gallery of old St Mary's Seminary. The printer and publisher was Jeremiah Moore, later to become a well-known Sydney bookseller. Other editors included William Bede Dalley, Daniel H. Deniehy, J.D. Delaney, Richard O'Sullivan, Edward Butler and Eddie O'Sullivan, the builder of Central Railway Station. The first Catholic paper in New South Wales was the *Australasian Chronicle*, founded and edited by William Augustine Duncan and published from 1839 to 1848. Archbishop Vaughan founded a journal, *The Express*, but it folded after some clashes with the *Freeman's Journal*. Vaughan had sought to set up a smart weekly with a Catholic flavour. He had the men in mind for the job: J. Haynes, J.F. Archibald and William McLeod, who were all Catholics. The Catholic magazine did not eventuate, but Haynes and Archibald co-founded *The Bulletin* in 1880; in 1886 McLeod became a joint owner and was business manager for 40 years.

The *Catholic Press* was founded in June 1895, when the Sydney clergy met to purchase Fr Joseph Bunbury's paper, the *Irish–Australian*. The *Catholic Press* was produced first at Lincoln's Inn, Elizabeth and Hunter Streets, then in 1896 at 336–38 Kent Street, and in 1899 at 26 Market Street. Tighe Ryan was 27 in 1897, when he began to edit the *Press*. He sympathised with the Boers and opposed conscription in World War I. The *Catholic Press* moved into a four-storey building on the corner of Campbell and Commonwealth Streets, Surry Hills, in 1930. The *Catholic Weekly* began its publishing life at the same address, appearing for the first time in 1942 after a merger between the *Catholic Press* and the *Freeman's Journal*. Responsibility for negotiating the merger was delegated to Monsignor James Meaney, who founded both Radio Station 2SM and St Michael's Golf Club. Mgr Meaney also organised the 1928 International Eucharistic Congress in Sydney. James M. Kelleher published the first issue of the *Catholic Weekly* on 5 March 1942, just after the Japanese forces had occupied Rabaul and were pushing south to Australia. Kelleher, with Fr James Murtagh of the Melbourne *Advocate*, co-founded the Catholic Press Association. He also founded the Catholic Journalists Guild. Brian Doyle, associate editor, was later to become manging editor of the Brisbane *Catholic Leader*.

Dean John Felix Sheridan

Dean Sheridan was the first Catholic parish priest of the Haymarket, 1867–88. This marked a significant shift from the Benedictine monasticism of Archbishop Polding to more urgent pastoral needs. Dr Polding selected St Francis de Sales, the gentle bishop who is the patron saint of journalists and best known for his spiritual treatise, *Introduction to the Devout Life*, to grace the name of the new church in the turbulent Haymarket. He blessed and opened the church on the site of the former town pound for lost animals. The pound site has seen some transformations, from the Belmore or Paddy's Markets, to the Tivoli Theatre, and currently the Department of Youth and Community Services building. Before coming to the Haymarket, Sheridan had served as rector of the short-lived Lyndhurst College above Blackwattle Bay. He was a great organiser and fund-raiser, with his violin if need be, a benefactor of the Good Samaritan Sisters at Pitt Street South. He was Vicar-General of the archdiocese when Archbishop Vaughan was overseas and was caretaker until the arrival of Cardinal Moran. He assisted the Sisters of St Joseph and lived his last days in retirement in a small cottage in Mount Street, North Sydney. He was buried at Kincumber beside the parish church near the site of the orphanage the sisters established there.

Belmore Markets.

Vaughan Fosters Alternatives to the State

Polding's successor, Archbishop Vaughan, clearly and precisely opted for the preservation and extension of the sacred via a Catholic education and welfare system. 'Earth worship' was the enemy. Archbishop Vaughan was a powerful preacher and in reply to his welcome by the clergy in 1873 he set out his priorities as the divine presence and religious education:

> There are two instruments, it seems to me, we have in our hands by means of which we may attack what I would call earth worship, and overthrow it. In the first place we have that which is a continual protest against earth worship, and that is the commencement of this magnificent Cathedral which is being built now, and which will for generations stand ... and proclaim ... that the Catholics ... manifest their true love to Him from whom all strength proceeds ... Within these walls we shall worship and praise Him ... And there is a second instrument, which seems to me to be that of Christian education.

In 1874 Archbishop Vaughan encouraged the Marist Brothers to rapidly expand their educational work. Disagreeing with the leading Catholic laity he consulted, who claimed there was not much poverty and such as existed was taken care of by the state, he wanted the St Vincent de Paul Society to come to Sydney and begin their work, which they did in 1881.

PERSONS AND EVENTS

Downtown Dairy

As a young girl Frances Lepherd had a milk delivery run from her parents' dairy at 203 Goulburn Street. The house stood in the midst of the Riley estate which comprised much of Woolloomooloo and Surry Hills. By the 1870s the estate was being subdivided and cut up into small building allotments. Investors saw the district as a boom area, and statistics bear this out: only 20 per cent of Surry Hills housing was owner-occupied in the period 1851–82, according to the Cook Ward and Fitzroy Ward rate Assessment Books held in the Sydney Council Archives.

Frances Lepherd wrote down her own experiences, disguised as fiction, in her *A Surry Hills Childhood, 1870*. She describes herself as eager to deliver wholesome milk to sick people and to babies. Surry Hills itself was not able to supply milk. The supply came from Woolloomooloo and Strawberry Hills. A report of the Sewerage and Health Board of 1876 lists 14 dairies, all in Woolloomooloo and Darlinghurst, as having a total of 93 cows in adjoining paddocks, and an average of six cows per dairy. The actual milk run described by Frances went from the Surry Hills reservoir to the Terry Hughes paddock, Prince Alfred Park, Redfern, Chippendale, Darlington, University Paddock, Arundle Terrace, Forest Lodge and George Street West. There were still plenty of paddocks and the young girl knew the short cuts. The difficulty does arise, however, as to how a girl of eight could carry sufficient milk for these deliveries. Perhaps milk was not drunk in large quantities and perhaps it was carried on a shoulder pole, as in England. A cart would not be suitable for crossing the paddocks. At any rate, Frances rose in the dark at 5.30 a.m. to begin her deliveries by 6.00 a.m. and then struggled to get to school on time. There was no street lighting at the time. The *Sydney Morning Herald* of September 1873 mentions the larrikins who frequented

Surry Hills. The Lepherd family moved shortly afterwards to another dairy at Paddington. But Frances Purcell, née Lepherd, has recorded an enduring tale of the rigours and hazards of her immigrant Welsh family over a hundred years ago.

Francis Dixon: Trade Unionist

Francis Dixon followed the same craft as his Yorkshire stonemason father. He was 32 when he arrived in Sydney in 1864 with his wife and two children, after five years in Victoria. From his experience within the Eight Hour System Extension League he proposed that a more suitable organisation, a Trades Council, be set up. By 1871 the New South Wales Trades and Labour Council had been established. After industrial action had failed to secure the desired eight-hour working day, Dixon advocated political action in the form of direct labour representation in parliament. This motion of 1874 had to wait until the action of P.J. Brennan led to the foundation of the Labor Party in 1889-91. Dixon was the chief organiser of Angus Cameron's election as the working man's candidate for West Sydney in 1875.

Dixon lived in Surry Hills where he and his wife Elizabeth raised their seven children. He guided and shaped the growth of the young union movement, preserved its identity, repulsed takeover attempts and brought an humane style to problems between workers and employers. In 1879 he chaired the first Intercolonial Trade Union Congress. One of the most central figures in the trade union movement of the nineteenth century, he died destitute in 1884, of lung disease.

Thomas Sutcliffe Mort

A young man of 22 when he arrived in Sydney in 1838, Thomas Sutcliffe Mort became a successful wool merchant, built a dock at Balmain, and was a pioneer of

Statue of T.S. Mort.

the frozen meat export trade at his Darling Harbour plant. This was located in Harbour Street and known as the N.S.W. Fresh Food & Ice Co. Ltd. Mort had earlier financed Eugene Nicolle and Augustus Morris in new ice-making processes in a shed in Dixon Street. Morris had been bankrupted and ridiculed in Victoria for his 'fanatical belief in the making of artificial cold'. Sadly, Mort died in 1878, just before his experiments were vindicated. A great benefactor of the Church of England, especially Christ Church at Railway Square, he was also the chairman of the meeting which set up the New South Wales Academy of Art in April 1871. This was the forerunner to the Sydney Art Gallery, which was finally established as the National Art Gallery of New South Wales. A public subscription was raised to enable a statue to be erected to his memory. The sculpture by Pierce Connelly, which was unveiled in Macquarie Place in 1883, is the only one in Sydney to honour a non-official man of business.

ENTERTAINMENT

Strange Animals in Town

When television personalities Bert Newton and Mike Walsh rode into the Sydney Entertainment Centre astride two pink elephants on opening night, it was not altogether something new for the Haymarket. One hundred years ago whichever circus was in town would pitch its big top on the site now occupied by the Capitol Theatre. The elephants would be off-loaded at the Darling Harbour wharves and parade in a line, trunk to tail, along Sussex Street to the circus site. When the film *Phar Lap* had its world premiere at the Hoyts Cinema Centre, the showbiz personalities had their thunder stolen by the 16 mounted police troopers and the equine star, Towering Inferno. However, only a few hundred metres away in Hyde Park the sport of kings and fools first saw the light of day in the colony. The first official horserace was held around the perimeter of the park. The nearby Australian Museum housed a tigress and several other animals in Hyde Park, and these living exhibits attracted more viewers than the exhibits inside. Other exotic beasts were housed in private zoos at Botany and Watsons Bay.

Sydney's first formal zoo was on the heights of Surry Hills in Moore Park. The animal pits may still be seen within the grounds of Sydney Girls' High School. On the Anzac Parade perimeter are two grotto-like bear pits. They are connected by an hibernation tunnel. The northern bear pit is adjacent Sydney Boys' High School and the southern pit stands in the grounds of Sydney Girls' High School.

The New South Wales Zoological Society was formed at a public meeting in 1879. The stated aim was the introduction and acclimatisation of song birds, game and other objectives. The annual subscription was one guinea. Two years later the City Council granted the society that area of Moore Park known as Billy Goat Swamp. The initial area was seven

acres, subsequently increased to 15 acres. An early president of the society, Walter Bradley, transferred all his family pets and birds from his Randwick home to the new zoo. He also imported skylarks, thrushes and blackbirds. An elephant came from the Calcutta zoo in 1883 and in 1888 Quong Tart donated a pair of Indian buffaloes.

If any one name deserves to be remembered with regard to zoos in Australia, it is the unusual name of Le Souef. The name is Huguenot in origin, but Albert Le Souef was born in Kent and educated at the Moravian Mission School in Neuwied, Germany, and also as a teenager on an Aboriginal protectorate station on the Goulburn River. He learned bushcraft from the Aborigines there. In 1870 he became secretary, and from 1882-1902, director of the Melbourne Zoological Gardens at Royal Park at £300 per year. Le Souef's son, Ernest, became a director of the Perth zoo and another son, Albert Sherbourne Le Souef (1877-1951), was director of the zoo both at Moore Park and Taronga Park as well as being president of the Royal Zoological Society of New South Wales.

On his arrival in Sydney in 1903 to take up management of the zoo, A.S. Le Souef found the gardens small, dusty and noisy. In 1907 he and Dr R.H. Todd were commissioned to inspect European zoos. They visited, amongst others, Hagenbeck's Tierpark in Hamburg and returned home determined to fight for a modern, more free-range zoo. Le Souef asked Colonel Vernon, the surveyor-general, if it was possible to have the military reserve on the north side of the harbour set aside for a zoo. Mosman property owners were antagonistic, and so was a majority of members of the Zoological Society itself. Wentworth Park and Maroubra were next considered. Wentworth Park was actually purchased as the new zoo site, but Le Souef fought against the proposal. At the society's elections a new council more favourable to Le Souef was voted in. Objections from Mosman Council concerning noise and safety were slowly overcome and by mid-1916 the new Taronga (Sea View) Park was ready to receive its new guests. Le Souef was in charge of Taronga until 1940.

Circus in Town

The names of Ashton, Wirth, FitzGerald, Bullen, Gill, Sole, Perry, and Silver conjure up the smell of sawdust and the excitement of the circus. Before the advent of television and lion parks, the circus was the most spectacular public entertainment. The equestrian James Henry Ashton, 1819–99, was one of the earliest performers, along with John Jones (pseudonym St Leon; 1825–1903). A central location in the city for convenient public access to a visiting circus was important and various venues were used—Belmore Park, Prince Alfred Park and Moore Park amongst them.

FitzGerald's circus can be seen in Arthur Streeton's 1883 painting of the old Sydney Terminal Station. It stood on the grounds formerly occupied by the Benevolent Asylum. One of the most distinguished guests to FitzGerald's Pitt Street Circus was the Archduke Franz Ferdinand during his 1893 visit. The most enduring site, though, was the Haymarket Reserve between Hay and Campbell Streets. The giant American Cooper & Bailey Circus performed at the Haymarket during its 1876–77 Australian tour. This circus later became part of the Ringling, Barnum & Bailey Circus, popularly known as 'The Greatest Show on Earth', which toured the U.S.A. by special train.

The Wirth Brothers built up in Australia a spectacularly large combination which also toured in special circus trains. Joachim and Johannes Wirth were band musicians who came from Bavaria at the time of the gold rush. One story from their pre-circus days was

that the whole Wirth clan was held up at Goonoo Gap near Tamworth by the bushranger Thunderbolt, who seized all the cash—about £20. The Wirths asked if they might perform for him. The bushranger agreed and after the show said that if things went well he would return their money. The Wirths were disbelieving but Thunderbolt is said to have kept his word.

Starting out in the circus world with Ashtons, the Wirths launched out on their own and prospered. They built a permanent structure on the Haymarket Reserve, called the Hippodrome. May Wirth, a child adopted into the family, could at the age of eight turn somersaults whilst driving a team of horses bareback around the ring. She was later acclaimed as one of the great international circus performers. Circuses were expensive to keep on the road, and the Wirths paid over a £1,000,000 to the Australian railways over the years. Costs would increase, but could not be passed on to the public. Perhaps the major setback was the terrible fire that destroyed Wirths Circus at the Olympia site in Melbourne.

In 1963 Wirths Circus closed and in 1968 Bullens followed suit. But Michael Edgley has since brought out the Great Moscow Circus several times. In Sydney it has performed at Wentworth Park and the Entertainment Centre.

The Gregorys and the First Test Match

Hyde Park was not only the first racetrack in Australia, but also the first cricket ground. David William Gregory, victorious captain of Australia for the first Test match against England, played at the Melbourne Cricket Ground in 1877, received his education at St James Model School, Hyde Park. His brother Edward James Gregory was also in the side. Their father, Edward William Gregory, arrived in Sydney in 1814 on the *Broxbornebury* with his parents and two brothers. However, the mother died and the father returned to England, so the three brothers were brought up in the Male Orphan Institute.[6] Remarkably, five of Edward William Gregory's eight sons played cricket for New South Wales, and 20 of his descendants represented the state in cricket and other sports. In 1878 Edward James Gregory retired from international cricket and became curator of the Sydney Cricket Ground, which was laid out under his supervision. He lived with his family in a cottage at Moore Park, alongside the ground. In 1879 David Gregory questioned an umpire brought by Lord Harris and his Englishmen in a match against a New South Wales XI. Play had to be abandoned when the partisan crowd occupied the pitch. The next day the *Sydney Morning Herald* claimed that two of the English players had provoked the demonstrators by calling spectators 'sons of the convicts'. In fact the cricket riot received more coverage in the newspapers than did the Ned Kelly gang hold-up of Jerilderie on the same day.[7]

Charles Bannerman was Australia's hero in the first Test. This Sydneysider, born in Kent, faced the first ball bowled (round arm), scored the first run, was the first to retire hurt, but not before he had made the first century (165 runs). Banjo Paterson said of Bannerman, 'There should be a statue to him on every cricket ground in Australia'.[8] But being a celebrity did Bannerman no good. He had disappeared from international cricket by the age of 30, and gambling and drinking were suggested as his downfall.[9] The New South Wales Cricket Association gave him a benefit match in 1922, which raised £490. This was the first game of cricket broadcast on radio in Australia. Charles Bannerman died in 1930 in Surry Hills, aged 80.

CRIME

The Sussex Street Butcher

One day in 1866, responding to a request for help from a stranger, young Edgar Weekes found himself before a narrow house at 403 Sussex Street, three houses up from the Hay Street corner. Inside was a large iron box, very heavy and with a very unpleasant smell. The two struggled along Sussex Street but the box was so heavy that at Goulburn Street another young man was hired to help. By Bathurst Street they gave up and were paid by the man for their service. There things might have remained had not young Jamie Kilpatrick been out with his dog, who began to scratch a pile of rubbish in a vacant block behind the nearby Sir Walter Scott Inn. The boy raced home to tell his father about the human skull he had seen. Mr Kilpatrick hurried up Druitt Street to Central Police Station. The police began a search of the hostelry and in the cesspit were found an arm and leg, which were washed and sent to the mortuary at the Benevolent Society in Pitt Street South. There Dr Renshaw reported that these and other remains were those of a woman who had been struck on the head and that, despite charring by fire, it was clear that the corpse had been dissected professionally, either by a surgeon or a butcher. A torn piece of cloth was identified as a woman's chemise. A few weeks later a journeyman butcher, William Henry Scott, was brought in from Paddington to Central Police Station for questioning. Scott was identified by the two youths who had helped him and charged with the murder of his wife, Annie Scott, née Ramsden. The trial was before Mr Justice Cheeke. Not even the eloquence of William Bede Dalley could save the accused, although he maintained his innnocence, even on the gallows.[10]

MAP 4
1880 – 1913

1 CENTRAL RAILWAY STATION
2 CHRIST CHURCH ST LAURENCE
3 GERMAN CONCORDIA CLUB
  (254 ELIZABETH ST)
4 GRAND NATATORIUM HOTEL & BATHS
5 HORDERN'S HAYMARKET EMPORIUM
6 LUTHERAN CHURCH – GOULBURN ST
7 MARK FOYS:THE PIAZZA EMPORIUM
8 MARKET TOWER
9 SALVATION ARMY TEMPLE –
  GOULBURN ST
10 ST ANDREW'S CATHEDRAL SCHOOL
11 SYDNEY TRADES HALL
12 YMCA BUILDING

4 The Great Years of Downtown (1880–1913)

POPULATION

The New Goldfields

Chinatown is a prominent part of downtown Sydney, but it was not always so. The first Chinese to come to Australia were on their way to the goldfields. Many of them came from the 13 counties around Canton. They referred to the Australian goldfields as the 'Tsin Chin Shan', meaning the new goldfields. 'Chiu Chin Shan', or the old goldfields, were California. Members of the same county had their own form of community life and would not shop or trade, in the early part of the twentieth century, with Chinese from other counties. According to C.F. Young:

> By 1901, most Chinese communities on the goldfields had disintegrated, but the Sydney and Melbourne Chinese continued to thrive mainly in tight communities known as Chinatown—in buildings which served both for living and business activities. In Melbourne and its suburbs, the Chinese population numbered 2,200 out of the 7,349 in the state, with a Chinatown centred in Little Bourke Street and its precincts. By contrast, Sydney and suburbs absorbed some 3,800 Chinese out of the 11,263 in the whole state; its Chinatown was located in an area bounded by Campbell, Goulburn and Wexford Streets. In these Chinatowns there were import and export firms, fruit shops, cabinet-making factories, laundry shops, grocery and greengrocery stores, eating houses, county association premises and club headquarters, as well as opium and gambling dens catering chiefly for the Chinese population.[1]

The Chinese had a hard time on the goldfields. The riots against them on the Buffalo River and at Lambing Flat (Young) were only the violent flashpoints of more widespread racial tension. The ill-feeling towards them lingered on and gave impetus to the development of the trade union movement and, later, to the formation of the White Australia Policy.

In Sydney, the Chinese Merchants' Defence Association came into being in 1904 as a response to the Anti-Chinese and Anti-Asiatic League of the Commonwealth which was formed by trade unions, traders and the New South Wales Labour Council. This organisation continued to defend the interests of the New South Wales Chinese merchants until the birth of the New South Wales Chinese Chamber of Commerce in 1913.[2]

An exciting venture for the Chinese in Australia and the South Pacific was the formation of the China–Australia Mail Steamship Line. After five meetings, evidently held in the headquarters of the New South Wales Chinese Chamber of Commerce at 52 Dixon Street, the line was established in November 1917.[3]

For offices a three-storey building in George Street was bought in May 1919 and named China House. The building cost £14,000. Two ships bought from the Australian government were the *Gabo* and the *Victoria*, while the *Hwah Ping* was chartered from the Beijing government.

Competition from the British and the Japanese shipping companies was fierce and, with lack of experience or sufficient backing, the venture collapsed in 1924.

The Chinese

Cardinal Moran had a vision of Australia as a missionary base for China: 'The Chinese represent an older civilisation than we have in Europe,' he said. 'If that civilisation could receive the impress of Christianity there is no doubt they would become one of the greatest powers and greatest people of the world.' *The Bulletin* dubbed Moran as 'The Chow's Patron'. The cardinal opened St Columban College at Springwood in the hope of its being the launching place for the Asian mission, but it was not to be. It was the Irish Columbans who went to China in 1918.

The Chinese in Sydney were associated with the markets. After the demise of the gold rush many of them turned to trade and market gardening for their livelihood. Campbell Street was the predecessor to the present Chinatown in Dixon Street. The most colourful Chinese personality to emerge in Sydney was very likely Quong Tart, who became famous for his tea salons, his support of charitable causes and his work in Australian–Chinese relations. He was recognised as a 'Mandarin' of his people.

Sydney Mandarin

One of the amazing characters of the nineteenth century was Quong Tart. Coming to Australia as a boy, he was befriended by and brought up in an Australian family before he tried his luck on the goldfields. He married Margaret Taggart, who defied her parents to do so. Quong set up a tea importing business and by 1899 had headquarters in King Street, a central depot at the Queen Victoria Markets, and three tea-rooms. However, not even the successful entrepre-

neur was safe from the malicious racism of John Norton's *Truth*, which noted, 'We don't want an almond-eyed Messiah; in fact we don't want any almond-eyed men at all'.

Nonetheless, Quong Tart was an upright citizen, who campaigned vigorously against opium-smoking and other social ills, as his biographer Robert Travers notes:

> The anti-opium campaigns which Quong Tart inspired and led throughout these years were naturally supported by the clergy of all denominations. When he spoke, he was usually accompanied on the platform by such stalwarts as Dr Steel, Dr Kelynack, and the Chinese minister, Rev Soo Hoo Ten. This preacher had himself been a tea merchant until he received the call and went into the Anglican Church. As the founder of a Chinese YMCA he was in a good position to argue against the use of the poppy amongst his own country-men. A great fillip was given to the work by the arrival in 1887 of Bishop Raimondi, the Roman Catholic prelate from Hong Kong. His expert advice and influence with some of the priests led to a wider spread of Quong Tart's ideas. The Bishop told Quong 'Any Chinaman known to use opium is not admitted to the Church'.

Chinese Consulate

In February 1903 Quong Tart played host to Dr George Ernest ('Chinese') Morrison, the famous Australian adventurer. Dr Morrison, when he left Australia, carried with him a petition to the Emperor requesting the appointment of a Consul in Sydney and recommending Quong Tart for the position. Quong Tart had long been a mediator and unofficial ambassador for his people. The petition was supported by a host of eminent Australians:

> Sir Edmund Burton; George Reid; Premier John See; Sir George Dibbs; Sir Julian Salomons; Thomas Hughes,

Lutheran church, Goulburn Street.

Concordia Club, Elizabeth Street.

Mayor of Sydney; and a full bench of judges, including George Simpson. With unusual haste the Imperial Court considered the request and, in July, the Emperor Kuang Hsu let it be known that he favoured the appointment. The necessary documents were prepared but were never processed, for at the very moment of achieving his ambition to serve as Consul-General for China Quong Tart died at his home in Ashfield.[4]

Germans in Sydney

By the 1880s a German communal presence had established itself in the Haymarket. The Concordia Club first assembled at George Street near the GPO in 1883, moving to 393 Pitt Street in 1885 and then to 180 Elizabeth Street in 1905. This position put it in close proximity to the Deutsche Evangelische Kirche of 1881, which still stands in Goulburn Street. By 1915 the Concordia Club had 500 members, but the club premises were shut down by police in that year and the building was sold in 1920 for £5,000. In 1925 new premises were bought in Albion Street for £5,000 and another £11,000 was spent in renovations.

The Austrian cruiser *Queen Elizabeth* called in at Sydney in June 1893. On board was the man whose assassination triggered off the First World War. It is not

known if Archduke Franz Ferdinand visited the Concordia, but the ship's officers did. After spending several weeks in Australia Ferdinand observed:

> It is a great pity that Australia has only made its presence felt in Europe through the growing influence of its already disquieting competitiveness in many economic sectors whilst its intimate features remain so unknown and unappreciated. This is hardly surprising because of the enormous distance. I would compare Australia with someone who is difficult to approach and who only shows the coarse sides of his nature. But to those who get to know him better, he unveils the charm of his excellent and engaging qualities.[5]

In 1897 the 11,000-ton *Friedrich der Grosse*, a Norddeutscher Lloyd steamship, visited Sydney. The mayor of Sydney, Isaac Ellis Ives,

> was pleased to be there to recognize the merit of the German citizens. In taking them by the hand, their fellow colonists were aware that they were only greeting their own brothers and sisters. Personally, he looked upon the Germans, not as foreigners, but as fellow citizens who had come here to benefit themselves, if possible, but also to help raise up an Empire in the Southern Seas. It was impossible for a man to forget the land of his birth ... it was equally appropriate that the Germans should hold a

festival to rejoice in their nationality. He was assured that the Germans were doing good to themselves, to their children, and to the colony.[6]

The Federation of the colonies into the Commonwealth of Australia was taken as opportunity to show public loyalty. It was a chance to allay the suspicion shown German–Australians during the Boer War and the fears aroused by the Tirpitz warship program. A federation triumphal arch in Sydney was hurriedly put together, consisting of an imperial German eagle, coat of arms and greetings.

The Concordia Club members must have been good drinkers. When the *Condor* made a friendly visit to Sydney port in 1906, 125 gallons of lager were consumed with the help of the midshipmen. The full onset of World War I was felt by the members of the club after the sinking of the *Lusitania* by a U-boat on 7 May 1915. Premier Holman condemned 'the thoughtless murder of women and children of friendly countries'. By the middle of May over 60 members of Concordia were interned behind barbed wire at Holdsworthy and Trial Bay, South West Rocks (Kempsey). The club was closed. At the time of the Armistice over 5,000 Germans were interned at Holdsworthy—the last were released in 1920. The orthopaedic specialist and German-speaking Jew, Dr Max Hertz, had rooms in Macquarie Street. Despite his progressive practice and enthusiastic following, he was one of the first to be interned. What went on in the minds of his medical colleagues? Hertz ministered to his fellow internees in both camps till his release in 1920.

Radical Sydney

An extraordinary situation prevailed in urban Sydney towards the end of the nineteenth century. Unemployment and a chronic housing shortage led to a high population density of unattached men and it is possible to describe the ebb and flow of itinerants, country visitors, immigrants, outcasts, and drifters as constituting a human tide, melting pot or transitional zone. By 1890 there were over 300 listed boarding houses squeezed into a corridor between the waterfront and the railway station.

According to Graeme Davison: 'The overlapping circles of secularists, republicans, land-reformers, feminists and socialists, which together comprised Sydney's infant "counter-culture", focused their activities on a small triangle of the "transitional zone" between the Town Hall, Hyde Park and Redfern Station'.[7] Davison states that the Sydney described in the writings of *The Bulletin* school is symbolic rather than factual. The horrors of the city are contrasted with the attractions of the outback or the 'Bush' to use the word given currency by Henry Lawson and Francis Adams. Lawson's verse shifted from urban themes to outback fantasies:

> We'll ride and we'll ride from the city afar
> To the plains where the cattle and sheep stations are.

In 1892 Lawson did make a journey to Hungerford near the Queensland border. This unhappy episode stripped him of his dreamy views of the outback.

> I am back from up the country—very sorry that I went—
> Seeking for the Southern poets' land whereon to pitch my tent;
> I have lost a lot of idols, which were broken on the track,
> Burnt a lot of fancy verses, and I'm glad that I am back.
> Further out may be the pleasant scenes of which our poets boast
> But I think the country's rather more inviting round the coast.
> Anyway, I'll stay at present at a boarding house in town
> Drinking beer and lemon squashes, taking baths and cooling down.

The socialists had two noteworthy centres. McNamara's bookshop and boarding house in Castlereagh Street near Liverpool Street was next door to the Australian Socialist League rooms. It was there that Lawson met McNamara's step-daughter, Bertha Bredt, whom he married. In 1893 William Lane, the driving force behind the New Australia experiment in Paraguay, set up a temporary centre in Chippendale. Lane describes the moral geography of George Street in his novel, *The Workingman's Paradise* (1892):

> There were no street-walkers in Paddy's Market, Ned could see. He had caught his foot clumsily on the dress of one above the town-hall, a dashing demi-mondaine with rouged cheeks and unnaturally bright eyes and a huge velvet-covered hat of the Gainsborough shape ... Then he had noticed that the sad sisterhood were out in force where the bright gas-jets of the better class shops illuminated the pavement, swaggering it mostly where the kerbs were lined with young fellows ... Nearing the poorer end of George Street they seemed to disappear, both sisterhood and kerb loungers, until near the Haymarket itself they found the larrikin element gathered strongly under the flaring lights of hotel bars and music hall entrances. But in Paddy's market itself there were not even larrikins. Ned did not even notice anybody drunk.[8]

The young country schoolteacher Mary Cameron, better known later as Dame Mary Gilmore, was also in Chippendale at this time, helping Lane organise his New Australia venture. As the depression of the 1890s lifted *The Bulletin* writers made their escape from the inner city to more congenial surroundings in suburbia. However, a myth had been generated, that the rural interior is the locus of Australian ideals, a projection onto the outback of values prized by alienated inner-city intellectuals. The Bush ideal was in part a creation of anti-urban feeling by the literary downtowners of the 1890s.

GOVERNMENT

Public Instruction Act

The state took responsibility by parliamentary legislation for all primary and some secondary education. State aid to church schools was cut off in 1882. The Church of England Blackfriars School, a magnificent Gothic structure built by G.A. Mansfield, was forced to close. Blackfriars was re-opened as a Superior (High) Public School and had 1,000 pupils by 1885. Surry Hills South Public School (Bourke Street) was built in fine classical style by the architect for many public schools, William Kemp. This school also had 1,000 pupils in 1885.[9]

Separate high schools for boys and girls were provided by the Act. In 1883 high schools were opened in Sydney, Bathurst and Goulburn. Sydney Boys' and Sydney Girls' High School occupied separate floors of the Greenway Building (1810) in Elizabeth Street, which had been St James' Church of England School until 1882. The boys moved out in 1892 but the girls did not move to the new Moore Park School until 1921.[10]

The Gothic chateau 'Palace' style was also seen to good effect in the Ultimo Public School of the 1880s. Meanwhile the new Board of Technical Education, established in 1883, took over Sydney Technical College. The Sydney School of Arts had hitherto run the college, which included an annexe in Sussex Street South (1869). The Board was in turn replaced by the Technical Education Branch. A new triple-storey 'Palace' building housed Sydney Technical College in 1891.

An educational reform followed the Knibbs–Turner report, which recommended pre-service courses for students who had finished secondary education and wished to be teachers. The training schools at Fort Street and Hurlstone were amalgamated in 1906 to become Sydney Teachers College and located in the Blackfriars buildings. There the college remained for the next 20 years, despite protests that it should be within the grounds of the University of Sydney. However, the Depression caused plans for a university-based teachers college to be postponed.

At Blackfriars, the Montessori principles of education were first put into practice with the Blackfriars Kindergarten in 1913. This led to a shift from the formality and regimentation of the nineteenth-century teacher-dominated classroom to a more free, informal setting with self-chosen tasks.

Women's Hospital

The Women's Hospital in Crown Street, closed by the Wran Government in 1983, had a very humble beginning in the Haymarket. It began its work directly opposite the markets in Hay Street. The place was a two-storeyed four-room boarding house, run by Mrs Mary D'Arcy, which stood near that corner of Belmore Park where the ramp goes up from Hay Street to Central Railway. These Hay Street premises are listed in the *Sand's Directory* of 1897, as 'The Women's Hospital & Dispensary—David Fell, Hon. Treasurer'. However, the 1897 *Directory* also states that David Fell is now also 'Hon. Secretary, corner Elizabeth & Reservoir Streets'. By 1903, the *Directory* records the Women's Hospital at Crown Street, with Miss McLeod as matron. The Women's Hospital served the inner city community for 90 years.

Centennial Park

Centennial Park had a planner, the Scottish botanist Charles Moore (1820–1905) who came to Australia in 1848 as first director of the Botanic Gardens in Sydney. He was a member of the Hyde

Park Improvement Committee, and founding trustee of the National Park, to mention only a few of his achievements. Centennial Park 'was dedicated to the Enjoyment of the people of New South Wales for ever on Thursday the 26th January, 1888'. All the governors of the other colonies were present.

Sydney Trades Hall

One important function of the Trades and Labour Council was the settlement of industrial disputes. The council grew in stature through its conciliation role with employers and its power to approve of strikes. One hundred years after Governor Phillip arrived with his motley collection of convicts and some marines to keep them in line, the foundation stone of the Sydney Trades Hall was laid by the governor, Lord Carrington. The building stands on the corner of Goulburn and Dixon Streets. Only two years later the Trades Hall was involved in the national maritime strike (August– December 1890).

Formation of the Australian Labor Party

In 1890, unskilled labourers in New South Wales had to work 12 hours a day, seven days a week. Women would toil the same hours for half the wages. Children would work in factories for no wages at all. The Labour Council vigorously challenged such conditions. On 7 November 1890 Peter Joseph Brennan, a prominent delegate, moved the following historic resolution: 'That the Parliamentary Committee be instructed to consider at its next meeting the advisability of bringing forward Labour candidates at the next General Elections, and the said Committee draw up a Labour platform and submit same to Council.'[11]

So was born the Australian Labor Party. At a snap election seven months later, 35 Labor candidates were elected, and so for the first time the Labor Party took its place in an Australian parliament, among the 141 members of the Legislative Assembly. In 1904, John C. Watson, a former president of the Trades and Labour Council became prime minister of Australia. In 1910 the first New South Wales Labor government was formed under Premier John S.T. McGowen. Also in 1910, the first stable Federal Labor ministry was elected under Prime Minister Andrew Fisher.

Downtown Dentistry

Dentistry has a long association with Sydney downtown. It all began in 1830, when Australia's first dental publication was printed by R. Mansfield in a George Street warehouse. The text, *Hints for the Preservation of the Teeth*, was written by Henry Jeanneret. The 'Father of Australian Dentistry', John Belisario, pioneered the use of ether in Sydney in 1847, only eight months after its discovery in Massachusetts. Dental practitioners gained their qualifications overseas. The need for local training became apparent and a private college was started by Dr Harry Peach. It was located in the Haymarket.

New South Wales Dental College. It is not generally known that a Dental College exists in Sydney. Dr. Peach, B.S., M.D., D.D.S., of Burwood is the principal, and the instruction given is being largely availed of by dental students. Mr. Henry Wilder Wells, Pharmaceutical Chemist of George Street, Haymarket, who studied at this College has received the following diploma:–

NEW SOUTH WALES
COLLEGE OF DENTAL SURGERY,
SYDNEY:

Be it known by these presents that Henry Wilder Wells having successfully completed the regular course of study and practice in this institution, and having passed satisfactory examinations in the following subjects—anatomy, pathology, therapeutics, materia-medica, anaesthesia, operative and mechanical

United Dental Hospital

dentistry and the practice of dentistry, he is therefore awarded this diploma as evidence of the same.

28th July, 1896
(signed) H. Peach[12]

Peach soon clashed with another forceful personality, Professor Anderson Stuart, head of the Faculty of Medicine at the University of Sydney. Stuart wanted dentistry to come under his control and Peach lost the ensuing political struggle. In addition there were two conflicting interest groups. There were the dentists who wish to provide free dental care to the poor and there were those concerned with correct dental education. The University Dental School was liaising with Sydney Hospital and faced endless administrative problems. Meanwhile, the Sydney Dental Hospital, established in 1902 at 319 Elizabeth Street, was experiencing difficulties with its private subscriptions. However, it took over the University Dental Hospital at the corner of George and Bathurst Streets in December 1903.[13]

The ultimate solution lay in amalgamation. A Union Bill was eventually passed in parliament in 1905. Between

1901 and 1904, 42,000 patients had been treated completely free of charge at the Sydney Dental Hospital. A site in Chalmers Street, a compromise location not pleasing to Professor Stuart, was chosen and the new United Dental Hospital was opened in 1912. However, the hospital aroused some criticism, which was aired in the *Sydney Morning Herald*:

> Students are at once, without examination, without training, and without even question allowed to start practising on the unfortunate individuals who, through poverty and the agony of dental disorder, are forced to seek the portals of what ought to be, to them, a sanctuary of alleviation. Everyone knows the discomfort endured when having a tooth drilled in the hands of an expert. What must it be like in the hands of a novice? If this is true of the dental engine, how much more so is it true of an extraction? ... I have personally known students, raw novices, to be engaged in a top room all alone extracting a tooth.[14]

The upshot was a censure motion at the annual general meeting in January 1911. The principal complaint was that 'the hospital had become too much of a dental school, and the wants of the suffering poor were neglected in the interests of students'.[15] The censure motion, moved by Mr F.G. Hardwick and seconded by Dr Deck, was lost—13 votes to 16.

INDUSTRY AND TRANSPORT

Horderns' Haymarket Empire

Australia had produced many millionaires, but one family dynasty at the turn of the twentieth century stood head and shoulders above most. This was the family firm of Anthony Hordern and Sons. The origins were quite humble. Anthony and Ann Hordern arrived in Sydney in 1824 with three small children. Another three were born in Australia. In the hold of the ship on which they were paying passengers were 204 male convicts and soldiers to guard them. Two of the convicts died on the voyage. Their ship, the *Phoenix*, was badly damaged on the Sow and Pigs reef inside the Heads and, refloated the following day, struggled into Campbell's Wharf at Sydney Cove. The ship was declared unseaworthy and was permanently moored as a prison hulk in Lavender Bay, named after Boatswain Lavender who was in charge of the hulk. Anthony Hordern, a coachbuilder, opened up a workshop in King Street. Ann opened a haberdashery shop alongside and prospered. When the gold-rush boom was on in the 1850s and 1860s, the second generation of Horderns had shops at Brickfield Hill and the Haymarket which prospered both then and later:

> During the 1880s and the 1890s the sale turnover [at the Haymarket] expanded tremendously, chiefly by the development of one of the biggest mail-order businesses in the world, arising from the wide circulation of 1,500 pages of itemised priced articles in such amazing variety that the firm's claim to be 'Universal Providers' was not greatly exaggerated! (One motto was 'Everything from a Needle to an Anchor'.) Another sound business principle was trading for cash only, which the founders correctly claimed enabled prices to be cut.[16]

A cluster of buildings, culminating in the Palace Warehouse, was located within the area of George, Hay, Parker and Barlow Streets. An electric fuse started a spectacular fire at 8.00 a.m. on 10 July 1901. The fire, whipped by a strong wind, spread quickly from building to building. But it did not defeat Sam Hordern:

> With characteristic energy, and thinking of his 1,200 employees, Sam Hordern set

to work to rebuild. The premises and stock were insured for £300,000, the biggest insurance claim ever made until that time by an individual insurer, and those claims were satisfactorily met. In various warehouses in the city, Horderns already had some £500,000 worth of goods recently imported. As a temporary measure, Sam Hordern hired the Exhibition Building in Prince Alfred Park, and there opened his store temporarily.[17]

Sam Hordern decided to build a new emporium on the Brickfields Hill site. It was where he had been born in 1849. After only two years in the building, the New Palace Emporium was opened in 1906. It was five stories high, complete with tower. Emblazoned everywhere was the firm's distinctive crest of the spreading oak and the motto, 'While I live I'll grow'. Other large city stores at this time were David Jones (George Street, 1887), E. Way and Co. (Pitt Street, 1891), Marcus Clark (corner of Railway Square, 1906), Grace Bros (Broadway, 1906) and Farmers (George Street, 1910).

Mark Foy: The Piazza Emporium

Francis and Mark Foy were the eldest and third son of Mark Foy, Snr. Francis was born near Dublin and Mark, Jnr, at Bendigo. Francis was a partner with his father in a drapery shop in Collingwood before he moved to Sydney. In 1885 the two brothers opened a shop in Oxford Street, commemorating their father.

In the era of great city stores, the Mark Foy Emporium was one of the last to be built. The grand chateau-style building was constructed in 1908. It was close to the route of the city railway which was to be extended from Central to St James with a stop in between at Museum Station, virtually beneath the store. The piazza store was modelled on the Bon Marché store in Paris. The piazza, the chandeliers, the marble and the opulent ballroom made the store the foremost in the fashion field. Sydney's first escalator

Mark Foy's Piazza Store.

and motor delivery service were also introduced by the store. Only two storeys were originally built, but after Museum Station was opened in 1926 four more levels were added in 1928.

Like the Horderns, who were influential patrons of the Royal Agricultural Show—in fact the Hordern Pavilion is testimony of that link—the Foys also had many other interests. Francis was a popular and flamboyant turf identity, with an Irish sense of humour. 'At his stud, The Monastery, near Parkes, His Reverence stood as chief stallion and he called a foal by Something Irish, The Christian Brother.'[18]

Mark was a keen sportsman, winning several medals for rifle-shooting in the U.S.A. In 1890 he founded the Sydney Flying Squadron which did much to popularise and brighten up boating in Sydney Harbour. In 1904 Mark constructed the magnificent Hydro Majestic at Medlow Bath, beyond Katoomba in the Blue Mountains.[19] It was built as a spa health resort in a splendid cliff-top setting. Huge boiler rooms were built for the resort's warm pools and interior heating system. There was a Swiss doctor and spa water from Baden-Baden in Germany.

Like Horderns, Mark Foy did not move into suburban growth centres, and eventually lost out in the battle with the more centrally located David Jones stores and the new regional centres. From being *the* store with quality second to none, it closed in 1980. Grace Bros re-opened the store for three years before it closed down again. Top floors are now occupied by the New South Wales Housing Commission and the Courts of Petty Sessions. The wealth of the Mark Foy enterprises was inherited by Mrs Juanita Nielsen, who from 1968 published a fortnightly newspaper called *Now*. The paper was critical of high-rise development of Victoria Street, Kings Cross. Mrs Nielsen was last seen alive on 4 July 1975, after leaving the Carousel Cabaret. On 15 August 1983, an inquest into her death began.

The six-person jury sat for 13 weeks and heard an extraordinary parade of witnesses, some of them alleged to be key underworld figures. The jury could not ascertain how, when and where Mrs Nielsen died but added the following rider: 'There is evidence to show that the police enquiries were inhibited by an atmosphere of corruption, real or imagined, that existed at the time'. Eddie Trigg and Shayne Martin-Simmonds were serving sentences at the time of the inquest, convicted on charges of conspiring to abduct Mrs Nielsen. The mystery remains to tantalise Sydneysiders.

Central Station

The original Sydney to Parramatta railway had its city terminus at Redfern. Over the next 61 years the railways penetrated further inland and along the coast, but when passengers arrived they had still to hire a cab or take the steam tram along Pitt Street into the city. The government therefore decided to build a new station on its own land one mile closer to the city. The main tract of land was the Sandhills cemetery. The remains of many of the pioneers had to be buried elsewhere. In Pitt Street South, the Benevolent Asylum,

Central Railway Station.

Christ Church Rectory and St Scholastica's all were demolished. The Government Architect was W.J. Vernon, described as a poet in architecture by E.W. O'Sullivan, the secretary for public works. The station was four years in the building; the clock tower was added later. Ironically there are now plans afoot to redevelop and roof over the railway yards. Historical plaques pertaining to Central Station may be found on the corner of Eddy Avenue and Pitt Street and also on a stone pillar opposite the Eddy Avenue Colonnades.

Market Tower

The market tower on the corner of Ultimo Road and Quay Street bears a foundation inscription dated November 1910. This is 100 years since Macquarie moved the markets from the western side of Sydney Cove to the site of the present Queen Victoria Building. Greenway built a domed market house there, but the sheep and cattle boom led to chaos in the streets and the Haymarket area was developed for the livestock trade. Governor Darling converted the market house into a police station and courthouse. In 1858 the Sydney Council united four market

Queen Victoria Building.

Hydraulic Lift, Queen Victoria Building.

buildings under one roof, with shop space in York Street for meat and poultry and flowers and fancy goods for the George Street shops. By 1869 easier cart access to the Campbell Street area led to three long open-sided market buildings being opened by Lord Belmore, known as the Belmore Markets. Soon fruit and vegetable growers used these markets as their main outlet. In 1893 George McCrae built a new Belmore market (later converted to the Capitol Theatre), which was a prelude to the city architect's masterpiece, the Queen Victoria Market. The Council wanted to create a classy shopping centre in the centre of the town, but the basement fruit and vegetable market turned out to be a failure. So once again new market buildings were erected, this time west of George Street at the head of Darling Harbour, Vegetable Market Nos 1 and 2

and the Fruit Market. In 1968 the Sydney Council lost its 126 years right to run the markets. The Sydney Farm Produce Markets complex at Flemington was begun in 1972 and officially opened in 1975. Much of the facade of the market buildings in the Haymarket has been preserved and incorporated in the Market campus buildings of the University of Technology and other redevelopments in the Haymarket.

Electric Light and Power

On 8 July 1904 the lady mayoress of Sydney threw a switch at the newly completed powerhouse at Pyrmont. The lord mayor, Alderman S.E. Lees, said the site had been chosen by his predecessor, Sir James Graham, and the powerhouse

View of the Haymarket showing the Tower.

was built under the supervision of Mr T. Rooke, the resident electrical engineer. This marked the beginning of electrical street lighting and power for homes, businesses and factories in Sydney.

In 1936 the State government took over the running of the power station. In 1949 the Labor government set out on a development program which resulted in another power station on the Pyrmont site known as Power Station B. Completed in 1955, Pyrmont B was the last coal-fired power station built in Sydney. I can remember looking at the prevailing wind with dread on washing day, to see if soot from the four Pyrmont chimneys was blowing towards the Haymarket.

First Australian Air Mail

A French airman, M. Guillaux, took off from the Melbourne Showgrounds on Thursday, 16 July 1914, with 1,785 postcards weighing about 40 pounds, several official letters of greeting and some private parcels, 'descending here and there to renew his petrol'.[20] Guillaux landed at Moore Park on Saturday afternoon, 18 July.

Grace Bros, Broadway.

Museum for Applied Arts and Sciences

The wonderful exhibits now so well displayed in the former Ultimo Powerhouse were originally on display in the Technological Museum in Harris Street. William Kemp was the architect of this building, opened in 1892. Premier Neville Wran recounted how on rainy days as a boy he would love to visit this old museum.

Grace Brothers

Joseph Neal Grace learnt the draper's trade in London and was about 21 when he arrived in Sydney in 1880 to begin work at Farmer & Co. After three years he obtained a hawker's licence and travelled with a horse and cart around the inner suburbs. He prospered so much he was advised to open a store. With his newly arrived brother Albert to help him, Grace bought the drapery of John Kingsbury at 5-7 George Street West in 1885. Other shops nearby were bought six years later. Buildings were put up. The clock tower, globe and electricity powerhouse were constructed in 1904. Removal and transport became a large business of its own. In 1917 all shares were owned by members of the family. For Joseph Grace, work was play. Perhaps 'workaholic' might be the word. In 1960 Grace Bros Pty Ltd became a public company and went on to acquire a chain of stores around Australia. Where else in Sydney in the early 1980s could I drive from the Haymarket for five minutes, park under cover, buy food and drink, have a haircut, order a carpet to be measured and laid, see Santa Claus and hear a choir, all while the car was being serviced? But alas by 1992 the imminent closure of the Broadway store was announced.

RELIGION

St Mary's Cathedral

The present St Mary's Cathedral is the third building on the site. The first church's foundation stone was laid in 1821, after a land grant by Governor Macquarie. At that time the site was beyond the inhabited part of the town, but handy to the convict barracks nearby. Dr Polding dedicated the chapel in 1836, which was enlarged in 1842 when he became archbishop. But on 29 June 1865 the shingle roof caught fire and the whole building was destroyed. A second temporary structure was also totally destroyed by fire a month later. The architect William Wardell, who also designed St Patrick's Cathedral in Melbourne, was asked to design a new cathedral. Polding laid the foundation stone of the present structure in 1868 and it was opened at a dedication in 1882. A temporary church building was used in the interim. Further additions were made during the days of Cardinal Moran and Archbishop Kelly. No more building was done after 1912, and the three towers are lacking their originally intended spires. The Cardinal Moran Roll of Honour found in the eastern transept of St Mary's Cathedral gives a list of fundraisers. The downtown members of this roll, both individuals and groups, were very prominent in raising funds for the construction during 1880-82.

Door Knock on a Rainy Night

In 1893, when a policeman knocked on the door of an Elizabeth Street house seeking shelter for a wet and bedraggled girl about to give birth, the benevolence of those within was clarified. The girl was taken in and gave birth within an hour. The following year Mary O'Brien and her companions opened the house as a refuge for destitute expectant mothers. Of the 32 admitted in the first year, 23 were unmarried. The St Margaret's Home which remained in Elizabeth Street till 1910 coined the slogan, 'A shilling a day keeps a baby a day'. Upon expiry of the lease, Mrs Gertrude Abbott, for that was the name Mary O'Brien adopted for her charity work, bought old St Aloysius College in Bourke Street. When she died St Margaret's passed to the Sisters of St Joseph. Mary had been associated with Mother Mary McKillop in Adelaide but had greatly developed from a young, fervent, would-be mystic to a champion-of-the-fallen. In the words of Fr R.J. Murphy: 'She continued the valiant work till her death in 1934 at the age of 88. She was a little Queen Victoria-shaped woman with a golden heart and her name should be written large in the Annals of truly Christian workers beside that of Caroline Chisholm, "The Immigrant's Friend".'[21]

Gertrude Abbott

Many of the Women's Hospital's services and patients were transferred to nearby St Margaret's Hospital. This hospital has important links with the scientist, priest and co-founder of the Josephite Order, Father Julian Tenison-Woods. A group of apostolically minded women headed by Mary O'Brien were hoping that Father Woods would help them become a religious community. The ladies supported themselves by sewing. Sydney's tailoring industry was located in the Surry Hills, St Peter's and Redfern districts and was staffed almost entirely by women who were paid less than the men and thus had to work 14–16 hours per day for mere subsistence.[22]

But the 13-room house they rented from the proceeds of their sewing work became unintentionally a hospice. It is now Strawberry Hills Gallery. Mary O'Brien and her companions became the founders of St Margaret's Hospital in 1890 and Mary O'Brien is commemorated in the district by a nursing home in Albion Street named in her honour and staffed by the Sisters of St Joseph. As she adopted the name of Gertrude Abbott for her charity work, the house is known as the Gertrude Abbott Home.

Julian Tenison-Woods

The story of Father Julian Tenison-Woods is too rich and complex to be dealt with adequately in this work. For one thing, he is regarded as the co-founder, along with Mother Mary McKillop, of the Sisters of St Joseph. (Mary McKillop is now well on the way to becoming the first Australian-born Saint.) For another, he travelled all over Australia in the course of his educational work and scientific research. He spent time in Europe as well, being employed as teacher of the Marist College headed at that time by Peter Julian Eymard, later to become founder of the Blessed Sacrament Congregations. (The Church at 641 George Street is named after St Peter Julian.) Fr Tenison-Woods spent his last weeks in a religious community of Sisters dedicated to adoration of the Blessed Sacrament. This house was in Elizabeth Street, Surry Hills. Although Fr Tenison-Woods had been a diocesan priest most of his priestly life, he desired to be reclothed in the Passionist habit he had worn as a novice with the Passionist Order. Two Passionist priests happened to be conducting a Parish mission at Surry Hills at the time.

Tenison-Woods was an honorary member of the Royal Societies of New South Wales, Victoria, Tasmania, South Australia, of the Linnaean Society of New South Wales, and of the New Zealand Institute. His scientific interests included the disciplines of geology, botany, palaeontology and zoology. Publications included *History of the Discovery and Exploration of Australia* (London, 1865) and *Fish and Fisheries of New South Wales* (Sydney, 1883).

Fr Tenison-Woods' grave in Waverley cemetery is a most distinguished one. His memorial contains tributes from various scientific bodies in Australia and New Zealand, and from the Sisters of St Joseph and the Sisters of Perpetual Adoration.

St Vincent de Paul Society

When Frederick Ozanam founded the St Vincent de Paul Society in 1833 he scarcely would have dreamt that it would fulfil an important role in Australia. The earliest knowledge of the society in the Southern Hemisphere was the foundation of a Conference in Christchurch, New Zealand, in 1867 by Father Castaigner, SM. The Society then came to Sydney in 1881 when

> two independent meetings, each unknown to the other, took place at St Patrick's Church Hill and St Francis' on Sunday, July 24, 1881. Fortunately there were still alive two members who had attended the respective first meeting— Father Piquet at St Patrick's and Mr T.J. Dwyer at St Francis'. The Superior Council was quite satisfied the first two Conferences were founded on the same day. The Society spread to Melbourne and to Adelaide in 1885, to Brisbane in 1884, to Launceston in 1899 and to Hobart in 1911.[23]

The first Matthew Talbot Hostel for Homeless Men began in the former St John's Church in Kent Street in 1938. There were 11 beds and 100 meals were served per day. The hostel moved to Young Street in 1952 and had 80 beds and served 400 meals per day. The third and current hostel has 550 beds and has served as many as 1,565 meals in a day.

An overview of the theory, philosophy, motivation and practical spirituality of the St Vincent de Paul Society at the turn of the century is provided in the lengthy extract from its centenary history. The society had to decide whether to commit itself to shelters for homeless and derelict men:

> St Vincent's Manual says that no act of

charity is foreign to the Society. While we have in Sydney an excellent Night Refuge for women, conducted by the Sisters of the Good Samaritan, which performs noble work and which has been the means of rescuing a great many poor creatures from a miserable and degrading end, there are many unfortunates, who never come within reach of its portals, and who never have the good fortune to come under the kindly and regenerating influence of the saintly nuns. Our Society is able to do something for those who have a home or shelter of some sort, but what of those who have no place whereon to lay their heads, though perhaps the fault be their own, and who are wandering the night amongst the streets and lanes of the city? Our duty on some occasions brings to our notice both men and women of this class. In a big city too, there are always fascinations which tempt many from their homes in the country. They spend their time in satisfying their curiosity, and incautiously prolonging their stay, they find their funds are exhausted and they have no place to go. Perhaps even young girls and women may be unhappy in this plight, and may be driven in desperation to seek shelter in the slums, or among the shadowed byways where they become easy prey for the night vultures who are ever alert haunting such places. How sad it must be if any Catholics should be placed in such a deplorable position! It is quite easy to imagine that some may be beguiled by those who would offer shelter that they might find themselves where their Faith might be jeopardised. And then the case of the poor derelicts, men and women, can nothing be done for them? Can nothing be done to help the poor creatures who drift about all night without food or shelter, in rags and tatters, with feet on ground, sometimes in the middle of winter in cold or wet; hiding like hunted animals at the approach of their fellows, for fear of being seen or known? Many of them have been respectable, perhaps fathers and mothers of happy children, and now through misfortune, or may be their own fault, are reduced to so sad a state. Must we pass them by?[24]

Origin of the Westmead Boys' Home

In 1891 the St Francis, Haymarket, Conference of the St Vincent de Paul Society decided to found an institution for orphan boys to assist them in learning a trade. The president, Brother Minahan, and the Haymarket Conference rented a small house in Upton Lane and later a house at 231 Riley Street, Surry Hills. The following year, St Aloysius Boy's home was established at Five Dock for 52 destitute orphans. Four years later it was transferred to Westmead where the Marist Brothers were appointed to run the institute.[25]

Charles O'Neill

Charles O'Neill (1828-1900) and his brother John helped found the St Vincent de Paul Society in Australasia. Charles O'Neill was an engineer who had been involved in the society in his native Scotland. When he went to New Zealand he founded the society. Archbishop Vaughan asked him to come to Sydney and form the society there. After 10 years O'Neill resigned as president in 1891. Twenty branches of the society had been established, one at Braidwood, and the first special work, the Home for Boys. His personal fortunes declined in the 1890s and he had to ask for assistance from the society he had founded. He died poor and unknown in 1900. His engineering work constitutes a story in itself, but of particular interest was his tender in 1885 to construct a tunnel under the harbour to North Sydney.

Catholic Schools and Religious Orders in Downtown Sydney

Broadway:
St Benedict's 1875—Marist Brothers
1883—Good Samaritans
(Business College) 1937
—Good Samaritans
Golden Grove:
St Kieran's Primary 1889?—Mercy Sisters

Haymarket:
St Francis' Primary, 1867 (Hay Street)—
Marist Brothers
1901 (Albion Street)—Good Samaritans
Pitt Street South 1862—Good Samaritans
St Scholastica's High School 1878
—Good Samaritans
Pyrmont:
St Bede's Primary 1883
—Good Samaritans
Redfern:
St Vincent's Primary 1893
—Good Samaritans
Surry Hills:
'The Surry Hills School' 1847
—P.M. Ryan, teacher
St Kilda—Boys 1879—Jesuit Fathers
St Kilda's Primary 1889—Mercy Sisters
Boys 1906—De La Salle Brothers
Sydney:
St John's Poor School (Kent Street)
—Sisters of St Joseph
Ultimo:
St Francis Xavier 1900—Good Samaritans

Perhaps nothing documents the vitality of the inner-city Catholic community at the end of the nineteenth century more than the numbers of its schools. Religious orders of brothers and sisters staffed the schools which were attended by children of Irish working-class families. The brothers and sisters did their educational job all too well. The children grew up, secured good jobs, bettered their parents financially and moved out to the newer suburbs of Randwick, Coogee and Ashfield.

Catholic Club

In 1913 Archbishop Kelly set the foundation stone of the Catholic Club in 179 Castlereagh Street. This club formed a social outlet for the life of the Catholic community. I myself attended several communion breakfasts there. The building was pulled down at the end of the 1980s for a new development.

Knights of St John

Two things distinguish the Order of St John, known popularly as St John's Ambulance. One, the organisation is the only one to be accorded the freedom of the city of Sydney; and two, the organisation has links with the Middle Ages, the Crusaders and the Holy Land in general and Jerusalem in particular. All this may seem very surprising when you stand in front of a modest four-storey building tucked away in Hunt Street, Surry Hills.

The ancient Order of St John arose after the First Crusade, which had led to the establishment of the Christian Kingdom of Jerusalem on Christmas Day 1100. There developed three classes within the Order—the knights, the priests and the brothers. All three classes wore the black monastic habit with the eight-pointed white cross. The military banner adopted was the flag of their patron John the Baptist, a white cross on a red field. However, the Order was expelled first from Jerusalem and then the island of Rhodes. Sanctuary was established at Malta, where the Order remained until Napoleon disbanded them. Priories of the Order were established throughout Europe, including England, from which the St John's Ambulance organisation in Australia was founded.

Louis Gille store.

The first ambulance station.

The improvers and reformers of the late nineteenth century gave the revived Order a sustaining purpose it had previously lacked. The Seal of Royal Approval came in 1888, when Queen Victoria became Sovereign Head and Patron of the Order. In the meantime interest in assisting the wounded of the Franco-Prussian war led to the establishment of an Ambulance Department. The attendants were walking 'ambulant', alongside the two-wheeled litter *en route* to the hospital. Despite early striving for a foundation in Sydney, the organising committee dithered and did not establish St John's Ambulance Association until 1890.

The Colonial Sugar Refinery plant at Pyrmont, the Australian Gaslight Company at Haymarket and the Fresh Food and Ice Company were some of the early participants in educational first-aid courses. The association enrolments rose dramatically in 1914, after the declaration of war. Indeed Ian Howie-Willis observes that disasters favour recruitment in a voluntary organisation like St John's, whereas peace and heavy 'Big Brother' government spending are detrimental to enrolment.[26]

When troops returning from Europe most likely brought back a virus, popularly known as 'Spanish' influenza, which killed 13,000 Australians across the continent between October 1918 and May 1919, the resources of the brigade were put at the disposal of the director-general of public health. The Newtown members manned an ambulance tram which shifted influenza victims from the city to the Coast Hospital at Little Bay, near La Perouse. The brigade's lady superintendant organised the production of face-masks for volunteer workers at the Railways Institute. In Sydney, 11,772 patients were transported by a coordinated ambulance system. As the population was about 892,000, it means one person in 75 was hospitalised.[27] The epidemic was one of the greatest disasters Australia has had to face. The Order certainly gave sustenance to its motto 'for the service of humanity'.

During World War II the brigade assigned 200 of its own instructors to train civilians required in the ARP (air-raid precaution) first-aid stations. It had already been training personnel for the State Emergency Services since 1936.[28]

Salvation Army

While the young Henry Lawson was envisaging 'an army of the streets' to launch a revolution, a different army was being established in Sydney's downtown. The members had a uniform, a flag,

Former Salvation Army temple.

officers, military bands and a war cry, for the Salvation Army had come to town. The enemy soon identified themselves— the city larrikins. In the streets around the Belmore Markets battles raged, the larrikins hurled refuse at the Army bandsmen, jeered at the preachers and with bold effort attempted to snatch the flag. On one occasion one of the 'Sallies' wrapped the flag around herself and defied the larrikins to take it. They retreated.

In 1893 the Salvation Army made the basement of their Goulburn Street building a refuge for homeless men. Soon 164 men crowded in each night. Greybeards of 70 and youths of 20, uncouth and cultured, up to 400 were accommodated by the following winter.[29]

The Salvation Army made a substantial investment of its resources in the greater Haymarket district, covering seven buildings at one stage.

Goulburn Street (1885) was for public worship. The present structure is the third Army building on the site and dates from 1911. It became redundant after functioning as a day centre for alcoholics and was sold in 1974.

The People's Palace (1899) at 400 Pitt Street was originally a temperance hotel for travellers and accommodation for the destitute. This function is served by Foster House for men and Winderradeen House for women and the Palace was sold in the 1980s.

By 1969 the William Booth Institute (56 Albion Street, Surry Hills) was a key link of the 'Bridge' program to rehabilitate alcoholic men. The original step of the Bridge Program began in the old Nithsdale Clinic in 1964 at the rear of Territorial Headquarters. A suburban house and several farms are also involved in the program.

Winderradeen House (348 Elizabeth Street) began as a hostel for working girls in 1910, then became a shelter for destitute women. A geriatric wing for women was opened in 1960.

The premises at 69 Goulburn Street (1914) began as a recreation centre for servicemen on leave. It was remodelled after the war to become temporary headquarters for five years until the new headquarters completed in 1926, and then sold.

Foster House (1923) was acquired to replace the Sussex Street hostel for destitute men, which was resumed by Sydney Municipal Council. In the heart of Foster House is the Knudsen Chapel, dedicated to Brigadier Knudsen who for many years managed Foster House.

Sydney Congress Hall and Territorial Headquarters (1926) are at 140 Elizabeth Street.

At present William Booth House, Winderradeen House, Foster House and the central Administrative Building continue functioning. In addition, the Army has hostels for teenage boys at 145 Commonwealth Street and for women at O'Loughlin Street, Surry Hills. There is a Family Welfare Centre, also, at 141 Commonwealth Street.

St Andrew's Cathedral School

The school was opened on 14 July 1885 in Pitt Street, opposite Central Street. Of the 27 boys enrolled, 22 were choristers. In its first 90 years the school was moved to nine different sites. In 1962 a master plan for the St Andrew's Square project was formulated by the architects Hely and Bell. It involved removal of existing buildings, construction of a pedestrian square between the Cathedral and the Town Hall, an office tower which was also to house the school and four levels of parking. In the meantime a school building of three levels was constructed in 1965 behind the Cathedral. A new method of precast concrete load-bearing wall units was employed, but this building was demolished in 1971. The present Noel-Ridley Smith plan of a nine-storey stepped profile was adopted in 1972 and completed in 1976, at a cost of $12 million.

Canon Newth, headmaster of the school, 1941-79, comments on the various development plans for the Cathedral School:

> Yet these attempts failed, either because the planning proposals were beyond the resources or the faith of the Cathedral Chapter, or because of the intervention of civic authorities; or because those who desired to develop the Cathedral site for the benefit of the Cathedral placed a sufficiently low priority on the function of the Choir School as to be prepared to either banish it to a suburban location or close it altogether.[30]

The canon laments the failure of consulting research experts to involve the school in feasibility studies.

The school now has an enrolment of 600 and is located on the top two floors. Commercial offices occupy the lower levels. The arcade contains 45 shops. There is parking for 300 cars.

The famous aviation pioneer Charles Kingsford Smith attended the Cathedral School in the early 1900s. The composer John Antill, who wrote special music for the Pope Paul VI ecumenical prayer service on St Andrew's Day in 1970 in Sydney Town Hall, had also been a student. Another chorister who became world famous as a French horn soloist and conductor is Barry Tuckwell.

The Cathedral School belongs to the World Wide Association of Choir Schools. This association is affiliated with the Royal School of Church Music, established in 1927. The school motto 'Via Crucis, Via Lucis' (The Way of the Cross is the Way of Light) was supplied by Archbishop Saumarez Smith, principal of St Aidan's Theological College, Birkenhead, U.K., for 21 years, with which it shares the motto.[31]

Parish of St Laurence

The Anglican Bishop Broughton preached a sermon in 1838 in the storeroom of the Terry Hughes Brewery at the corner of Elizabeth and Albion Streets. Assembled was a congregation named after this temporary 'church' of St Laurence. In 1839 Rev. W.H. Walsh was appointed pastor. On 1 January 1840 the foundation stone of the present church was laid by Bishop Broughton. This makes it one of the oldest church buildings in the city. The spire and tower are the work of the architect Edmund Blacket, who soon began work on the neighbouring Christ Church School. The parish buildings are located on a large block bounded by George and Pitt Streets and Rawson Place. One of the notable worshippers in the 1850s and 1860s was Lucy Osburn. Trained in nursing by Florence Nightingale, she took up the position of first 'lady superintendent' of Sydney Hospital, where she nursed the Duke of Edinburgh back to health after the abortive assassination attempt at Clontarff in 1868. Lucy Osburn 'was severely censored at a Commission of Enquiry by witnesses who complained of her habit of attending early Communion at Christ Church with some of her nurses'.[32]

The verger's house at the intersection of George and Pitt Street became in turn a police watch-house, ambulance station, Marcus Clarke building and State Lotteries Office. In exchange for the verger's grounds, land was given on the east side of Pitt Street, where a large parsonage and gardens were established. All that survives today is a Moreton Bay fig tree opposite the taxi rank outside Central Station. Christ Church School, which stood amid green grass and fields, extended along Pitt Street to the Australian Gas Light Company building. When financial difficulties resulted on the withdrawal of a government grant, Thomas Sutcliffe Mort paid £1,500 for the school buildings.

Even before the church was built, the pastor was criticised in the secular press for wearing a surplice. Objection was made to a Greek cross reredos built in 1869. The Rev. C.F. Garnsey began the practice of daily Eucharist, with cross, candles and vestments. However, in 1910-11 Archbishop Wright forbade the use of vestments. An ornate chasuble is mounted on the rear wall in a glass case. It provides silent witness to the painful observance of the edict. However, incense, Gregorian chant, and the Feast of Corpus Christi (1924) have all been introduced.

The history of Christ Church St Laurence has been documented by three of its parishioners: Laura Allen, L.C. Rodd and John Spencer. By and large they tended to see themselves as isolated within the Anglican archdiocese, indeed even 'under siege'. The entry of Rev Makinson, Rev Sconce and the Rev Broddenham, curate at Christ Church, into the Catholic Church may have played no small part. Makinson and Sconce had been at the Anglican school at Lyndhurst nearby. Canon Walsh, Broddenham's superior, is commemorated by a plaque in St Andrew's Cathedral, but no mention is made on the plaque that he had been Rector of Christ Church for 28 years![33]

The rectorship of John Hope from 1925 to 1971 did not make for good relations with St Andrew's. Hope was a committed Christian socialist, which would have set him at odds with the establishment, and he caused further episcopal wrath by having Stations of the Cross and a Confessional erected in the church. He received a 'please explain' after advertising a High Mass at Easter in 1933 in the *Sydney Morning Herald*. Hope began a Healing Service, which was, however, also later introduced at St Andrew's.[34] One of his associates, Fr W.A. Clint, began Tranby Aborigines' Co-

Operative Training College in an old home in Glebe.[35]

Christ Church was regularly attacked by the principal of Moore College, Archdeacon Thomas Chatterton Hammond. Rodd maintains Hammond 'brought with him the bitterness of Ireland's religious feuds'.[36] Moore Theological College, established in 1856 on the estate of the late Thomas Moore at Liverpool for training Anglican clergy, was relocated at Newtown in 1891. Hammond was its principal from 1934 to 1953 and also Rector of St Phillip's, Church Hill.

Thomas Moore (1762-1840) was a sailor who settled in Sydney in 1796 and was made master boatbuilder. He became interested in farming and was given land grants in the Georges River area in what is now Liverpool. A deeply religious man, he assisted in the building of churches in the Liverpool district. When his wife died without issue, he drew up a will leaving all his considerable land and wealth to the Church of England. He had already given land to Bishop Broughton in The Rocks area for a cathedral site. The monies from that site assisted in the eventual building of St Andrew's Cathedral.

John Tooth, the founder of the Kent Brewery, appears in the St Laurence baptismal register on the occasion of the baptism of four children during the 1840s. The Benevolent Asylum across Pitt Street was a key factor in the life of the parish. The inhabitants were disadvantaged and contrasted strongly with the more well-to-do parishioners like the Tooths. The chief justice, Sir Alfred Stephen, represented the parish at a Diocesan Conference in 1857.[37] Laura Allen mentions that Hordern, Bull, Metcalfe, Woolley, Palmer, Greville, Armytage, Ackroyd and White all appear frequently in the baptismal register.[38] A fall in the number of baptisms, marriages and burials that had begun in the 1860s is attributed by Spooner to the expansion of the outer suburbs.[39]

The Rev. C.F. Garnsey introduced the militant Guild of St Laurence in 1883. The guild donated a credence table, eucharistic banners, formed a literature committee, and in 1889 supported the introduction of the Sisters of the Church for working with the poor of the parish.[40] Foundlings and Chinese appear in the registers, indicating a shift to a church of the disadvantaged.[41] This development holds the key to survival of Christ Church against all odds.[42]

Of the prize-winners of St Laurence's School, 11 out of the 26 winners between 1911 and 1923 were Chinese.[43] In 1927, the Guild of St Laurence was discontinued and became part of the Confraternity of the Blessed Sacrament.[44] Christ Church became less and less a church for baptisms and weddings and grew as a centre for Eucharistic worship, especially at Christmas and Easter. Of the 458 listed parishioners in 1980, no more than 10 lived in the originally defined parish.[45]

Apart from a bias to the academic field, the present parishioner of Christ Church represents the normal cross-section of society.[46]

PERSONS AND EVENTS

Christopher Brennan

One of Haymarket's greatest native sons was the poet and academic Christopher Brennan. Brennan's parents were both Irish. His father worked at the Castlemaine Brewery in Hay Street. Christopher, named after his father, was born on 1 November 1870, in Harbour Street. His surviving siblings were Agnes Ellen, Teresa Mary, Philip Benedict (who served in World War I and to whom *A Chant of Doom* was dedicated) and John Felix, named after Dean Sheridan.

The family was very Catholic, with the father presiding over family prayers every night. This did not prevent the enjoyment of card games, horseracing, smoking or a drop of spirits. When Chris was five and the family was living in Quay Street, next to the brewery where his father worked, there was a fire. As recorded by the *Sydney Morning Herald*: 'The boy was hastily wrapped in a blanket and carried to the house of some friends, in Hay Street'. Brennan recalled that 'The sparks were showering and I asked if the stars were falling? When I was put to bed I was too excited to sleep and got the ebony elephants from the clock to play with.' He was sent first to St John's Poor School in Kent Street (he was one of the few to wear shoes) in 1877. Then in 1879 he started at the Haymarket parish school of St Francis. But in 1880 he went to the Good Samaritan School in Pitt Street South, run by the Sisters, opposite Christ Church St Laurence. The family attended mass at St Francis' Church and Chris became an acolyte there. But on moving to the Good Samaritan School:

> I was taken out of the rather rough company of the St. Francis' altar boys and set apart as single in my kind ... I was surrounded by dedicated women except thus far ... Now hither came the Magdalens as well and, as they came past, they would pat my cheek and say 'Ain't he a little love' ... I early gained perceptions of delicate ritual beauty ... What change it was from the black soutanes and snuffy taper-smelling surplices of St Francis to a red soutane, lace cotta, watered silk sash, blue cord and tassel and buckled shoes.

There was no going out after dark (despite dim gas lamps) except to church and together. When he was 11 Chris made his way across to the new Jesuit school of St Kilda in Woolloomooloo Street (before it was relocated in Bourke Street as St Aloysius), which had only opened in 1879. Brennan took to English and Latin with gusto, acquired the basics of French and German and did well at chemistry. He was taught singing for nine years by an eccentric German, Hugo Alpen, who had a gift for cajoling hidden musical talents from his pupils. In 1883 the school was in Bourke Street—the building was later to become St Margaret's Hospital. Brennan was encouraged by his parish priest, Dean Sheridan, to apply for the Riverview Scholarship, the purpose of which was to assist students in their study for priesthood. Cardinal Moran, who had established the scholarship, remained on good terms with Brennan after he had abandoned his vocation.

Brennan went from success to success, from brilliant poet to classical scholar, from the University of Sydney to Europe (Berlin) and then back to take up professorship in German at Sydney. After being separated for four years, the Prussian Elisabeth Werth came out to Australia and six days after her arrival the couple was married in St Mary's Cathedral. Her mother and sister came to live with the Brennans three years later. But the Great War and the alcoholic demon could not be restrained!

> Brennan ... the finest flower of European culture in Australia was by then on the way to joining Lawson on the scrap heap of human endeavour. Possibly in revenge for the terrible delusion that a woman's love might stifle the sorrow deep in his heart, he seized on the outbreak of war as an opportunity to savage his wife's people. The bully boy of intellectual discourse announced to audiences of wine bibbers in Sydney that the British had a chance of settling the world's bully! A terrible descent into hell had begun.[47]

In 1917 his daughter, Anne, intellectually, emotionally and artistically most like him, fled the tempestuous family residence. Though only in her late teens, she lived on the streets and was known as 'German Annie'. Her preferred location was outside the Australian Museum, where she would tell everyone she was Brennan's daughter.[48] One of Anne's haunts was the Café la Bohème, at 5 Wilmot Place in the city. Run by Betsy Matthias, the separated wife of an IWW organiser, it was a meeting place for artists, writers, actors and mountebanks.

Brennan himself sometimes would stay there instead of Bateman's Hotel, at 432 George Street.

In 1925 Brennan suffered the misfortune of being convicted in court of adultery *after* the death of his mistress with whom he had lived in Paddington for several years. A short time later he was dismissed from his professorship by the senate of the university. Still, he fared better than Henry Lawson, thanks to his friends and to the Marist Brothers and Charity Sisters of Darlinghurst. The disgraced and impoverished old scholar and poet made his peace with the Church of his youth. Before his death in 1932 he had returned 'to the religion he had learned in his family at the Haymarket—the crucifix next to the heart; the belief in the healing power of the Blessed Sacrament'.[49]

Peter Joseph Brennan

In 1883, aged 40, Peter Joseph Brennan settled in Ultimo after coming to Melbourne from Liverpool in 1868. Brennan worked as a steward on sail and steam ships and was appalled at the conditions in which ship cooks and stewards worked—60 hours a week, often without adequate meals and berths, for the sum of 2*d*. an hour. In 1884 Brennan founded the Stewards and Cooks Union and affiliated it with the Trades and Labour Council. He also formed in 1889 the Amalgamated Slaughtermen and Journeying Butchers' Union and in 1891 the Hotel and Caterers' Employees Society. He became president of the Trades and Labour Council in 1890 and the subsequent Australian Labour Conference. Though a trade union leader rather than a politician, his historic motion of 1891 led to the formation of the Australian Labor Party.[50]

Frank Clune: The Little Larrikin

Popular author Frank Clune, though

properly from Woolloomooloo, used to roam, as young inner-city urchins did, through the Haymarket district. George and Pitt Streets were paved with wood blocks which came from the jarrah forests of Western Australia. These blocks would be piled up by the roadside when the streets were blocked or repaired. As wood was the normal cooking fuel for the poor people nearby, and the poor were many and so were the children, they all had billy-carts which came in very handy to take a load home to feed the family oven.

After dark, the larrikins would have another picnic. They enjoyed smashing the street gas lamps by hurling stones at them. Clune recalled that during the bubonic plague outbreak in 1900, free disinfectant was available at the Sydney Town Hall. He collected a few dozen bottles and peddled them back in Surry Hills for profit, until the officials woke up to the dodge.

But the most gruesome memory is left to last. The occasion was the removal of Devonshire Street cemetery to Botany. The urchins kept a sharp eye after the disinterment. 'It sounds ghoulish,' Clune wrote, 'but a boy has no qualms when gold glitters in the clay. I found more gold in Devonshire Street Cemetery than my absent father ever found on the diggings in the West.'

Little Frank went to the Marist Brothers at 'St Benno's' (St Benedict's, Broadway). Blackfriars Public School was next door. Fights were a-plenty and sectarian insults traded between the 'Prodoppers' and the 'Cattleticks'. The star pupil at St Benno's was Norman Gilroy, who was invariably at the top of the class. 'Little did we know that Norman would finish up as Archbishop of Sydney.'[51]

Jack Lang

Another of Haymarket's greatest sons was Jack Lang. The baptismal register of old St Francis reads:

JOHN THOMAS LANG, BORN 21 DECEMBER, 1876 of J.H. Lang and

Jack Lang.

Mary Whelan of George Street—
Godparents:
J.J. Gilchrist and Mary Gilchrist,
Baptised 1 January, 1877.

'I was born in a house on Brickfield Hill at the corner of Union Street, where the Plaza Theatre now stands,' Lang wrote.[52] His father, James Henry Lang, was a Scottish Presbyterian who became a zealous convert to Catholicism at the time of his marriage to 'an easygoing Irish woman, who never attempted to impose her beliefs on anyone, but remained rigidly loyal to her church'. Lang's father later opened a watchmaker and jeweller's shop on the George Street site where his son had been born.

Lang was the sixth child in a family of 10. J.H. Lang prospered in his jewellery trade but constantly moved his shop. *Sand's Directory* provides the following trade entries for J.H. Lang:

1873	10 Park Street
1875	86 Market Street
1880	24/20 Goulburn Street
1882	617 George Street
1883/4	710 George Street

1887	28 Wexford Street (residential only)
1893	70 Macquarie Street South (residential only)
1894/5	70 Macquarie Street South (resumed trading)

Jack Lang was to recall:

> The streets were illuminated by gaslight, and each night about dark, the lamplighter would walk around with his crooked stick lighting the lamps. Another well-known character was the bell ringer, who was the travelling advertising man, announcing the auction sales, meetings, tent shows and theatrical performances in ringing tones so that all could hear, with the traditional 'Oyez ... Oyez ... Roll up'. Behind George Street in the area from Hay Street to Rawson Place, on the site where the Australian Gas Light Company headquarters now stands, there was the blacks' camp, where the aborigines gathered around their camp fires at night, had their sing-songs and performed their tribal dances.
>
> I attended school at St. Francis, a Marist Brothers school, surrounded by Hay, Campbell, Castlereagh and Elizabeth Streets, where the city railway now goes overhead into the underground railway.[53]

However, rheumatic fever struck down Lang's father and left him bedridden. 'We were forced to leave our very comfortable residence in George Street and go to a poverty-stricken house in the slum area of Wexford Street (now Commonwealth Street).' Lang's mother hawked jewellery from door to door; one of his sisters became a servant and Lang sold papers on a beat from Market Street to Circular Quay: 'I had my regular customers to whom I delivered the *Sydney Morning Herald*, its afternoon publication called the *Echo*, and its weekly, the *Sydney Mail*, the *Evening News* and the weekly, *Town and Country Journal*'.

Jack Lang courted Hilda Bredt, daughter of Herman Bredt, a German-born citizen who was shire clerk of Bairnsdale. When Bredt died his widow married W.H. McNamara, who opened a bookshop in Castlereagh Street, next to the fire station. Henry Lawson married Hilda's sister, Bertha. Lang was first attracted to the shop because of the Bairnsdale connection—he had been sent to an uncle's property there and went to school in Bairnsdale, where he was chastised by a Fr Verlin for something he hadn't done. 'Then for the first time I realised that I had a rebel streak in me.' Mrs McNamara later became the founder of the Women's Central Organising Committee of the Labor Party.

On 14 March 1896 Lang married Hilda Amelia Bredt at St Francis' Church, Haymarket. They had four daughters and three sons. Lang became a real estate agent at Auburn, was mayor of that municipality and entered state parliament as MLA for Granville. He was treasurer, 1920 to 1922, party leader from July 1923, founding director of the *Labor Daily* (January 1924) and treasurer and premier 1925 to 1927, and again from 4 November to 13 May 1932, when he was dismissed by the Governor of New South Wales, Sir Philip Game. 'The Big Fella', as he was known, established his paper *Century* which he edited until his death on 27 September 1975, aged 98. Lang published five books after his dismissal and was Federal MHR for Reid from 1946 to 1949. After Requiem Mass at St Mary's Cathedral he was buried at Rookwood Lawn Cemetery.

Arthur Calwell regarded Lang as the first folk hero of the city. Lang was always a fighter and left behind many achievements, such as child endowments, widows' pensions, the Main Roads Authority and Government Insurance Office.

Henry Lawson

As a youth of seventeen, Henry Lawson was living with his mother, the early feminist Louisa, in Phillip Street. He had to get up at five to catch the workers' train from Redfern at six:

> There were times when I would have given my soul for another hour's sleep. I used to make bread and milk over a

little spirit lamp before leaving home, but sometimes I'd be so weak and worn out with overnight study and want of rest that I'd go out in the yard and be ill before starting for Redfern. I walked through Hyde Park, Elizabeth Street, and Belmore Park to the railway station, and it was then that the faces in the street began to haunt me. The faces, and the wretched rag-covered forms on the benches, and under them, and on the grass. The loafers and the unemployed used to sleep under the verandahs round the old central markets, and under the eaves of the sheds of Circular Quay on wet nights ... I remember one morning, seeing a horrible old bundle of rags and bones, that had been a woman, struggle up from the wet grass and, staggering, try to drink from an empty bottle. I don't know why she sticks in my memory picture.

Lawson and Daughter.

But the faces in the street were passing all the time. The worn faces and the gaunt figures in the pitiful clothing. Meeting me and passing, and catching up and passing, and seeming to turn momentarily, hopelessly, fearfully, resentfully, appealingly, as though looking at me for help or sympathy— or guidance—for something—I don't know what. And my face was one of them and not the least pale and pinched nor my figure the least gaunt or meanly clad.

I used to haunt Paddy's Market— about the only place I went to on a Saturday night.[54]

Lawson drew quick literary sketches of these city people, unlovely and unloved, the haggard and bedraggled women loaded with groceries and toddlers. It is ironic that the man whose portrait was for years on the ten-dollar note was the man who once proposed 'red revolution' as the answer to poverty, misery and sorrow, and who challenged 'the apathy of wealthy men' and 'Mammon slaves'.

While Lawson was no saint, for he destroyed his own life and could not support his wife and children, he could be generous. The story is told of how in Hyde Park he swapped his new boots for

some battered ones belonging to an unemployed married mate of his with a family with no chance of a job.[55] Lang described how he spent his weekly pay to take a drunken Lawson home with him to Dulwich Hill, and how he had to gag Lawson when the cabbie objected to Lawson's shouting.[56] Lawson died aged 55 and was buried in Waverley cemetery. The latter part of his epigraph on his grave is painfully true: 'No heart, can take of thee a tame farewell'. His wife Bertha lived for another 35 years and died in 1957, aged 81.

George Ardill

Another of the Haymarket's notable personalities was George Edward Ardill. Born into a Baptist family at Parramatta in 1857, while still in his twenties he devoted himself full-time to charity organisations and evangelism. Preaching at late-night street meetings he came across destitute and homeless women. By 1884 he had opened an All-Night Refuge and the Home of Hope For Friendless and Fallen Women. Other homes were opened for discharged prisoners and unwanted children. By the 1890s Ardill was organising creches in the city and was director of 12 societies. In 1885 he married Louisa Wales at the Baptist church in Bathurst Street. The matron of the Home of Hope hospital, which was renamed South Sydney Women's Hospital, Louisa died in 1920 but the hospital continued till 1939 without government subsidy. Despite effort and ingenuity, and his quarterly magazine *Rescue*, Ardill found it difficult to pay his many expenses, mortgages and salaries. He was reprimanded by the 1898–99 Royal Commission on Public Charities for his leniency to recidivist women (second illegimate child) and failure to pay employees. Government subsidies were withdrawn. Ardill became a member of the Aboriginal Protection Board in 1897. He removed children from the Aboriginal community into his care to make them 'useful members of the state'.

Ardill was a founder, and in 1890 secretary, of the N.S.W. Society for the Prevention of Cruelty to Children. He lobbied successfully for an act of parliament establishing a woman's right to support from the putative father of her child before its birth and for the establishment of a children's court. Ardill and his wife were ecumenically ahead of the times, and he helped organise missions in the early years of the century which drew audiences of 50,000 to 100,000. Fittingly awarded an MBE in 1934 for community service, he died in 1945 at Stanmore, aged 87. He was buried in Waverley cemetery with Anglican rites.

Ardill had to resist public slander and criticism, successfully in the case of the labour newspaper, the *Australian Workman*, which in 1891 had damages of £300 awarded against it for misrepresentation of his work. He accepted £120.[57]

The *Sand's Directory* of 1910 lists the following institutions under the directorship of 'G.E. Ardill (J.P.), 403 Sussex Street', between Goulburn and Little Hay Street on the western side:

Sydney Rescue Work Society
Society for Providing Homes for Neglected Children
Our Children's Home
Jubilee Regis
Home of Hope
Open All-Night Refuge
Our Boys' Farm Home
South Sydney Women's Hospital
Society for Prevention of Cruelty to Children
Babies' Home
Discharged Prisoners' Mission
Hon. Secretary Aboriginal Protection Association

Lest anything be left out it should be stated that Ardill was 'a founding member of the Social Purity Society in 1886 and later Secretary of its viligance committee on public morals'.[58]

John Norton: The Anti-Wowser

In 1884, aged 22, with a European walking tour behind him, John Norton migrated to Sydney and made a mark with his journalism on the *Evening News*. He had already worked as sub-editor with the *Levant Herald* in Constantinople. In 1886 he represented the Trades and Labour Council at a Paris Conference. He joined the newly established *Truth* in 1890 and six years later was editor and sole proprietor. 'He had a flair for pungent phraseology, published divorce news under the caption "Prickly Pairs in the Garden of Life", constantly attacked what he regarded as puritanism, and has often been credited with introducing the term "Wowser".'[59]

John Norton was also a politician, being elected member for Surry Hills in 1898. He accused W.A. Holman (premier of New South Wales, 1913–20) of corruption in July 1906 and actually nominated for Holman's electorate of Cootamundra, but later withdrew. Norton lost his own seat of Surry Hills but gained Darling Harbour instead, 1907–10. He died in 1916 in his fifty-fourth year.

George McCredie: Unsung Saviour

Human history has had to endure many disasters, but what can equal the terror of bubonic plague? Sydney experienced such terror in 1900.

Conditions in the workingmen's houses around the shores of Darling Harbour had long been atrocious. Inadequate sanitation, forgotten by absentee landlords and health authorities, was exposing the city to great risk. The fuse was lit a long way off, but as Max Kelly records, slowly it crept closer:

> Plague outbreaks were first recorded in the town of Liao Tchou in Kwang Si Province. Bubonic plague was then officially declared in Hong Kong, May 1894, Bombay in 1896, Mauritius in February, 1899, Noumea on December 24, 1899, Adelaide on January 15, 1900 and Sydney on January 19.[61]

Arthur Payne was the first to be transferred to the Quarantine Station, but it was 1 March before a poster appeared both in English and Chinese: 'Plague is present in Sydney. It has been introduced by diseased rats and there is a great danger of its spreading still further'.[62] Between 19 January and 9 August 303 persons contracted the disease, of whom 103 died.

An architect and a consulting engineer, George McCredie, whose offices were in the Mutual Life of New York Building in Martin Place, was appointed by the government to take charge of all cleansing operations. He started work at 4 p.m. on Friday, 23 March, more than two months after the first death from the plague and amid protests about his 'outside' appointment. His first task was an inspection of the plague-infected areas. A shocking indictment of the neglect of the public health on the part of the City of Sydney Council was the outcome:

> the house to house inspection showed that the Board [of health] had fallen into a deplorable state from long continued omission of the local authority to execute the ample powers to preserve the public health ... under its own Act of Incorporation, 1879, and under the Public Health Act, 1896. The result of this maladministration—now for the first time revealed to the general public, though

well known in several quarters—was that where though there are good laws, there is an executive authority over a part of it which is at once uninstructed, indifferent, unguided by the routine of an efficient organisation, and ungoverned by strict principles of action.[63]

McCredie quarantined a district at a time and, as it was difficult for him to find volunteers, he began to recruit those who lived within the quarantined areas. Local residents had to remain within the barricaded area as the work of cleansing (with carbide water), limewashing (walls and fences), burning, and in some cases demolishing progressed:

> Cleansing continued from March 23rd to July 18th. The extent of the work is conveyed by the following. 52,030 tons of silt and sewage was dredged from the front of the wharves. 28,455 tons of garbage was taken out to sea and a further 25,430 tons was burned. 3,808 premises were inspected and cleansed. 17,000 rats were destroyed in the normal course of the work. At the quarantine depot 27,548 rats were destroyed, having been caught by rat catchers. 1,423 dead animals were taken from the Harbour and burned. Between 1,000 and 3,000 men were employed. The total cost was £63,935.[64]

The areas of sub-standard housing stretched along the western shore of Darling Harbour to Kent Street, and from The Rocks south to Chippendale. They also included the area east of old St Francis' Church. Certain parts of Woolloomooloo, Paddington, Redfern and Manly were also affected. Lang and Lawson's mother-in-law had written rather prophetically:

> Four small rooms, a little backyard, a few feet wide, a few feet long and, perhaps a little garden. Yes, I say garden, because it is of favoured Australia, the working man's Paradise, I am speaking. Though I may add, if Australia at present presents the Working man's Paradise, I should hardly care for a glimpse even of the Working man's Hades.[65]

The aftermath resulted in a reformation

of the Sydney City Council in 1901. William Morris (Billy) Hughes, the local MP, was the driving force. A state body, the Sydney Harbour Trust, was established. It was given power over all docks, wharves, warehouses and areas adjacent to the harbour. Large tracts of land along Darling Harbour were resumed at the direction of the chairman, R.P. Hickson.

Slum demolition campaigners emerged. Prominent were R.F. Irvine and the Rev. Boyce, rector of St Paul's. Boyce insisted that 'people should have room to live'. Exeter Place, off Wexford Street, was only 11 feet wide. The Chinese population had 300 households in these sub-standard houses, but only nine of them were Chinese-owned. The Chinese who died from the plague were interred near the Coast Hospital at Little Bay. The headstones, with Chinese characters inscribed, still stand within a military enclosure there.

The quarantined houses and the men, women and children, native-born and Chinese, who lived in them were all captured on film by McCredie's anonymous photographer. McCredie himself appears in the photos, wearing riding boots and philosophically smoking his pipe. He is perhaps the unsung hero of the whole episode and could, with some justification, be named the saviour of Sydney.

George McCredie was born in Pyrmont in 1859. He went to Fort Street School, which he left at 14, and gained a professional education by evening study. After his successful business career he also became mayor of Prospect, local magistrate and local member for Central Cumberland. A presentation was made to McCredie by the people of Sydney in gratitude for his cleansing work. Tragically, he died in 1903, at the age of 45, from an illness attributed to the effects of the plague. He left behind a widow and eight children.[66]

Surry Hills Childhood

Early this century the sea-chests, telescope, sextant, sou'wester, sea-boots and coat of Captain Rodd found a permanent home in a former prison warder's cottage at 362 Bourke Street, Surry Hills, opposite St Margaret's Hospital. The captain had lost his savings in an investment debacle and he now received an invalid pension of 10s. a week. On this he had to support his wife and three children. The rent alone for the single room they lived in was 4s. a week. The captain would sit by the fireplace in a sagging cane chair, smoking his pipe and dreaming of the time when a cataract operation on his eyes would permit him to return to the sea. Pictures of ships he had skippered hung over the mantlepiece— *Kosciusko, James Craig, Mary Moore* and *Dominion*. Shortly before Christmas one year two ladies from the Benevolent Society came and said the family was worthy of their charity. Packets were left on the table—no words were spoken—the women left. The father started up, asked for the packets and hurled them after the women. The wide-eyed young Lew, named after his father, went outside later and noticed the packets of charity had gone save for the cocoa package, its royal coat of arms torn and a crimson trail symbolic of a triumph of the spirit.

The young boy witnessed the transition of the Convent of the Sacred Heart to Mary O'Brien's Home for Unmarried Mothers, later to become St Margaret's Hospital. One afternoon after the iron wheels of the young Rodds' billycart had thundered down Flood Lane for an hour, a portly brothel madam appeared and loosed her full fury on the boys for disturbing the rest of her good hardworking girls!

Elder brother John was sent to the dying parochial school of St Michael's for threepence a week. Young Lewis would shop nearby at Mr Mullens' grocer's on the corner of Short Street. Butter would come from the ice-box served up on paddles, sugar, salt and flour from sacks and everything would go on the scales. Eggs were wrapped in newspaper. Kerosene would be filled in a bottle from a pump at the rear of the shop. The shopkeeper would often pour boiled sweets into a papertwist as a bonus. Harry King, the Chinese grocer on Crown Street, would give each customer at Christmas a pottery jar from Canton full of ginger.

Known for his generosity was Doctor Sampey, who lived in Devonshire Street. Whilst consultations were 2s. a visit, the poor paid only 6d. and the destitute received free advice and medicine. After the doctor died, the shops in Crown Street closed for the funeral and women cried as they told of his kindness.

At night the family gathered around the light of the kerosene lamp. The father sat in a dark corner, smoking his pipe. Books would be read aloud, everyone taking a turn: *The Pilgrim's Progress, The Swiss Family Robinson, Robinson Crusoe, A Christmas Carol* and *Oliver Twist.* Card games were played and folk tunes sung.

Ugly poles with stark bulbs replaced the elegant gas lamps. Tarred wood blocks were set on concrete foundations to provide a non-bluemetal surface. Tree guards enclosing plane tree saplings appeared. When the bell tolled slowly on Sunday morning it was not for church at St Michael's but for prayers for a man about to hang. The family stopped their breakfast as the mother said a silent prayer. The awesome gaol was visited after the Holman Government announced it would be converted into a technical college.

Crown Street Boys' School was a bitter experience for sensitive young Lew. His only joy was skating down the six levels of the polished bannister rail and skirting board. Fear of the class teacher's anger and punishment caused him to stay away from school and at times caused actual sickness. He took a dislike to the wartime patriotic jingoism and patriotic songs at school. His snobbish teacher humiliated him because of his patched clothes and all he learnt at school was the meaning of poverty. In the late afternoon from the nearby zoo, the roars of the lions at feeding time could be clearly heard from the family home. A back room for the boys was now rented and the two rooms cost 6s. a week. The young Rodd went to Sunday School at St Michael's with 180 other pupils. Young Lew would often read out racing tips and slip out to the Beresford Hotel to place a bet for his father. When the captain's health failed, there was no going to hospital. The boy fed his father pieces of orange and removed the dried sections from his mouth. Two officious aunts were told to clear off by the dying man, who patted the boy's head to reassure him after the unexpected display of passion.[67]

In later life Lewis Rodd married author Kylie Tennant. A teacher by profession, he wrote a history of Christ Church St Laurence parish, of which he was a member. His early years provide a deeply felt experience of the inner city.

ENTERTAINMENT

Theatrical Crowd-Pleasers

Across Campbell Street, so named after one of the first merchants of Sydney Town, adjacent to the Mick Simmons Store, stood the Alhambra Music Hall. It provided entertainment with its vaudeville shows such as 'Stiffy and Mo' and exhibits such as exploits of the daring Aboriginal Jimmy Governor. Further down and off George Street, the Cyclorama opened in 1889 with *The Battle of Gettysburg*. The battle was accompanied by lectures and war songs sung by a hidden vocalist. At Eastertime a spectacular Jerusalem scenario was presented in similar dramatic fashion.

Swimming Place

Championship sport at the highest

international level is not readily associated with Sydney's downtown. There are, however, historical links between the two. For example, in 1888 the architect Thomas Rowe formed the Sydney Bathing Company Limited. On the corner of Pitt and Goulburn Streets, 400–08 Pitt Street, a large teetotal Grand Natatorium Hotel was built. It met a need. Bathing in the open on sea beaches in or near Sydney was prohibited by law until 1902. Some enclosed swimming baths, for men only, had been established on the shores of the Harbour in Woolloomooloo Bay. Frank Clune recalled:

> The Natatorium had two large concrete pools, each thirty-three yards long, in its basement. They were filled with sea-water, which was pumped from Woolloomooloo Bay, and not from nearby Darling Harbour, where Rowe considered the water was too stagnant to be healthy. The experiment proved to be successful, and led to the formation of the New South Wales Amateur Swimming Association in 1892, to control championship races. Outstanding among the swimmers who trained and raced at the Natatorium were W.J. Gormley, Percy Cavill, Dick Cavill, and 'Freddy' Lane. In 1899 Freddy Lane went to England and won championships there. Then he went to the Paris Olympiad in 1900, and won the 200-metres swimming race and title of World Champion ... (This was the first Olympic Gold Medal won by an Australian in Swimming.) ... After the bank smash of 1893, Tom Rowe lost money heavily, and eventually the Natatorium was sold to the Salvation Army and converted into the People's Palace, and the baths were closed.[68]

Trumper's Mystique

Victor Thomas Trumper was born in 1877 in Darlinghurst, one of eight children. He went to Crown Street Public School, where 'At lunchtime and before and after school, the boys played cricket, with the boy who dismissed the batsmen next in. Trumper once batted for six weeks. When his father

asked how he was going at school, he simply said, "I'm still in".'[69]

The *Wise Postal Directory* of 1905–07 lists a sports depot under the name of Trumper and Carter at 108 Market Street (later at 124). It was at this shop that meetings were held to discuss the N.S.W. Rugby Union's purchase of Epping Racecourse (Harold Park) while players injured received no compensation. James J. Giltinan and Harry Hoyle, MP, were among those who attended. In 1908 the breakaway N.S.W. Rugby League was formed with Hoyle president, Trumper treasurer and Giltinan, after whom the Sydney Rugby league competition is named, secretary.

On one occasion Trumper was late for a match and without a bat. He got a new one out of his stock, made a century with it and returned it to the shop, marked down at half price because it was second-hand! In 1901–02 Trumper took an office job which involved night work. His eyesight was affected and his cricket suffered. Trumper was recognised as a scruffy genius, a man who hated self-promotion and cared little for his appearance:

> His cricket bag was a mess of dirty clothes, mud-spattered bats and pads and grubby socks. He was a soft touch for cadgers and those down on their luck, a teetotaller and non-smoker who never kept late hours, worshipped his wife and family, but died in great pain from Bright's disease, aged 37.[70]

Hampden Oval in Paddington was renamed Trumper Park.

Another local cricketer was Frank Iredale, who was born in Surry Hills in 1867 and toured England with the Australian cricket team of 1896 and 1899. He was a journalist and his book, *Thirty-Three Years of Cricket,* gives the following assessment of Trumper: 'To be near him seemed to me to be an honour. He was one of those natures which called to you, in whose presence you felt it good to live. I never knew anybody who practised self-effacement as much as he did.'

On one occasion Trumper smashed 335

runs in 160 minutes at Redfern Oval. Sir William McKell remembers how the local Chinese shopkeepers rushed to put shutters over their windows when Trumper started hitting out. Another future N.S.W. premier, James McGowan, stopped playing bowls on a nearby rink as the Trumper barrage began. Six cricket balls were lost that day in 1903.[71] McKell recalls:

I remember, once, when Victor had set up a sports-goods shop, going with all my other cobbers to buy what we called a 'compo' ball. It cost a whole sixpence. Victor sent us on our way with a whole cricketing set, two bats, stumps, bails, pads, the whole lot, and all it cost was the sixpence for the 'compo' ball. No wonder he was our hero! We venerated him.[72]

Haymarket's Australian Cricket Captain

Monty Noble, Australian Test cricket captain in 1903–04, 1907–08 and on the 1909 tour of England, was born in the family home in Dixon Street in 1873. His father was a grocer who named the youngest of his eight sons Montague Alfred. This led to his being nicknamed 'Mary Ann' by some. Watching him lead New South Wales into the field, his mother heard this conversation: 'There's Mary Ann'. 'Where?' 'Out in front!' Maria Noble told her son that night: 'My boy, had I know they would call you that name, I'd have given you different initials!'[73] However, on a tour in England, her son hit up 267 runs and destroyed Sussex with his swerving spinners, claiming 6 for 39. One commentator waxed, 'What a performance! What a M.A.N.'[74] The 'Bodyline' English manager, Sir Pelham Warner, regarded Noble as Australia's best captain.[75]

In his farewell appearance, Noble was run out for 37 when his runner, the youthful Ted Adams, later town clerk of Sydney, made an error of judgment. When commentating one summer night before air-conditioning became available,

Noble was overheard to say, 'It's so hot they should call it not 2GB but 2KB'. The staff of Kent Brewery sent two dozen chilled bottles of KB to the studio for Noble and his colleagues.[76] When the bank he worked for refused him leave to play interstate cricket, he switched to dentistry. Noble studied for his exams between matches:

He liked to keep young cricketers in order in his later days and warned them against late nights during matches or drinking during the day. No wonder a fine grandstand at SCG was named after him, for martinet or shrewd psychologist, he was dedicated to Australian cricket in a way few Australians have ever been.[77]

Sir William McKell unveiled the Noble stand at the Sydney Cricket Ground in 1949.

Wharf Cricket

Famous Australian cricketing all-rounder, Charles George Macartney, nicknamed 'The Governor-General' or simply 'the GG', had a Test career spanning 19 years. Along with Bradman and Trumper, Macartney remains among the few Australians to score 100 before lunch on the first day in a Test against England. But the GG's beginnings were not so distinguished. At 16 he worked as a junior clerk for a produce store in Sussex Street, Sydney. 'At lunchtime the staff played cricket on a nearby wharf, using a bag of chaff as a wicket, a lump of packing case for a bat and potatoes as a ball.'[78]

Googly Champion from the Sandhills

Arthur Mailey was born in 1886 in the sandhills district of Redfern.

His parents simply put up another room of hessian as each offspring arrived. Arthur had a life-size portrait of Victor Trumper on the wall in front of his bed and when the wind blew across the sandhills at night, it seemed that Trumper played his drives straight down the room in the moonlight.[79]

The war interrupted his cricketing career, but aged 32 he was the best googly bowler in the world, surpassing Bosanquet and H.V. Hordern. Mailey describes touchingly how he clean bowled his idol Victor Trumper with a googly in his initial first-grade match: 'I felt like a boy who had killed a dove'.[80] Mailey finished with 4 for 362 when Victoria scored a world record 1,107 runs in an innings. He complained:

'A chap in the crowd kept dropping my catches' and 'I was just finding a length when the innings finished'.[81] When Mailey appealed to the umpire for a decision, it was not an extroverted performance, but 'an apologetic whimper'. Mailey was a cartoonist and commentator, but he retired after the Australian Board of Control objected to his dual role of commentator and player. He turned to writing a humorous book of memoirs entitled *Ten For 66 and All That*. Mailey did actually take 10 wickets for 66 against Gloucestershire.

CRIME

Great Baby Farming Case

During the depression of October 1892, some labourers digging drains in the backyard of a two-storey house in Macdonaldtown discovered the remains of two decomposed infants. The occupants of the house, John and Sarah Makin, were arrested. A check on a house in George Street, Redfern, where the Makins had lived for five years, revaled another 15 to 20 corpses. Some of the infants had been stillborn but others were as old as 12 or 14 months. The coroner arraigned the Makins for trial in February 1893. Found guilty, John Makin was hanged and his wife sentenced to life imprisonment.[82]

Rape at Mount Rennie

In 1886, a young orphan girl from Bathurst accepted a lift from a horse-drawn cab in Sussex Street near the corner of Goulburn Street. The cabbie took her out to Moore Park and climbed into the cab to join her. Before long the pair noticed four youths watching them, members of the Waterloo Push. When two men tried to rescue the screaming girl, 18 hooligans attacked them. A phone call was put through from Redfern police station to Darlinghurst and three mounted troopers arrived at the small hillock called Mount Rennie (then still covered in bushland, whereas today there is golf and grass skiing) to find Mary Jane Hicks in a distressed state. At her hospital bedside the police jotted down details. It seems she had been raped by eight to 12 youths. A squad of detectives found plenty of people in the densely populated district of Waterloo willing to talk and many arrests were made. Initially, 15 larrikins and the hansom cab driver were arrested. Four were discharged. The remainder were sent to trial before Judge Windeyer. The first day lasted 14 hours. At the summing-up the judge did not adjourn proceedings until nearly 2.00 a.m., while on the following day he spoke for 10 hours, finishing at midnight. Nine youths under 21 were sentenced to death by hanging. At a subsequent trial, the cabbie, Charles Sweetnam, escaped with a sentence of 14 years hard labour and two floggings. On 7 January four young men under 20 were hanged at Darlinghurst Gaol.[83]

Baby-Minding Murderers

Baby-farming was a form of baby minding offered by 'professional' baby-minders, usually older women, for poor and unmarried working girls. These girls, much like Fantine in *Les Misérables*, handed over their babies in the hope that this would only be for a short time. Often, though, the baby-minder would sell the baby to a childless couple and move without leaving an address.

In September 1893, only one week after being asked by the Victorian Police Force for the whereabouts of Frances Knorr, born Minnie Thwaites, Detective Keating from the Sydney CIB knocked on the door of a house in Brisbane Street, Surry Hills. 'All right Mr Keating, I know what you have come for,' said Knorr. The bodies of two babies had been dug up in the backyard of a house in the Melbourne suburb of Brunswick and a third nearby. After a trial of five days, Knorr was found guilty and sentenced to death by Judge Holroyd. The hanging was to take place in the Old Melbourne Gaol but the hangman, Thomas Jones, who had hanged 15 men, found the thought of hanging a woman too much for him. An alcoholic, he cut his throat two days before the execution. Despite Jones' demise and a citizens' protest meeting and march on Government House, the prisoner had to meet her fate. 'The executioner and his assistants, wearing false beards and spectacles', made no mistakes and the prisoner fell more than seven feet to instantaneous death.[84]

ARTS

The First Great Novel of Sydney

Louis Stone's novel *Jonah*, published in 1911, records the bustling life in the area of Sydney around the Redfern and market areas. Above all, he captures all the larrikin gangs of the turn of the century. He does this by weaving the story of two larrikins, the hunchback Jonah (Joseph Jones) and the streetfighter Chook, as they get married and get jobs to support their spouses. Chook marries the woman he loves, Pinkey, and is lucky at two-up, winning enough to buy a horse and cart for his vegetable shop. Jonah is successful in business, but unhappy in his marriage to the alcoholic Ada. The omnipresent Mrs Yabsley does the washing and ironing and comments on events—for nothing is hidden to her— much as the chorus in a Greek drama. The novel contains such vignettes of Sydney life as the stalls of Paddy's Market on Saturday night lit by the glare of gas-jets, the carts of produce arriving early at the Haymarket, the slum wedding where extra guests turn up necessitating extra jugs of beer from the pub, and the boot-shop discount war.

Live Theatre

As Sydney grew, theatres began to move southwards. An Academy of Music began in Castlereagh Street next to St George's, was renamed the (Catholic) Guild Hall in 1880, and finally became the Gaiety. Another academy was opened up at the Haymarket in 1884. After one year it was renamed the Alhambra Music Hall, under which name it enjoyed a long life. The Criterion Theatre opened in 1886 on the corner of Pitt and Park Streets, and six years later the Lyceum opened in Pitt Street. The Adelphi (1911) is given special mention in the next chapter. The earliest theatre in downtown Sydney seems to have been the Haymarket at Brickfield Hill, which opened in 1874. However, it lasted only a year.

MAP 5
1914 – 1945

1 CENTRAL RAILWAY
2 CHIPPENDALE
3 HOTEL SYDNEY
4 HYDE PARK

5 HYDE PARK WAR MEMORIAL
6 SURRY HILLS
7 PYRMONT

5 Hours of Battle, Days of War, Years of Hunger (1914–45)

POPULATION

Chinese Nationalism

In 1911 the Manchu dynasty in China was brought to an end by the revolutionary movement led by Dr Sun Yat-sen. But it took 10 years before symbolic expression was given in Sydney to this momentous change. The many Chinese market gardeners simply continued to bring their produce to the new Municipal Markets, now located at the western end of Hay Street, where many other Chinese acted as agents for the sale of the produce. The Kuomintang Building in 58 Ultimo Road, Haymarket, became the home of the Chinese Nationalist Party of Australia and the South Pacific. In 1937 the Chinese General Pao Chun Chien had his offices on the second floor at 635 George Street,

adjacent to the Haymarket Post Office.[1] When in 1975 the wholesale and retail markets were relocated to Flemington, the Chinese character of the Haymarket developed further and broadened from importing warehouses, to restaurants and tourism as a distinct 'Chinatown'. The Consulate of the People's Republic of China is located in Elizabeth Street.

Closure of Concordia and Internment of Members

The fourth site of the Concordia Club was at 207 Albion Street, Surry Hills. For the fiftieth anniversary of the club in 1933, the German Cruiser *Köln* tied up at Circular Quay from 7 to 16 May and the

Concordia Club (Durham Hall), Albion Street.

Club's hospitality prompted a grateful letter of thanks from the captain. This was the first German warship to sail into Sydney Harbour after World War I. The ship was on a world voyage and had to adjust allegiances midway, when Hitler rose to power.

Solo aviatrix Elly Beinhorn on a round the world flight was another guest at the Concordia in April 1932. Another German aviator guest was Hans Bertram, who had to make an emergency landing in the north-west, and was discovered by tribal Aborigines after three weeks disappearance.

The renaissance of the club occurred in a small restaurant run by former club steward, Hermann Mortel. A covert club life began amid card games, coffee, pastry rolls and family evenings. During World War II over 100 Concordia members were interned at Tatura (Victoria), where Willi Haack built a short-wave radio set out of spare parts from a car wrecked in a smash by the camp commandant after a party, and other bits from a film projector and an electric iron. The radio was never discovered.[2]

During World War II the club was converted to a recreation centre for American servicemen. Officialdom, anxious to clean away any vestige of Hitler's racist propaganda, dedicated the centre to the Negro educational reformer and writer Booker T. Washington (1856-1915), who had been principal of Tuskegee Institute in the U.S.A.

GOVERNMENT

Industrial Workers of the World

The Industrial Workers of the World (IWW), popularly known as the 'Wobblies', were formed in Australia in 1907, two years after their foundation in Chicago. The ideology of the Wobblies included aggressive socialism, militant industrial action and the formation of one big union (OBU) to cover all unionists. Such ideas did not find favour with the majority of the Labour Council delegates who favoured the path of elected constitutional power. Driven by rival factions right at the beginning, the Sydney chapter of the Wobblies numbered only 14 members in 1912 and confined itself to propaganda work. The IWW head-quarters were in an old gospel hall in Castlereagh Street. A key member was Tom Barker, who had emigrated from England in 1909 to New Zealand, which he fled after being arrested for sedition for IWW activities. Seventeen months after his arrival in Sydney he produced one of the most controversial Australian posters of World War I. It read:

TO ARMS!!
Capitalists, Parsons, Politicians, Landlords, Newspaper Editors, and Other Stay-at-Home Patriots,
YOUR COUNTRY NEEDS YOU IN THE TRENCHES!

On 3 September 1915 two detectives arrived at the IWW headquarters and arrested Barker for publishing a poster prejudicial to recruiting under the N.S.W. War Precautions Regulations. Eleven days later Barker was tried at Central Police Courts and sentenced to £50 or six months gaol. Barker appealed on the grounds of being charged by State regulations on a matter of Commonwealth law. The judge upheld his appeal and Barker was free. But before long Barker was in trouble again. He took responsibility as printer and publisher of an issue of *Direct Action* which featured a cartoon by Syd Nicholls, which depicted a soldier crucified on a cannon with his blood dripping into a 'War Profit' skull held by a grinning fat man. Barker was sentenced, after an initial Crown withdrawal on account of incorrect police procedure, at Central Police Courts to either £100 or 12 months hard labour. Barker chose gaol, but he served only three months as the governor-general reduced his sentence.

The Arson Conspiracy Trial

In the meantime, five fires were set in city retail shops, causing damage estimated at £340,000. After Barker's release another 13 fires in city premises were lit but were most quickly extinguished. These fires occurred in the first 12 days of September. On 15 September the police offered a £500 reward for information on the outbreaks. On the information supplied by F.J. McAlister and Louis and Davis Goldstein, nine warrants were issued on 22 September 1916. The next day 30 police raided the IWW headquarters, now at the southern end of Sussex Street. Four members of the IWW were immediately arrested. Another eight of their colleagues were similarly charged with arson, conspiracy to secure the release of Tom Barker and conspiracy to prevent the introduction of conscription. Three of these arson attempts had been against Mark Foys and one of them, set in the Mark Foy bulk store, was successful.

Mr Justice Street was the presiding judge at the trial but Ian Turner charges that the real conspiracy had been that of the Crown: 'Of the twelve, three, perhaps four, had been involved in arson or preparations for arson (although the Crown case against the twelve was largely faked and bore little resemblance to anything that these three or four had done)'.[3]

Tom Barker had meanwhile been deported to Chile. The 12, however, remained in gaol. In 1920 the Labour Council, after a Labor government took office, resolved that: 'having given consideration to the case of the IWW men, we are convinced that they are the victims of a frame-up. We consider that a further inquiry will serve no good purpose and demand that the present Government release the men forthwith.'[4]

Ewing Royal Commission

In his memoirs Jack Lang said boldy, 'When a Government decides to set up a Royal Commission, its first job is to get the right Royal Commissioner'.[5] No judge could be found and eventually Justice Ewing came from Tasmania to head the commission. After 15 days, 30 witnesses and 7,000 questions and answers, Mr Justice Ewing found that of the 12 men, six were innocent, five guilty of seditious conspiracy and only one guilty of conspiracy to commit arson.

When Premier John Storey made public the Ewing recommendations, declaring the releases would take place as soon as possible, the *Sunday Times, The Bulletin* and the Melbourne *Argus* bemoaned this administration of justice.

> The New South Wales Cabinet met to consider Mr Justice Ewing's recommendations on August 3, 1920. The Minister for Justice, W.J. McKell, an IWW sympathiser, and later to be Premier of his State and Governor-General of the Commonwealth, minuted the decision: 'Cabinet has given careful consideration to the report of Mr Justice Ewing ... [and] has decided to recommend that all of the prisoners, with the exception of Reeve and King, be released forthwith.'[6]

In his Annual Report of 1921, the Labour Council secretary, Jack Garden, wrote somewhat fervently: 'The agitation for the liberation of the twelve IWW men is one of the greatest acts for the liberation of political prisoners that has been accomplished in any country in the world'.[7]

It must be remembered that Garden was at that stage a leading member of the Communist Party, which was formed in Australia in October 1920, three months after the first 10 of the IWW men were freed. Two of the 12, T. Glynn and J.B. King, became Communists. Glynn was the first editor of the party's paper but both he and King broke with the party in 1922, disillusioned with the Bolsheviks' failure to realise their slogans.[8]

Origins of 6.00 p.m. Closure

In February 1916 another batch of recruits for the Great War, not quite so eager as the first volunteers, rebelled against their harsh training. From their camp they stormed into nearby Liverpool, commandeered the liquor supply of a hotel, and then boarded trains travelling to Sydney.

> Noisy, drunken soldiers arrived at Central Railway Station in train after train, and marched through the city overturning fruit carts and smashing windows. Meanwhile a group of about 500 soldiers was confronted by an armed military picket at the station; several shots were fired, killing one rioter and wounding six ... The Commonwealth Government responded to the disturbance by ordering six o'clock closing of the hotels under the War Precautions Act and no further incidents of this kind occurred.[9]

It was not till a referendum in 1954 that 10 o'clock closing of hotels was restored. 'The tradition of the "six o'clock swill" endured, however, as bars were still required to close for one hour at 6.30 p.m. This unhappy requirement was abolished in 1963 by the Liquor Amendment Act.'[10] Many of the hotels in the Haymarket were early openers, operating from 6.30 a.m.

to 6.30 p.m. to service the wholesale fruit and vegetable markets. The other patrons were the homeless and destitute who made a beeline for these hotels at sunrise after a night in a squat, a dosshouse or one of the many hostels in the Surry Hills/Darlinghurst area. With the introduction of Sunday trading and the repeal of the Summary Offenses Act, the alcoholic comforter became available all the time, provided no-one was hurt or offended.

Lang gives this version of what happened on the soldiers' platform on Central Railway Station where the trains left for Liverpool:

> It was about 11 p.m. The grille on the eastern end of the assembly platform was closed. The military police had by this time been issued with arms and ammunition. They called upon the soldiers to halt. The soldiers turned a hose on them. A few pressed forward. Rifles rang out. A soldier of the 6th Light Horse fell dead on the platform, shot through the eye. A number were wounded. That was the end of the riot. Bullet holes in the roof, and one in the ticket office wall, provided reminders of the Battle of Central for years.[11]

War Memorials in Downtown

Numerous memorials are to be found in downtown Sydney paying tribute to those who gave their lives on active service in World War I. Among the earliest was the memorial (1917) at the start of Anzac Parade (Moore Park). Other close-by suburbs which erected memorials included Pyrmont (Harris Street), Surry Hills (Bourke Street School) and Redfern (Redfern Park). A simple plaque was put up in Eddy Avenue in 1925 to commemorate the New South Wales troops who marched to fight in the war. The cricketers at Moore Park put up a special fountain in memory of their fallen comrades. The fountain is on the corner of South Dowling Street and Cleveland Street.

In Hyde Park South is located the

War Memorial, Hyde Park.

major war memorial of Sydney and the Pool of Remembrance. Anzac House was located directly opposite the memorial (it is now in Kent Street). While the Cenotaph was constructed in Martin Place in 1926, it was not till two years later that an act of parliament gave legal sanction to the 1923 suggestion of the Institute of Architects that a memorial be erected in Hyde Park.[12] In 1929 a competition for the design of the Memorial attracted 117 entries. The first prize was won by Mr O. Bruce Dellit. Construction began in July 1932 and was completed eight months later. The memorial was officially opened by His Royal Highness, the Duke of Gloucester, on 24 November 1934. Architect Dellit was only 31 when his design was chosen. Sydney-born, he had studied at Sydney Technical College and the University of Sydney. Dellit asked Rayner Hoff to create the sculptures for the memorial. Despite the European name, Hoff was born on the Isle of Man, grew up in Nottingham, served in the war, came to Australia in 1923 and died tragically in 1937. Hoff was an instructor in drawing and sculpture at Sydney Technical School. His central sculpture in the Hall of Silence is the body of a young man borne on a shield by his mother, sister, wife and child. On 30 November 1984, the Governor of New South Wales, Sir James Anthony Rowland, rededicated the Anzac Memorial to all Australians who have served their country in war.

The Influenza Epidemic

The worldwide epidemic of pneumonic influenza reached Australian in 1919. Half the deaths, 11,552 in number, occurred in New South Wales, mainly among the young and middle-aged. About 36 per cent of Sydney's population was estimated to have contracted the disease in virulent form. The Holman State Government made a special appeal to the people that 'Everyone shall wear a mask'. Face-masks were worn when people went out

Masked volunteers during flu epidemic.

shopping or travelled in trams and trains. Churches, libraries, theatres, hotels and racecourses were closed. Churches and schools outside Sydney were allowed to remain open at the discretion of the local authorities. The critical period was one calendar year from February 1919.

Milk in the Schools

The major milk distributors used to have their bulk warehouses in Ultimo (Dairy Farmers Co-Op Ltd) and Darling Harbour (Peters Milk Ltd). In 1921 the milk companies began to distribute milk free of charge to infant schools in the poorer parts of Sydney. This move met with a favourable response from parents. By the end of 1923, over 5,000 children were paying a nominal penny a day for half a pint of milk.[13]

The Great Depression

At sunset in the worst days of the Depression, those men who had no jobs, money or shelter for the night would leave the soup kitchens and market areas of downtown for the nearby parks. The Domain was a popular area. Billies were boiled, newspapers unrolled as blankets, even makeshift bag humpies were put up.

Balfour Street flats (first inner-city public housing).

These humpies incurred the wrath of respectable citizens, the police and the Bavin Government. During 1931 many families relied on the sustenance provided by the state in the form of a weekly dole of cash, food vouchers or free issues of shoes and clothing. This was living on 'susso'.

Tenants who could not pay rent were often evicted by landlords. The most noteworthy clash occurred on Friday, 19 June 1931, at 143 Union Street, Newtown. This is often referred to as Bloody Friday, when the Communist-led Unemployed Workers Movement and other anti-evictionists clashed violently with the police, who had been sent in by the Lang Government. Fourteen anti-evictionists and 13 police were injured. Thousands watched this clash. In a demonstration at Railway Square, the speeches were of a revolutionary nature and the crowds were close to violence. In the event, three massive windows at Grace Bros were cracked, and three at Anthony Horderns. A rock was hurled through the window of the *Labor Daily* office in Brisbane Street, off Oxford Street, narrowly missing staff working there.

In July 1931 Eric Campbell, a retired colonel with a DSO and then a Sydney solicitor, called a meeting in Sydney Town Hall. The outcome was the formation of a paramilitary organisation of returned servicemen, known as the New Guard, for the purpose of protecting the community from Communists, anarchists and wreckers. By September the police estimated that effective strength was about 36,000. The New Guard was thought to resemble the Italian Fascist movement, while the method of breaking up Communist meetings resembled that of the German Nazis. At his inaugural address, Campbell advocated strong government, minimal taxation, radical reduction of civil servants, public services to become self-supporting, unemployment only solvable by stimulation of industry not by hand-outs, the banning of Communism and the deportation of Communists.[14]

At Darling Harbour during the Depression there was a hostel housing 400 unemployed men. The men had to be out by 9.00 a.m. Lights out was 9.00 p.m. There were also unemployed girls sleeping in the parks and doorways of the city. Sydney Labor women were concerned. Premier Lang referred the matter to the Repossessed Buildings Commission and part of the MLC Building on the corner of Elizabeth Street and Martin Place was used to house 40 homeless women. During the years 1931–32 the *Sydney Morning Herald* featured 18 leaders and 24 special articles on aspects of unemployment:

> During recent months the growth of begging in Sydney's streets has been a feature of the city's life. Many of those who have swelled the ranks are obviously victims of the financial crisis, honest unfortunate beings reluctantly driven to the quick charity of the passer-by as a last resource ...
>
> Most of their tales are as old as begging—tram fare to a job, sick wife, last square meal a week ago, war injury. Some are true; many false.
>
> Lurking in an alley-way, a man pushes his stunted child forward to offer onion pickles, home-made toffee. 'Has the gentleman a coin? ... sick mother ... please sir!' Thin faces dart from doorways—ties, handkerchiefs, face cream, shoe laces, posies, fish that waggle fins; unshaven chins, unwashed necks, collarless, shirtless, sockless, tense faces:

'Buy, buy, buy, give, give, give'; fierce whispers, the failure, the dart back to cover, the next prospect, "ere y'are sir, very cheap sir"; eager thrusting tenacious imploring.

Some offer nothing, some sing, make pretence at playing violins, clarinets, anything. Some just stand and look with hunger in their eyes. When the sun dips, the still lower orders rake the garbage tins—hooking, stirring; 'nothin' 'ere Jack'; banging of lids, the prowl beyond the lights. By the time the theatre crowds are home, they have all gone—somewhere.[15]

Teachers

Arthur McGuinness was born in New Zealand in 1878, grew up with his grandparents at Bathurst and became a teacher, one of his early positions being at Crown Street Public School. He became involved in teachers' politics and served on the executive of the N.S.W. Teachers' Federation from 1928 to 1945. A popular and fearless leader, he served as president of the N.S.W. Teachers' Federation, 1929–32, 1935–36 and 1940–45. McGuinness brought about a major change in the former multiple classification system of grading teachers from 3B to senior principal, 1A. Progression, which had been dependent on a system of departmental examination and thesis writing, was replaced by the criterion of professional competence alone. McGuinness died in 1970, aged 93. A tribute to him is found outside the Teachers' Club in Sussex Street.

Preparation for the Worst

In 1942, exactly 100 years after its incorporation as a city, Sydney was facing a very real possibility of invasion. A Japanese submarine shelled Rose Bay a few days after three midget submarines penetrated into Sydney Harbour and caused a night of chaos on 31 May 1942. The federal minister for home security

published Civil Defence handbooks pertaining to rescue and demolition. The State government set up the National Emergency Services (NES). The minister for labour and industry and social services, the Hon. Hamilton Knight, MLA, was in charge of civilian evacuation and detailed contingency procedures were drawn up. It was conceded, however, that evacuation of large residential areas was not practicable. The Sydney City Council published *Standing Orders and Instructions, with full explanation of the City of Sydney National Emergency Services Organisation.* Included were official instructions for air-raid wardens. A.M. Pickford, chief warden, signed the orders on 15 November 1942. Fifteen first-aid posts were established within the city, along with five stretcher party bases.

I stumbled on the Disasters Centre in my walks around downtown Sydney. The locality of the centre is not widely publicised for strategic reasons. The archives section was a treasure-trove of information.

Wartime Food Rationing

Rationing of goods did not start in Australia until the middle of 1942.

By mid 1944, severe drought further restricted each person to 2 oz. (about 60 gm) of tea, 1 lb. (450 gm) of sugar, 6 oz. (170 gm) of butter and two and a quarter lb. (1 kg) of meat each week. Sausages, fish, poultry and bacon were not rationed and special arrangements were made for young children, pregnant women and the sick. Each piece of clothing needed a given number of 'coupons' if you wanted to buy it: thirteen for a dress, six for a hat, twelve for a shirt. Detachable collars became popular again. Daylight saving was introduced from 1 January 1942 for the summer months of 1942, 1943 and for the first half of 1944 but ended then.[16]

While the Australian basic wage was £4 13s. 0d. a week and Australian troops earned 6s. 6d. a day, American GI's were paid £60 a month.[17]

INDUSTRY AND TRANSPORT

The Foundation Industry

Fred R. Burley, along with Horderns and the Foys, was another successful draper connected with downtown Sydney. He was born in 1885 and bought a half-share in a corset shop in Market Street in 1910:

> At that time the population of Australia was four million, of whom at least one million were women wearing corsets or 'stays' imported from England or France. These were cumbrous contraptions reinforced with whalebone strips, tight-laced to give the 'female form divine' a straight-laced appearance.[18]

Before long Fred, with the help of his family, opened a corset factory in Wilmot Street. By 1917 there were 60 employed in the factory and larger factory premises were obtained in Liverpool Street. In 1919 the trademark Berlei was adopted and the company name was changed to Berlei Limited. In 1920 the staff had grown to 280 and in 1921 to 384. In 1922 the factory was moved to Berlei House in Regent Street. Forty years later the total staff was 1,253, scattered across four outside manufacturing plants. Today Berlei is a multinational company.

Burley took advice from medical specialists concerning the design of women's foundation garments.

> In 1926–27, at his instigation, the Department of Obstetrics at the University of Sydney undertook an extensive anthropometrical research—the first of its kind in the world—coordinating the measurements of thousands of women, to obtain data ensuring that women's foundation wear would be not only fashionable but also anatomically designed on scientific principles, for health.[19]

In 1923 Burley became the first president of the Australian-Made-Preference League, to counteract the propaganda of those importers who stated local manufacture was inferior. In 1939 Berlei began manufacture in Britain, becoming one of the first Australian industries to open a subsidiary plant in Europe.

> Fred Burley was prominent in public and philanthropic work. He was associated with the Chamber of Manufactures, the Young Australia League, the Boy Scouts' Association, the Father and Son Welfare Movement, the Big Brother Movement, the Rotary Club and the YMCA. He made generous donations to and was appointed Life Governor of the Crown Street Women's Hospital and Royal Prince Alfred Hospital, Sydney, the Alfred and Women's Hospitals, Melbourne and the Geelong Hospital.[20]

Seventy years later Berlei U.S.A. recorded a more infamous milestone: the first nude TV commercial in that country. This occurred on two cable networks which reached 15 million subscribers. The saleable top and panties totalled $25; the commerical cost $40,000 for 30 seconds. From family thrift down to international sexploitation is a sad and sorry export progression.[21]

On the Sydney Buses

Apart from trains, trams driven by cable, steam and electricity, together with horse-drawn buses and hansom cabs, were the principal form of public transport. The internal-combustion engine saw horseless carriages restricted to 8 mph in the central city. After World War I motor buses multiplied. Initially they ran on solid tyres—pneumatic tyres came in the 1920s. By 1930 there were 219 privately owned bus services in Sydney using 587 combustion-engine buses. The government passed an Act in 1931 to rationalise these many bus services and began operating its first bus services in 1932. The first double-decker buses appeared in 1934. A trolley bus, double-deck, ran along Liverpool Street through Kings

Cross to Wylde Street from 1934 to 1948. Buses began to replace trams before World War II. The Leyland double-deck diesel arrived in 1946 and double-deckers were in use until 1976, when the unions fought and won against their one-man operation. They are now only used on express routes where the driver does not collect fares. The first Mercedes-Benz single-deck went into service in 1977. After fare-collecting conductors were phased out in May 1981, the centre doors of buses were opened for exit only in May 1982.[22]

The ABC

In 1923 a broadcasting licence was given to Farmer & Co., Sydney, station 2FC, and Broadcasters Sydney Ltd was given a licence for 2SB (later 2BL). The next year a system of 'A' and 'B' licences was introduced. A-class was financed by licence fees and B-class by advertising. 2FC became an A-class station. In 1928 all A-class stations were nationalised and 2FC and 2BL came under the New South Wales Broadcasting Co. The following year the Australian Broadcasting Company was formed and won the tender to take over all A-class stations. In 1932 the Australian Broadcasting Commission Act was passed and the ABC began operations with eight metropolitan stations and four regionals. The headquarters were in Sydney, and the first radio transmission of the ABC (Australian Broadcasting Commission; later Corporation) was made in Sydney on 24 July 1932. The actual location was 262 Pitt Street, in church offices next door to the former Congregational Church. The projector booth of the theatre on the first floor contained the original studio. The only remaining sign of the ABC's presence is a humble coir mat at the entrance of the building. The yellow characters 'A.B.C.' are clearly to be seen.

The chairman of the ABC at its formation was W.J. Cleary, but for 50 years the commission lacked the physical presence of the BBC, on which it was in many ways modelled:

> However closely the makers of the ABC might want to copy the BBC, distance and the federal compact imposed local peculiarities. This country would see no building like Broadcasting House, the great temple of wireless in London, which affirmed the BBC's presence at the centre of the imperial capital. The ABC has taken over from the Company a collection of studios and offices whose inadequacy became a regular theme in reports by Commissioners and grumbles by users; but ideas for improvement did not include a monumental headquarters building. There was no need for one, as long as programmes were fashioned separately in each State; and nobody could say for certain where an Australian Broadcasting House should be put.[23]

The headquarters staff was lodged in Sydney but commission meetings were held in both Sydney and Melbourne. During World War II the Pitt Street basement of Broadcast House was sandbagged to make both an air-raid shelter and a broadcasting studio. 'On the site intended for a new Broadcast House in Forbes Street, Darlinghurst, a suite of underground studios was built with a thick concrete roof.'[24] Dr H.V. Evatt, minister for external affairs, told W.J. Cleary that the ABC must counter the propaganda of BBC relays on the European war by putting Australia and the Pacific first. ABC controller MacMahon Ball discovered that Australia 'had only two or three people competent to eavesdrop on enemy transmissions or broadcast idiomatically in Japanese'.[25] He became an advocate for the study of Asian languages in Australia. The emphasis on local as opposed to European news imposed by the Labor government led the ABC to replace the introduction to the news bulletins ('The British Grenadiers') with 'Advance Australia Fair'. Top management had to endure much criticism for the change. South Australians were more disappointed that their own tune, 'Song of Australia', was overlooked. 'During the months of siege, people used the radio as never before: a poll in June 1942 disclosed that half the population were listening more often than they had done a year earlier, most of them to hear news of war.'[26]

What a turn-around it would have been if the ABC had been relocated on the corner of George and Liverpool Streets in one of three tower buildings on the block designed by Japanese Architect Kenzo Tange. The plans for the new ABC headquarters were, however, switched to the Dairy Farmers site in Harris Street, Ultimo, in order to house an organisation which has grown in 60 years from 12 radio stations with a staff of 256 to a staff in excess of 6,300.

The grey exterior of the new ABC headquarters, opened by Prime Minister Bob Hawke on 22 June 1991, conceals a vast ultra-modern array of atriums, bridges, tubes and lighting and houses ABC departments that were previously scattered around 11 buildings in Sydney. The new centre was designed by architect Ken Woolley and can house 1,200 employees. The floor space makes it the fifth-largest office building in Sydney. New technology is incorporated, such as

Ernie Warman in 1930s tramways uniform.

computer-based digital broadcasting, and four studios once housed at King's Cross—namely 2BL, Radio National, Triple-J and ABC–FM—are now in residence.

Riding the Footboards

I travelled out to Randwick to interview Ernie Warman in his home on 14 August 1984. Ernie and his wife made me welcome. He showed me a photo of his tramways uniform of the 1930s—it had to be buttoned up to the neck according to the regulations, and the same uniform was worn winter and summer:

> There was a white celluloid collar inside—a button and two little hooks. If you eased it off in summer and one of the 'curlers' caught you, he'd report you. You'd be reprimanded and disciplined. The uniform was navy blue with brass buttons which you had to polish. The brass button featured the initials 'G.R.' [George Rex] surmounted by the Crown. The words 'N.S.WALES Tramways' were embossed around the perimeter. The reverse side of the button bore the inscription 'Stokes & Sons, Melbourne'.
>
> When the Stevens Government got in our wages were cut in half—£7 a fortnight and one in six was put off work ... Do you want to know the names of the trams? *(Yes.)* There was a 70-seater which had an open seat on the front, five people could sit up front with the driver and they were called an 'N' car. And then there was a combo that was an open section where you sit with the driver and two open compartments and then there was a corridor and there was the same at the other end and the driver's section. They were always coupled together. Then they brought in the 'LP' cars, they had the footboards and instead of the open doors that the 'O' cars had they had a blind that you had to pull up and down. It was terrible when you were working on them as when it was raining, you had to keep pushing them up and down. And then there was the 'O' car; it had five doors on it with what you would call a

saloon. It had four compartments on it. Both ends had two compartments which were called 'smokers'. They had a big blind which used to come down. I tell you what, when you used to come and collect the fares and it was raining, you used to let the blind go up and walk away and leave it up and the people used to go crook. They were in more of a position to pull the blind down than we were, out on the footboard. Yes, it was dangerous. I was riding the footboards from 1927 to 1942 and then I was an acting driver, that is driving and conducting and I was appointed a driver in 1945. So I was 18 years on the footboards. *(Did you ever have a tumble?)* No, thank the Lord, cos if you had a tumble it was mostly the only tumble that you ever had, unless you were lucky enough to pick a soft part, or soft ground, but mostly when you hit the ground in hot weather, the ground was hard. *(Some of your friends must have been killed?)* Oh yes. There were a few, but not that many. I suppose there at Dowling Street [depot] there would only have been six or seven.

The depots were at Ultimo (mostly Erskineville run with the N cars) right out to Ryde and Gladesville and from Drummoyne over to Canterbury station across country. There was Rozelle [depot]. They did all Abbotsford, Leichhardt, and Balmain, Glebe Point, Lilyfield. The Fort Macquarie [depot] did mostly the city, between the Quay and the Railway. There was Waverley, they did Bondi, North Bondi, Bronte, Waverley, Bondi Beach via Bellevue Hill—they were the 'Jumping Jacks'. The Jumping Jacks were the trams that had only two sets of wheels, one near the front and the one near the back. They would rock as they went along. Past St Vincent's Hospital, you went over a bridge and did a sharp right-hand turn into Brown Street. Any amount of times if you weren't careful hanging on, you'd finish up on the other side of the road and you'd have to run and catch the tram which you could easily do because they weren't travelling that fast. They had to do away with those Jumping Jacks. (The sharp curves could only be taken by the two-wheel and not the four-wheel trams.) Waverley looked after the run from Bondi

to Coogee across country. Rushcutter's Bay depot—they all had Jumping Jacks. It was the only one to have a single line. They used to run from Erskine Street Wharf out to Watson's Bay. Sometimes the tram would only go to Dover Road, Rose Bay, Vaucluse, the Lighthouse or Watsons Bay. And then Dowling Street did Henderson Road, Alexandria Bay Street (Botany), Botany, Matraville via Botany and Daceyville via Waterloo. The Dowling Street Depot was on the corner of Dacey Avenue and Dowling Street where the Brambles depot is now. On this side they did Railway—Clovelly, the Quay to Clovelly, Coogee to Railway. Same with Maroubra to Railway and Quay to La Perouse. The trams went out to Mascot and you would either walk or get a taxi to Kingsford Smith airport. It was only in later years that buses went out to the airport. Now there's a yellow bus that does nothing but go out to the airport (route 300). It's a goer though, mind you. I've got a nephew that's a driver on it. And then there was a depot, in the steam days, up in Ritchie Street, that done from Kogarah to Sans Souci and Sandringham . . .

On the service from La Perouse and Maroubra Bay to the Quay they always had a timetable so that there was always a four- or five-minute service from Maroubra Junction to the Quay. When I first started here at Dowling Street, you would pick up your passengers here at the White Horse Hotel Kingsford and there'd be practically no more pick up till you got to Maroubra Junction and then no more pick up till you got to La Perouse. (Maybe one or two.) There was a bus from Henderson Road, Daceyville, Botany, etc. They all got to Raglan Street and from there it was a two-minute service to the Quay and they had officers out to see you weren't early. They had various inspectors out along the route. They had the same uniform as us only a gold braid around the cap. The sub-inspector only had a crown. Women didn't come in until the war. First they had the O car and then they had the P car. The P car had doors that opened and shut with canvas. The O car had glass doors. The P car had windows that pushed down and up. Then they got the 'R' type on. Well, over at Dowling

Street they used to get the large amount of 4 pence an hour as danger money for walking the footboard. But they'd sooner work a footboard tram than an R tram. *(Why?)* Well you had that little bit of footboard to yourself. But in the R tram when it was packed full, you had to fight your way through. Most preferred the footboards. Those that didn't went to depots where they had the R cars. They first came in at Rushcutters Bay and Circular Quay. We never got the R cars at Dowling Street till right to the last job. The ladies did not ride the footboards. They worked the R cars. My job at Dowling Street in the later years used to be stationed at the Showgrounds.

I used to 'make and break'. In the peak hour, I used to couple single cars in sets and then they come back after peak hour and broke them down again. (From two cars back down to single units.) Each car had its own conductor. It was only on the Jumping Jacks, where a conductor crossed from one car to another. *(Now which tram did you enjoy working on best?)* Oh, that was the O car. It was easier to walk along the footboard. *(And driving?)* Again the O car. They had small handles, a little control handle, whereas the R car had a large controlling handle.

The cars had two power poles. Only the N car had a single pole. When you got to the terminus you had to swing it right around. It used to cause a lot of friction. If it was a fraction out going across an intersection, it would go up in the air.

On the La Perouse run the trams would get up a bit of speed and one night we heard some terrible squealing. A hare had been hit. So we stopped the tram and we ran around in the dark trying to catch it and put it out of its misery.

From George Street West to Broadway

The postal authorities, the banks and business houses and the churches switched over to the new name of Broadway readily enough when George Street West was widened in 1940 to upgrade Sydney's main traffic outlet westward.

Archbishop Gilroy notified Dean Norris at St Benedict's that the parish would be known henceforth as Broadway.[27] The road-widening necessitated rebuilding the northern wall of the church and the demolition of the presbytery. Dean Norris arranged for a duty priest to remain in residence on site while the other two priests would reside at the Hotel Sydney. The church could be reached by tram in five minutes from the hotel and parish visitation could also be made from the trams which ran down Cleveland Street, City Road and through Broadway to Glebe. The three priests ate at the Hotel Sydney and had a common private sitting room.[28]

These expenses and the building costs for the church and the new presbytery were eventually met by the compensation money paid the Church by the State government. The Church had first to establish a special trust fund before an act of parliament was eventually passed to grant the compensation. Father Slowey moved the Catholic Education Office away from Roma House in George Street, opposite Central Station, to the Abercrombie Street School building. The Church was desperately attempting to keep up with the postwar baby boom and the children of immigrant families which were severely taxing resources and personnel of the Catholic school system. The westward spread of the younger families, regionalisation of the archdiocese, and the stringent new fire regulations applied to the old buildings, resulted in the closure of the old school complex by the beginning of 1983.

The Pastoral Year of Studies for newly ordained priests was also located at St Benedict's, as were courses for catechists teaching in the State schools. Monsignor W. Murray was in charge of pastoral formation as well as being the official spokesman for the Archdiocese. He was appointed Bishop of Wollongong in 1974.

The newly founded Brothers of Saint Gerard Majella taught secular subjects to prospective candidates for the priesthood at St Benedict's.

The Mirror Established

Ezra Norton continued his father's newspaper publishing activities, Truth and Sportsman Ltd. In May 1941 he established the *Daily Mirror*. Ezra was not the hell-raiser his father was. In fact, he became a convert to Catholicism from his Jewish religion. In 1958 he sold his interest in the company.

RELIGION

Downtown Catholics in World War I

In general terms, Australian clergy welcomed war in August 1914, believing that Australians would be weaned from materialism and learn the value of sacrifice and devotion to duty. Hundreds of clergymen served as chaplains in the AIF. But the grim reality of war led to no reform and renewal on the front, or at home, and frustration frequently resulted in sectarian outbursts. After the initial enthusiasm for war subsided and the terrible loss of life at Gallipoli, opinion over the introduction of conscription was bitterly divided. Fr Maurice O'Reilly was rector of St John's University College. He had been an ardent patriot and written a poem to celebrate Australia's war effort. 'He became, however, a passionate anti-conscriptionist and castigated Catholics who supported conscription as wealthy associates of the Liberal party who had as much love for labour as they had for Beelzebub.'[29] Defending Sydney's Catholics against Protestant attack, Fr Forrest compiled a list of recruits from each Sydney Catholic high school and the rewards they had won, among them 19 Military Crosses, one Victoria Cross and numerous other distinctions.[30] The list was published in the *Freeman's Journal* of 18 July 1918, which had adopted a pro-conscription stance in 1916. Its rival, the *Catholic Press*, had taken an anti-conscription stance and doubled its circulation at the expense of the *Freeman's Journal*.[31]

Prelude to the Boree Log

At St Francis Presbytery, Haymarket, in 1921, George Robertson, co-founder of Angus and Robertson, listened to a number of poems read by a newly ordained curate, Eris O'Brien (later to become an historian and Archbishop of Canberra and Goulburn). The poems were written by an outback priest, Patrick Hartigan, who had in the course of his duties attended a sick call from old Jack Riley who had been immortalised by Banjo Paterson in 'The Man from Snowy River'. George Robertson wrote immediately to Fr Hartigan: 'These verses are the best we have come across since *The Sentimental Bloke* happened along and we want to publish them. The tenderness and the humour of the verses have made me a friend for life.' C.J. Dennis also wrote to Fr Hartigan, urging him to publish. 'The contract was signed—and almost torn up when the firm's reader wanted to change the original title: *The Little Irish Mother and Other Verses* to *The Little British Mother*. The compromise was *Around the Boree Log* by 'John O'Brien' (pseudonym). The edition was immediately successful and still ranks with *The Sentimental Bloke* as a continuing bestseller in Australian verse.

The Irish Scholar Prelate

Michael Sheehan was a distinguished scholar and apologetic writer and, most importantly, vice-president of Maynooth. I can still remember grappling with the doctor's learned text, *Apologetics and Christian Doctrine*, in fourth form. The concepts of 'ex opere operato' and 'ex opere operantis' were more alien to our inquisitive minds than Mars or Venus.

When Dr Sheehan was appointed coadjutor archbishop of Sydney in 1922, with right of succession, rumblings of discontent among advocates of an Australian priesthood became public. Members of the Manly Union of Priests viewed with dismay the prospect of another 20 years of Irish episcopal rule. Fr Joseph Cusack, parish priest of Haymarket from 1912, wrote to the Melbourne *Catholic Press* that the principle 'Australia for Australians' had been ignored. He quickly found himself in a remote country parish. Dr Sheehan took up residence at St Benedict's, George Street West Parish. Not one who sought the public eye, in 1937 he resigned the coadjutorship and returned to Ireland. This opened the way for another coadjutor, Archbishop Gilroy, who had grown up in the George Street West Parish.

Marist Brothers High School

This school run by the Marist Brothers from 1875 to 1968 has as its motto 'Servo Fidem' (I Serve the Faith). The school was opened at Harrington Street, transferred to the grounds of St Mary's Cathedral in 1887, and then to Darlinghurst in 1911. Though the school does not strictly fall within the parameters of this study, there are many connections. Of the 22 pupils who were admitted to the school in 1875, one was E.J. Dwyer, who later was to establish an ecclesiastical retailing house. The firm of E.J. Dwyer operated in Kippax Street, Surry Hills, and is the publishing arm of the Australian Catholic Episcopal Conference. It recently moved to Alice Street, Newtown.

Captain of both the senior cricket and football teams of 1938 and 1939 was Ray Lindwall, later to become one of Australia's best fast bowlers:

In 1942, because of the threat of invasion by the Japanese, plans were mooted for transferring the school to Bowral, but these were shelved when the authorities advised that this was not necessary. However, the precaution was taken of erecting an air-raid shelter. The Old Boys Union and the Ladies' Committee raised the £535 to cover the cost. In addition, there was an increase in numbers in the senior cadet detachment which had been formed the previous year.

Other former students who went on to figure prominently in public life include Most Rev. John Toohey, DD, Bishop of Maitland, and three future Lord Mayors of Sydney: Patrick Darcy Hills, John Armstrong and Harold Jensen.[32]

Catholic Apostolates

The Newman Society was launched in the University of Sydney in 1928, partly to offset the anti-religious polemics of Philosophy Professor John Anderson, but also to provide for university representation at the Eucharistic Congress Procession.

The Catholic Club, founded in 1905, was by the 1930s a focus for social and intellectual activity. The Knights of the Southern Cross emerged in the 1920s as a powerful lay organisation which was popular and non-intellectual in character—a fact which, Patrick O'Farrell has noted,

> may be illustrated from the composition of the Southern Cross Library established by the Knights in Sydney in 1929. Over three quarters of its book stock was fiction: in the Catholic Library in Melbourne, this proportion is reversed, three quarters of the books were non-fiction.[33]

St Barnabas Church

Slaughterhouses lined the creek which ran

from George Street West into Blackwattle Bay in the middle of the nineteenth century. The men who worked in the slaughterhouses were a tough lot. Drinking and fighting took up much of their spare time. Thomas Smith was charged with forming an Anglican mission to the working men. While a church was being built, services were held in a room at the Marine Hotel at the top end of Bay Street. Bishop Barker set the foundation stone at St Barnabas on 28 August 1858. The church building, which cost £2,000, was enlarged three times on account of the successful preaching ministry of Thomas Smith.

Among later clergy, the Rev. R.B.S. Hammond is outstanding not just for the length of his sojourn (1918–43), but for the nature of his work. This temperance ministry through his Men's Meetings led to 4,000 decisions for Christ, while the housing settlement of Hammondville, near Liverpool, is a living memorial to his concern to provide housing for the poor and the elderly. On the other hand, it must be noted that no love was lost between the archdeacon and the rector of Christ Church St Laurence, the Rev. John Hope.

On Broadway there has been a long war of words between the billboard of St Barnabas on the west side, such as, 'Come to me all you who are heavily burdened' and the tavern opposite, which would chalk up a reply, 'And I will give you bread and wine'.

The Lutheran Church

In 1928 a more Australian grouping emerged from the Goulburn Street Lutheran Church worshippers. It was called the Trinity Congregation of the Lutheran Church and sought to make provision for 'An English Service' in addition to 'German Services'. The Congregation consisted of 'Australians, Estonians, Finns, Germans and others'. By 1932 the Estonians had formed their own Lutheran Congregation of St John. In 1936 the Trinity and St John's

St Barnabas' and billboard.

Congregations 'together rented and completely remodelled the centrally situated premises known as "Central Hall", 758/60/62 George Street ... and [these] were retained until 31st May, 1960'. A new Lutheran Church Centre was opened later that year in 17 Valentine Street, near Railway Square. A previous attempt to build a new centre opposite the Children's Court in Albion Street began in 1950 but was abandoned in 1956. 'A Master Plan was prepared but every effort to build was frustrated, due to the standing Landlord and Tenant's Act.'

Central Hall played an important role after the war when many refugees and displaced persons from Europe received their first welcome and assistance there:

> For many Lutherans it was a tremendous experience to be welcomed in a strange land by Lutherans in a language they all understood. Soon Mrs Stolz and Pastor Stolz were visiting 20 hostels and camps ... and a team of Specialist Consultants were prepared to give their time and their help without remuneration.[34]

Baptist Church

The Central Baptist Church in George Street, south of Goulburn Street, was opened in 1937. Before that time the

Baptists congregated at their Bathurst Street church, behind St Andrew's Cathedral. The premises there were not large enough to house the various departments of the Baptist Union. In 1933 a property in Harris Street was offered to the Union on the requirement that its headquarters be established there. The offer was declined but the State government resumed the Baptist site with the St Andrew's Cathedral Act, and so it passed to the Church of England.

The Government undertook to find a satisfactory alternative location and to pay the Church the sum of £10,000 towards the new building. The present site, 619 George Street, Sydney, was decided upon eventually and the Stone Unveiling Ceremony took place on September 19, 1936. It was fitting that one of the stones was unveiled by Rev Henry Clark, who, as Commissioner for the Church House, had contributed so much in earlier years. The other stone was unveiled by the Minister of the Church, Dr W.L. Jarvis.[35]

However, even at the opening, criticism was made that office and committee space was inadequate and that the auditorium was not large enough for the assembly meetings. This led to the 1953 decision that the Union and the Central Church should occupy separate buildings. In 1961 plans for a multi-storey building on the site were considered.[36] The centenary in 1968 passed without any resolution. Eventually the Union moved to premises in 58 Parramatta Road, Glebe.

PERSONS AND EVENTS

The Rise of Billy Hughes

Hero or villain? The enigmatic Billy Hughes (1864–1952) remains as controversial a figure as Jack Lang. The dilemma can be stated like this. When Hughes, aged 20, first arrived in Australia he boarded in a house in Flinders Street, Surry Hills, where he met and married his landlady's daughter. Another 30 or so years later he named the continuation of the street where he had boarded 'Anzac Parade', for Hughes as prime minister of Australia had to come to terms with a war for which nearly a tenth of its population had served, with one in two being wounded and one in five killed.

Hughes was a political survivor. Having failed as an outback teacher, he arrived in Sydney with nothing. He spent three nights in a cave in Sydney Domain with homeless men. He passed himself off temporarily as a cook and worked at the Golden Gate Hotel on Brickfield Hill for 15s. a week. When he charred the mutton and brittled the jam tart he got fired. He attended the Australian Socialist League in rooms at Leigh House, George Street, on Brickfield Hill. After working as a Labor Party organiser Hughes was selected as candidate for the electorate of Lang, named after the fiery patriot and preacher, the Rev. John Dunmore Lang. It was an era of great poverty with a mix of warehouses and workmen's cottages, tightly packed together and very run-down, taking in Darling Harbour as well. It was the area where bubonic plague broke out in 1900. In 1899 Hughes, with a group of organisers, enrolled 1,300 men into a Wharf Labourers' Union and later the Trolley, Draymen and Carters' Union with Hughes as president. He became first president also of the National Waterside Workers' Union. Hughes shifted from a position in 1894 that Australia needed no armies, to a democratic militia for self-defence, to the War Precaution Act (newspaper censorhip, discouragement of disloyalty to Empire, and building alien internment camps), to the promotion and championing of conscription for the defence of the Empire.[37]

Hughes was lionised on his trip to

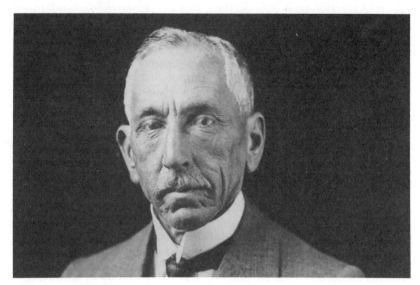

Billy Hughes (1864–1952)

London in 1916 and his printed speeches were taken back to Australia and heralded as a nation's 'coming-of-age'. But on his return Hughes found the Labour Council was against conscription, as was indeed his own personal power base, the Sydney Wharf Labourers' Union. A split in the Labor Party followed. Hughes left the party and continued to govern with opposition support. Queensland Premier Ryan's refusal to have demonstrators at a conscription rally arrested led to establishing the Commonwealth Police, now housed near Hyde Park. For many years Hughes would view the Anzac Day procession from Martin Place. Perhaps David Low's comment sums Hughes up: 'He was too small to hit, too deaf to argue with, and too tough to chew'.

The Rachel Forster Hospital

Who was Rachel Forster and why was a hospital named after her? The story is well worth telling and is firmly located in downtown Sydney. From its beginnings in 1885, the Medical School of Sydney Hospital was open to women students.

But once the women graduated they found it virtually impossible to further their hospital experience by becoming resident medical officers (RMOs). Hospital boards of management were not sympathetic to having women working in what had been a man's domain. 'The women doctors undertook Health Department lecturing, went interstate for their Residency or worked at the Sydney Medical Mission in Elizabeth Street, established by philanthropic people for treatment of the poor.'[38]

Six women doctors resolved to set up a hospital. They were: Dr Lucy Gullett, the first RMO at the Women's Hospital in Crown Street; Dr Harriet Biffin, 'the first Sydney medical woman to establish a suburban practice (Lindfield)',[39] Dr Constance D'Arcy, first woman RMO at the Royal Hospital for Women (Paddington); Dr Margaret Harper, first woman RMO at the Royal Alexandra Hospital for Children; Dr Susie O'Reilly, first woman RMO at Sydney Hospital (but unable to take up her appointment for lack of 'suitable accommodation for a lady doctor'); and Dr Emma Buckley, medical superintendent of Royal North

Shore Hospital. Their inspiration was the Queen Victoria Hospital in Melbourne, a hospital staffed by women for women and children.

The six decided to establish their hospital in a depressed area for the poor and thereby provide training for younger medical women unable to find positions in other hospitals. One thousand pounds was raised to purchase a very dilapidated terrace house in Lansdowne Street, Surry Hills, near the rear of St Peter's Church, and in 1922 the hospital was opened. The doctors themselves pitched in to do the cleaning, painting and mending. The house had been condemned and only lightweight patients could be put upstairs, so shaky was the upper storey. The little hospital was only meant for outpatients, as both the Womens' Hospital in Crown Street and the Royal Hospital for Women were not far away. During that first year 2,412 patients were treated, 773 being children.

The first annual general meeting was chaired by Lady Forster, who had herself begun a medical course in England. She was a friend of Emily Pankhurst and had worked to improve conditions for under-privileged women in London. The daughter of Lord Montague of Beaulieu, she married Henry William Forster in 1890. In 1920 she came to Australia when her husband was appointed governor-general. The couple were attentive to the social duties of office, travelling tirelessly around Australia, very often dedicating war memorials. They had lost both their sons in the war. Lord Forster was a founder of Toc H in Australia and also promoter of another charity, the Big Brother Movement. Rachel Forster was a Dame Grand Cross of the Order of St John of Jerusalem.[40]

The Forsters were only intending to stay for two years, but were prevailed upon to remain for another three. They returned to England in 1925, where Lady Forster died in 1962, aged 93.[41]

As the original hospital in Lansdowne Street was inadequate, a large house in George Street, Redfern, was acquired in 1924 and extensively renovated. Upstairs bedrooms were turned into a ward for in-patients, although only four adults and two children could be accommodated. Lady Forster allowed the hospital to be named after her in 1925.

Early fund-raising included 'shilling' drives, 'egg' collections, annual fetes and the Hyde Park Carols by Candlelight. By 1934 a new building had been opened, containing an operating theatre and beds for another 20 in-patients. Further expansion was necessary. An old stone house in Pitt Street adjoining the George Street premises was purchased. It turned out to be the former home of Dr William Redfern. (The good doctor, after whom the suburb is named, had arrived as a convict in 1801 for being involved in a Naval mutiny. He was pardoned after a year and became assistant surgeon, first at Norfolk Island and then at the newly constructed Sydney Hospital. Redfern was a friend of Governor Macquarie and a key figure in the struggle of emancipated convicts for social recognition.[42]) Various clinics and nurses' homes were added. A major change occurred in 1967 when the hitherto all-female hospital opened its new male ward. The first male patient was a beaten-up gangster found on the doorstep.[43]

Barnardo's Motto

Tiny Wilmot Street houses the headquarters of the Barnardo's organisation.

'No destitute child ever refused admission' was the charter of Dr Thomas John Barnardo. Arriving in London from his native Dublin, the young Barnardo had left a wealthy family business to become a missionary with the Church of England in China. It was 1866 and the squalor of the Industrial Revolution in London appalled the young idealist of 21. As he was studying medicine by day and discovering waifs in alleys by night, he perceived his mission field was right where he was. So began the work of Dr Barnardo's Homes for Children. The

Australian chapter of the Barnardo story began in 1883, when nine Barnardo boys arrived in Fremantle on the ship the *Charlotte Padbury*. Barnardo's in Australia based their centenary date on this event. In 1921, at a public meeting in Sydney Town Hall, the Governor-General, Lord Forster, launched an Australian branch of Barnardo's 'so that the sons of British Servicemen who had died in World War I could be given a fresh start in Australia'.[44]

On October 1921, 47 Barnardo boys disembarked on the SS *Berrima*. This same ship had taken the first volunteers of the Expeditionary Force to Europe in the early days of the Great War.[45] In 1960 a policy was made to extend Barnardo activities into the Australian community. There was also a move away from large institutions with 50 or more children to family-group homes dispersed in the general community. The majority of children coming into the care of Barnardo's are from broken homes, and aged from nine to 12. In the past, the children who came into foster care were babies or preschoolers. The organisation does not proselytise but respects the faith into which the child or its parents have been baptised.[46]

John Smith Garden

J.S. Garden, popularly known as 'Jack' Garden, came from Scotland and practised as a clergyman on the North Coast after his arrival. He rose quickly through the Sail Maker's Union to the staff of the Trades and Labour Council. When Jack Lang was leader of the Labor Party in 1923, Garden was leader of the Communist Party. They clashed bitterly. Lang described Garden as intelligent, quick, volatile, but a 'born showman and a show-off', 'a most effective mob orator ... with a calculating brain'.[47] Lang claims Garden left the Communists when he saw there was no future in it for him. Garden rejoined the Labor Party and won a seat in Canberra in 1934. In so doing

he lost control of the TLC and his political power base. Garden's habit of coining slick slogans often embarrassed his friends more than his enemies—e.g., 'The water is deep, the sea is damp and dead men tell no tales', 'We have only to pull the switch [at Yallourn] and there will be a night of darkness', and the famous 'Lang is greater than Lenin'. Garden had visited Moscow in 1922 and met Lenin. However, by the early 1930s Garden was anti-Communist and the Communists hated him for his turnabout.

The Langton Centre

In 1931 Dr W.D. Langton opened a community hospital opposite Moore Park on the site now known as the Langton Centre. Before 1931 a private clinic had existed there, and before that the site had been used as a residential quarters for nursing sisters working at St Margaret's Hospital in Bourke Street. Dr Langton obtained the lease from the sisters. The Endowment Board in the Langton Centre on the ground floor shows the support for the new community hospital. They include City Tattersalls Club, N.S.W. Fire Brigades, Mrs J.C. Williamson, Mr G.E. Adams, Berlei Ltd, Frank Packer and the *Women's Weekly*.

The Langton Clinic began treating alcohol-dependent patients in 1959. Detoxification facilities and 20 beds were provided. By 1967 there were 50 beds and drug-dependent patients were also treated. It was found that drug and alcohol users could not be successfully treated in common rehabilitation and therapy programs, so in 1979 a decision was made to offer only detoxification for opiate users. The clinic has never used 'cold turkey' (unmedicated withdrawal), however methadone and other opiates are not used.

Two important organisations working in conjunction with and under the umbrella of the Langton Centre are the New South Wales Centre for Education and Information on Drugs and Alcohol

(CEIDA) and the Bourke Street Drug Advisory Service. CEIDA is located on site at the Langton Centre. The Drug Advisory Service is located at 703 Bourke Street, Surry Hills. Silver Lining House, a halfway house which functions as a therapeutic community at North Bondi, has maintained an excellent recovery record. The Bennelong's Haven program for alcoholic Aborigines is also part of the outreach of the Langton Centre. In 1981/82 the Langton Clinic became the Langton Centre.

A City Barmaid

In 1943 and with a three-year-old child, Marge King counted herself lucky to get a job as a barmaid at the Bourke Hotel on the corner of George and Goulburn Streets. The hours were long. The hotel opened at 6.30 a.m. and closed at 7 p.m. The beer would be brought in large wooden barrels in carts pulled by draught-horses. Clientele came from the nearby Haymarket post office, from the Anthony Hordern store, the markets and the Trades Hall. The Bourke was run by the MacMillans, an elderly brother and sister from New Zealand. Three barmaids, wearing ordinary clothing, did the serving, two of them living in. Another dozen boarders lodged in as well. No meals were provided. Logan's restaurant near the Baptist Church provided a three-course meal for 1s. 6d. Purchases could be made at Paddy's Markets on Friday afternoons without using coupons. Prices were cheaper, too. A broom might cost 10s. in a shop but 4s. 6d. at the markets. Miss MacMillan might have been in her seventies but she knew her economics. She sent her staff for produce from Stanley's in Sussex Street, whose prices were the cheapest. A butcher was handy in George Street and 1s. 3d. would fetch three pounds of Wolf's sausages. Marge's wage was £2 11s.0d. There wasn't enough money to buy a radio. If there was any spare time, a book was read. It was a short tram ride to St Benedict's for Mass. A treat on Sunday afternoon would be a walk to the picture theatre.

Marge grew up in the Fitzroy Falls region and married Tom King, a guard on a construction train, at St Paul's, Moss Vale. The Depression hit them both hard. They would go anywhere for a job, picking peas at Moss Vale or digging potatoes near Fitzroy Falls. They lived in a 14 by 16 foot tent and fly at Mount Murray, near the top of Fitzroy Falls. Lino covered the wooden floorboards. The stove was a camp oven. Marge lived in the tent for 18 months, nursing her baby. Empty kerosene tins would be heated up for washing. Light was provided by a 'rabbit lantern', a hurricane lamp.

After her husband's death, Marge moved and stayed in the city. She was to spend 30 years working in city hotels: Twelve years at the Bourke, three at the Star, five at the Trades Hall, three at the Vicar of Wakefield and a few more in the snack bar at the old Wentworth.

She put her boy through school and he obtained a good position in the aircraft industry. Marge herself remained bright and alert. She cares for people and, despite her years, there is a vitality and sparkle that speaks of an indomitable spirit.

Another Side of the Thirties

The small hotels that are found on so many intersections of downtown Sydney belie some of their earlier glory. The exteriors even boasted original artwork!

Artists of the calibre of Tom Woodman were in demand for colour posters in the 1930s advertising beer. Elegantly attired couples would be shown drinking ale and lager in lavish ballroom settings. The Town Hall Hotel daringly even had a woman tennis player enjoying a beer on her own! This was the age when the Trocadero Ballroom, now Hoyts Cinema Centre, was in full swing.[48]

The drive behind the beer paintings came from Jules Rousel, who had studied painting in London and Sydney. He had a business called Rousel Posters in Oxford Street and persuaded the management of Tooths' Brewery to give beer advertisement paintings a try. He even sold the idea of having the paintings displayed on the *outside* of the hotel. The posters were 3 × 4 feet on transfer paper which was protected by ¼-inch plate glass. Tooths paid Rousel about £25 to £30. The artists Henry Hanke, Tom Woodman, Walter Jardine and Stan Denford received £12, but they were rarely permitted to sign their paintings.

Sir William McKell

After growing up in Redfern, William McKell was apprenticed as a boilermaker at the Eveleigh Railway Workshops. Before long he had formed a union of apprentice boilermakers. He rose quickly in the Trades and Labour Council and was a member of the committee which established the Workers' Educational Association. McKell was persuaded to stand against J.S. McGowan, who had changed to anti-Labor at the height of the conscription debate. He won the Redfern seat, which he represented from 1916 to 1947, when he was appointed governor-general. 'Redfern had been a major and happy part of my life. This is the area that elected me to be its representative in Parliament for thirty years and these are the people I have known and loved for a lifetime.'[49]

Like Lang, McKell experienced injustice during his childhood. As a young man working to support his widowed mother, he was shocked when the landlord called in and said the rent had been doubled. Despite having been good tenants, the McKells were given notice to quit. This meant that after seven days all their belongings could be put on the streets. Later, when McKell became minister of justice in the Storey Government, he amended the law to give tenants greater security and prevent such inhuman behaviour having the sanction of the law.

McKell also proposed building a technical college on the site of the old Darlinghurst gaol. Mutch, minister of education, was enthusiastic and the project went ahead.[50]

McKell became leader of the State ALP in 1939, when it was still hopelessly split in the aftermath of the Lang dismissal of 1932. McKell helped to spark a revival in country areas and after two years won office as premier of New South Wales, 1941–47.

During World War II 800 defence projects were handled by New South Wales. Among them were the construction of aerodromes in New Caledonia by the Department of Main Roads. It was from such airfields, built at breakneck speed, that U.S. aircraft operated for the decisive battle of the Coral Sea which saved Australia from invasion. Other projects included establishing the world's largest rice farm at Wakool, situated between Swan Hill and Deniliquin, and construction of the Captain Cook Dry Dock and the boom across Sydney Harbour (which saved Sydney from a more devastating attack by Japanese submarines).[51] Other notable McKell initiatives included the formation of the Joint Coal Board, the gift of Admiralty House to the governor-general as a city residence, the proclamation of the Free Municipal Libraries Act.[52]

McKell clashed with the chief justice, Sir Frederick Jordan, over closure of 30 nightclubs in the city and suburbs. Defence intelligence had tracked the loss of shipping to information gathered from ships' crews in such clubs. The club owners protested, but McKell had loopholes in his special wartime powers closed.[53]

After the war McKell had a long struggle with the British Labour government over the appointment of the first Australian-born governor of New South Wales, Sir John Northcott, in 1946. The following year saw continued political storms over McKell's appointment as the second Australian-born governor-general by the Chifley Government.

McKell initiated the formation of a Factory Welfare Board, introduced a miner's pension, formed the Government Insurance Office, amended the Workers Compensation Act to extend to workers injured going to and from work, established the Newcastle State Dockyard, created the Housing Commission of N.S.W., passed an Act providing holidays on full pay for all workers—the first legislation of its type in N.S.W.[54]

McKell's leadership, like Lang's, was radically reformist but it was non-abrasive. McKell's friendship with Ben Chifley played a major part in the formulation of the Snowy Mountains Project.

A tower building erected in George Street in the 1970s and named after McKell houses the Departments of Health and Agriculture. In 1981 McKell was the special guest of honour at the 110th anniversary dinner of the foundation of the Labour Council. He died in 1985, aged 93.

ENTERTAINMENT

From Grand Opera to the New Tivoli

Sydney's original Grand Opera House stood at the Castlereagh Street end of the old Belmore Markets. Efforts had been made to brush up the Haymarket's image. At nearby Brickfield Hill was the Anthony Hordern Emporium, while the People's Palace, the Great Southern Hotel and Hotel Sydney vied for the custom of train travellers. But as the Depression bit, the grand and imperial themes began to wane.

The Grand Opera House first saw the light of day as the Adelphi, opened in 1911 for anything from melodrama to pantomime and grand opera. It was the first theatre to be built according to parliamentary safety requirements for theatres and public halls, Sydney's theatres having an appalling record of fires in the nineteenth century. The theatre also was the first to have its galleries constructed on the cantilever principle. It was licensed to seat 2,400, and had 15 dressing rooms on one side and the props and sets on the other.

At the end of a performance in the Grand Opera House in 1930 an actor gave an impromptu diatribe against the new American talkies. Anger wasn't enough to save most theatres from the new invention, but in 1932, at the height of the Depression, Mike Connors and Queenie Paul reopened the Grand Opera House as the New Tivoli. They stayed open by charging 1s. for matinees and no more than 3s. at night. Mo, otherwise Roy Rene, otherwise Harry van der Sluys, and Sid Beck were the star comedians.

Mick Simmons and Sport

In the early 1980s as you entered the Mick Simmons Store in the Haymarket and before passing the electronic surveillance box, a pig-tailed teenager greeted you from a wall poster. It was Andrea Jaeger, the young tennis star almost biting her tongue with concentration as she winds up to deliver a sweeping ground stroke. Inside the store was a rich variety of colourful wet-suits, sail boards, exercise machines and athletic gear of all kinds. But alas, the store is now closed and the building faces demolition.

The original merchandising at Mick Simmons was very different—tobacco products. In fact the store had its own tobacco factory. It was the men who were catered for. There were five chairs in a hairdressing department. Guns were a big seller and a gunsmith shop was set up in the rear of the premises, where the guns could be test-fired. Fishing tackle was another popular item. Oceanic cycles, built by Bruce Small of Malvern Star fame, were also on sale. In fact Bruce Small had a shop of his own across the road.

In the 1930s there was a staff of over 100 working on different floors at the Haymarket store. Ten smaller stores were also in operation. Nineteen vans delivered supplies to suburban tobacconists and hairdressers. These vans would drive in from the rear entrance up to the second floor.

Back in 1874 Mick Simmons began his business career with a five-pound note, when he bought a property in Sussex Street and became a tobacco manufacturer. When he died in 1894 the premises on the corner of George and Campbell Streets had begun operations. By the 1920s the store advertised itself boldly as 'The World's Greatest Sports Depot' and the 'Home of Sport'. The building looked like a Greek temple, with pillars running up to the third storey which was surmounted by a stone colonnade along the roof. A special feature on the ground floor was a soda fountain and confectionary counter. Upper floors were graced with cafes, lounges and hairdressing salons. The greatest novelty of all was the roof-top sportsground. This included a full scale tennis court, a golf practice area and a shooting gallery.[55]

Mick Simmons employed many sporting heroes. One of the stars was Lionel Bibby. Inspired in his youth by Colonel Cody (Buffalo Bill) and other exhibition shooters, Lionel mastered stunts such as hitting aerially thrown targets and 'ejected shell' shots. Bibby could shoot off the head of a match and split a piece of paper in half at a distance of 10 feet. He could shoot out a profile of Don Bradman from a distance of 30 feet.

In fact Don Bradman and Stan McCabe also worked at Mick Simmons during the Depression.[56]

When he set off for his first trip to England (1930), Bradman had left real estate for a job with Mick Simmons Sports store, the shop in which he had chosen his first cricket bat, his mother's reward for the 300 he had made for Bowral against Moss Vale (1927).[57]

Like Bradman, Stan McCabe came to Sydney from the country. He played for St Joseph's College first XI at 14, for New South Wales at 18 and for Australia at 20. His parents had never seen him play in a big match, so he invited them down from Grenfell for the first Test against England at the Sydney Cricket Ground in 1932. As Jack Pollard described it:

McCabe had to go to the wicket with Australia 3 for 82, after weeks of newspaper criticism of England's bodyline tactics. His main worry was his mother, an excitable woman. 'Dad, if I get hit out there today, you keep Mum from jumping the fence,' he told his father. Then he went out and played one of cricket's great knocks, hooking the first ball he received from Larwood to the fence in front of deep square leg. He kept hooking balls off his eyebrows as if the bat was a magic wand, casting an occasional glance at where his mother was sitting.

'The crowd really shaped the innings,' McCabe wrote years later. 'With them yelling and cheering, my reaction was to hit at almost every ball. It was really an impulsive, senseless innings, a gamble that should not have been made but came off against all the odds. Vic Richardson helped me add 129 but when he was out Australia was in trouble again. I was hit once or twice about the shoulders by bouncers but not painfully or hard enough to bring Mum in over the fence.'

England's captain Jardine brought 'Gubby' Allen on and McCabe struck him for three handsome fours in a row. Jardine demanded that Allen bowl to his packed legside field but Allen refused. 'You can take me off,' Allen said. In the end Jardine dropped the leg-side attack and brought on Hammond, Verity and the other English bowlers to bowl orthodox stuff. Not out on 130 that night, McCabe scored a further 57 next morning, 49 of them for the tenth wicket in a partnership of 55 with Tim Wall. McCabe's 187 not out took 240 minutes but Australia lost the match by 10 wickets. 'Larwood took 5 for 96 and 5 for 28, with Australia all out for 164 in our second innings, so it was really Larwood's match not mine,' McCabe said.[58]

McCabe left Mick Simmons to open his own sports store at the other end of George Street, near Cricket House. Foot trouble shortened his brilliant cricket career.

Yabba, the Rabbito

Stephen Harold Gascoigne (1878–1942) trundled his cart around the streets of inner Sydney. He rang a bell and bellowed out 'Rabbie, wild rabbie' as he hawked his rabbits to the housewives. An army of cats would follow Yabba, as he was known, for they knew when a sale was made he would skin and gut the rabbit. That would not be enough to have him remembered, perhaps, but for 30 years he was a stalwart spectator at the Sydney Cricket Ground. He always went to the Hill, opposite the Members Stand. In his hamper he carried his bottles of beer. He championed the underdog and his voice carried loud and clear to all parts of the ground. He was a big man, 14 stone and close to six feet tall. Yabba was the main reason why the Hill had, in pre-television days, a reputation for informed spectatorship. In one match the English bowler Tate changed his boots three times. As the last pair was brought out, Yabba convulsed the crowd as he cried out: 'Eh Maurice, thank goodness you're not a centipede'.[59]

Paddy Pallin

Frank Austin Pallin was born in the north of England in 1900 and arrived in Australia in 1926. He started off as a share farmer but soon realised that without capital there would be little future. In Sydney as a clerk he was put off work in

Paddy Pallin (centre).

1930 as the Great Depression began to be felt. He resumed his youthful love of walking and the Boy Scout movement and began to explore the bushland around Sydney. He noted that there was a lack of lightweight camping equipment and began making oiled or chapara ground-sheets. From a suburban garage, Paddy moved into premises at Circular Quay, and in 1933 to the first floor of 312 George Street. By now canvas ruck-sacks were also being made, and in 1934 Paddy published the first edition of *Bushwalking and Camping*. That year the search for a lost hiker in the Blue Mountains led to the formation of a search and rescue organisation with Paddy as convenor. He held this position until 1976. His friend and first assistant Oliver Wulf was a great support when, after World War II, a fire destroyed the George Street building. A shop was set up in the basement of the CENEF building in Castlereagh Street and a workshop in a disused factory in Harris Street.

As a young bushwalker I first met the legendary Paddy Pallin in 1970, when his shop was located directly above a cafe on the corner of George and Bathurst Streets. From there his shop was set up in Liver-pool Street opposite the end of Kent Street. There are now Paddy Pallin stores right around Australia. I can certainly vouch for the spirit shared by every bushwalker in the title of Paddy's memoirs, *Never Truly Lost*. Paddy Pallin died on 3 January 1991, aged 90.

CRIME

The Mystery of Hotel Sydney

In the midst of an election result dispute over the Federal seat of Barton between Thomas John Ley, attorney-general in the State Fuller Government, and the sitting member, Fred McDonald, the latter simply vanished without trace. McDonald, a comparatively poor man, recently married, had claimed that Ley, an ambitious wealthy man with powerful friends, had attempted to bribe him not to nominate for the poll. The case was due to be heard in the High Court on 22 April 1926. Jack Lang received a letter from McDonald on 30 March in which McDonald speaks of being 'on the verge of the grave'. McDonald left his room in Hotel Sydney on 16 April and was never seen again. Was it suicide? His body and a briefcase containing his personal papers were never found. Frank Green, clerk of the House of Representatives, states: 'Ley contacted McDonald suggesting an appointment. McDonald agreed to meet him at the time and place suggested by Ley, and that was the last ever heard of McDonald.'[60]

Ley was unsuccessful in Federal politics and subsequently went to London, where some years later he was tried for the murder of a barman, Jack Mudie, who was his mistress' son-in-law. The unfortunate Mudie had been buried in a chalk pit by Ley's two accomplices. Ley was convicted and sentenced to death, but three London specialists declared Ley insane and he died in 1947 of a seizure, three months after being admitted to a mental asylum.

The McDonald disappearance has never been resolved.

Kate Leigh

The 'Bonny Belle from Dubbo', Kate Leigh, had a lifelong association with Surry Hills. When the drinkers' thirst became too strong on Sundays, Kate could be relied upon to provide the liquor. She was one of a number of sly grog merchants in the 1930s. Often she would come into a hairdressers' shop nearby and say she had to look her best at 'the picture show at 10.00 a.m. tomorrow'. This meant that Kate would be in court on someone's behalf, sometimes her own. Her second husband, 'Shiner' Ryan, was handy with a brush and while in gaol he painted 'The Good Shepherd' surrounded by a lot of black sheep. Kate proudly hung the painting in her front room.

Kate could always be relied on to help a family in need with groceries and food supplies, but while she had a heart of gold, it was wiser not to ask too many questions. In her latter years she noticed her hairdresser had a medallion, 'In case of an emergency call a Catholic priest'. Kate also acquired one, which she wore to her dying day. A priest did give her the last rites.[61]

When Kate died she was bankrupt. In fact she still owed the Taxation Department £6,000. Licensed clubs and 10 p.m. closing had ruined her. Born in Dubbo, she came as a young girl to Surry Hills, at that time a hotbed of criminal activity. She received her first prison sentence for perjury when trying to provide an alibi for 'Shiner' Ryan, who was a member of the Riley Street Push. Another time Kate was defending her house in Lansdowne Street during an underworld feud. As a bunch of hoodlums came up the stairs Kate fired a rifle and one of them, Prendergast, fell dead. The mob bolted. Kate was acquitted after pleading self-defence.[62]

Kate was popularly known as 'The Queen of Surry Hills' and her charity to those in need earned her this title. Her specialty was the annual Christmas party for the children of Surry Hills. Her flair for publicity in the media was equal to that of any politician. One year she rang the editor of a Sunday newspaper saying she had no Santa Claus. Could the editor supply one? The editor sent one of his best journalists dressed as Santa, and a photographer as well! On another occasion Kate was in Long Bay gaol when the governor and his wife were making an official visit. Lady Game tasted one of the scones Kate had just cooked and declared she did not get as good in her own home.[63]

Kate's first visit to hospital was her last. She died in 1964, aged 84, in St Vincent's Hospital. Among her mourners at St Peter's Catholic Church were Tilly Devine, the notorious brothel madam from Woolloomooloo, the former deputy commissioner of police, W.R. Lawrence, Major John Irwin from the Salvation Army and Mr P.N. Roach, a city solicitor who had defended Kate for many years in court cases.[64]

ARTS

Christina Stead and Kylie Tennant

Christina Stead was a novelist with an international reputation, who was credited with putting Sydney on the literary cosmopolitan map with her 1933 novel, *Seven Poor Men of Sydney*. She wrote not about low level or working-class life found in the inner city of Sydney but mainly around the Watsons Bay area where she lived until going overseas. However, some references are made in that novel to the inner city. Consider the nocturnal alienation: 'Seven miles away signs swing and windows rattle in the city, the boats strain at their anchorages, the poor people who sleep under the wharves in Ultimo move their rags closer to the bank, and rats leave their holes'. The lot of the seven is, to put it somewhat crassly, dullness, manipulation, escaping to Europe, socialism, suicide, Communism and psychosomatic paralysis.

Kylie Tennant's husband, L.C. Rodd, grew up in Surry Hills and his childhood was described in Chapter 4. Three of Kylie Tennant's novels are set in the inner city. They are *Foveaux* (1939), *Ride On Stranger* (1943) and *Time Enough Later* (1943). *Foveaux* covers the years from 1912 to the '30s and contains descriptions of life among the poor and unemployed; of hostels for the unemployed and unlicensed home-made wireless sets of the occupants; of 'mean' houses with their gas rings and penny meters and solitary tap in the back yard; of the 'Slum Abolition League' and its crusading parson; of one of the women searching for accommodation and finding one bug-infested, in another a landlord beating his children until they screamed, and another landlord who propositioned her.

A Poet of Sydney

The poet Kenneth Slessor (1901-71) notes that his father changed the family name from Schloesser to Slessor at the beginning of World War I. His mother's ancestry was Scottish, but his grandfather's grandfather was an innkeeper in Darmstadt. The German heritage was Jewish, though more cultural than religious. His great-grandfather, Louis Schloesser, was a pupil of Beethoven. Grandfather Adolphe Schloesser moved to London to take up the position of professor of pianoforte at the Royal Academy of Music. While still at school Slessor had poems published in *The Bulletin*. Slessor did not succumb to the charms of 'Bohemia' but earned his own living as a journalist for various city newspapers, starting with the Sydney *Sun*, *Smith's Weekly* (1927-39), and again at the *Sun* (1944-56) and then the *Daily Telegraph* (1957-70). He lived in the inner city and eventually became president of the Sydney Journalists' Club, located in Chalmers Street. He wrote many poems about Sydney, especially the Harbour. His poem 'Five Bells', an elegy to cartoonist Joe Lynch who drowned in a ferry accident, is regarded among his best. This poem also inspired the John Olson painting which decorates the lobby of the Concert Hall at the Sydney Opera House. I enjoyed his youthful poem on the *Emden* memorial in Hyde Park, 'I sing the Epic of those valiant souls', because after studying so many plaques around Sydney, here was a poet satirising the local officials who often dominated them at the expense of their true subjects. During World War II Slessor was for a time the Commonwealth Official War Correspondent. He also wrote a poem, 'Beach Burial', which is regarded as one of the finest poems to come out of the war. His friend Alexander Macdonald regarded Slessor as 'perhaps the finest and certainly the most individual poet that Australia has produced'.[65] Be that as it may, it remains a mystery why Slessor did not write any major poetry during the last 27 years of his life. Was the Journalists' Club more powerful than the Muse? Was the passion spent by his failure as war correspondent, by his lack of international recognition as a poet, and by his penchant for cigars and alcohol?

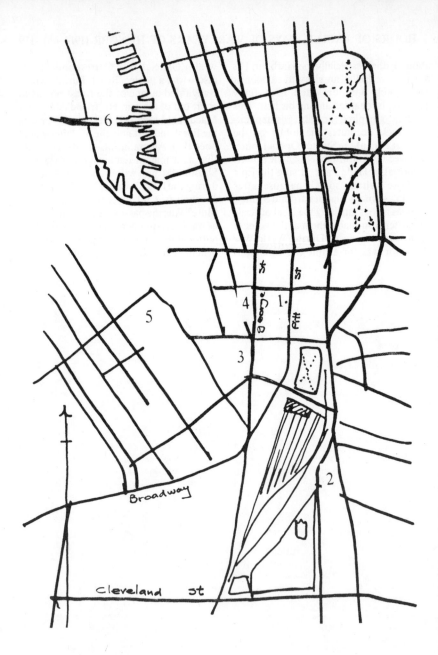

MAP 6
1946 – 1961

1 CHEQUERS NIGHT CLUB
2 IRISH NATIONAL ASSOCIATION CLUB
3 MARX HOUSE(695 GEORGE ST)
4 ST PETER JULIAN'S CHURCH
5 ULTIMO POWERHOUSE
6 PYRMONT BRIDGE WHEELHOUSE

6 Immigrants, Artists and Politicians (1946-61)

POPULATION

Mum Shirl Comes to Downtown

On first settling in Sydney, the Aboriginal welfare worker Mum Shirl moved into a house in Caroline Street, Redfern. Indeed she was soon to become a Caroline Chisholm to her own people. She recalls coming upon an excited rally in Redfern Park and asking what it was all about. 'The fellow answered angrily, "Can't you hear? You're not that ignorant—we're at war!" The only thing I remember thinking was, "Thank God, Laurie is in gaol!"'[1] Laurie was her brother.

During World War II captured Japanese soldiers were imprisoned in a compound in her home town of Cowra. Fences were not unusual for her. Her own Erambie Mission had a fence around it. The blacks did not know where the Japanese had come from or what they had done. She learnt about the mass killings of the Japanese prisoners at the time of the break-out from her two uncles, who were both returned servicemen. She noticed how some white people were cheating with their war coupons:

> What bothered me about this was that it didn't seem like all white people were really caring about each other, with some up on the front lines getting killed and others trying to get rich by buying illegal coupons. The other thing that bothered me was that this whole business of cheating with coupons was called the 'blackmarket' and there weren't even any Blacks involved in it.[2]

A professional boxer who fought under the name of Darcy Smith became her husband. They moved into a small house in Albion Way, Surry Hills. 'We lived in a two-bedroom house, with a little yard and kitchen, a little verandah in front and toilet out in the back garden.'[3] Heating and lighting were by gas. There was no bathroom. Their first child, a boy, 'died from suffocation on the labour table with me taking an epileptic fit'.[4] She remembers with affection the remarkable black women she has met: Mother Williams (Coe), Mrs Piedy, Granny Goolagong, Granny Robinson, Aunt Bunny Hinton from Lawson Street, Aunt Ellen Boney, Nana Jessie Ping who married a Chinaman and Granny Waters from Caroline Street.[5]

The Gaol Walkabout

From visiting her brother in prison Mum Shirl saw the great value, benefit and hope that the visits gave to those inside. Not long after the war she began a prison apostolate of visiting blacks in gaol. Gradually her visitation work grew and as she became known she was in demand as a speaker:

> My work, and the work of the other Blacks who are doing things in a similar sort of way as I do, is very hard to talk about, probably because it is not a job, it is a way of life. We don't start at any particular time in our lives, or at any particular time of the day. If the door knocks in the middle of the night, we

Mum Shirl.

open it. If the phone rings, we answer it. Saturdays and Sundays run into each other. We can be up all night talking with some person who has that sort of problem, out at the prison at early morning, back at the Children's Court in the afternoon, at a meeting to talk with some people about what we are doing in the evening, and likely as not, another meeting in the night. Then we get home at maybe midnight, there can be another phone message asking us to be somewhere urgently, or even someone sitting in the front room waiting all evening for the chance to talk. How can we say what we do?[6]

In 1976 she received an invitation to meet Mr McGeechan, the head of the Corrective Services Department. It was to be a dinner with Mr McGeechan and Fr Allan Mithen, the Catholic Aboriginal Chaplain, to celebrate her receipt of the 'Gold Pass' to all prison institutions—it was without expiry date—a pass for life[7]—but sadly a later administration replaced it with one based on annual application and renewal. The Department of Corrective Services is presently housed in the Roden Cutler Building in Campbell Street, Haymarket.

Once Mum Shirl was asked by an ex-prisoner, Kevin Gilbert, 'Who is an Aboriginal?' She replied: 'I'll tell you. An Aboriginal is everyone that knows what it was like down on Erambie Mission,

West Cowra, thirty years ago. An Aboriginal is anyone that lived down there with me, that knew what it was like.'[8]

Mum Shirl has a strong devotion to the black Latin American saint, Martin de Porres. She herself has been called the Saint of Redfern. If that is so, she is a saint with a difference, for she will not hesitate to use bar-room language with the best of them. She is open about her faith. There was a break with the Church about 20 years ago, when a priest refused her communion on the assumption that she hadn't made her first confession and communion. 'Since then I have come back to being a Catholic, which to me, means a Mad Roman Catholic like my Mother, or a Mad Roaming Catholic because either of them is me.'[9]

Immigration

The Chinese impact on the Haymarket region began with the aftermath of the gold rush. The civil wars in China and Indo-China led to a greater influx of Chinese immigrants. In addition, large capital investments resulted in major real estate purchases such as the old Hordern's Emporium by a Singapore company. The new revitalised Chinatown owes much to trading and family connections in Hong Kong. Other migrant groups who established an early presence in the Haymarket region were the German Lutherans (Valentine and Goulburn Streets), the Italian Club (established in 1948 in George Street opposite Rawson Place), the Spanish (a variety of restaurants, including a club). The Irish have their links with the Haymarket. The markets now survive only through the Paddy's Market, which operates twice a week at Redfern. The St Patrick's Day Parade traditionally starts in the markets and moves up George Street. The Irish Club, hotels and societies still remain around Central Station. It seems that the volatile and changing face of the Haymarket provided the best opportunity for a central toehold. The Circular Quay end of the city, impregnable with its Establishment institutions such as banks, insurance and government buildings, reflects the conservative and enduring marks of Australian society. The Haymarket allows the 'little people' to grace the stage—indeed its volatile, artistic, flamboyant tradition is symbolised in the new Entertainment Centre, opened in 1983.

Jews in Sydney

Between eight and 14 Jews were among the convicts on board the First Fleet. The first Jewish organisation to be set up in Australia was a burial society set up in Sydney in 1817. It was then that young Philip Joseph Cohen conducted services in his house in George Street. The first rabbi was Aaron Levy and the first synagogue was opened in York Street in 1844. Isaac Nathan, who arrived in 1840, is called the father of Australian music. He composed the first opera in Australia, *Don Juan of Austria*, and studied, recorded and described Aboriginal music. His talents were prized at St Mary's Cathedral. Jewish girls came to Australia via the work of Caroline Chisholm, who may doubly be called 'a second Moses in bonnet and shawl'. The Great Synagogue in Elizabeth Street was opened in 1878. At a centenary dinner which also served to commemorate 150 years of Jewish communal life in Australia, Premier Neville Wran remarked:

> The presence of His Excellency the Governor-General is itself powerful evidence of the significance and distinction of the Jewish contribution to Australia. With the exception of modern Israel itself, only one nation in more than 2,000 years has called upon Jews to be head of its armies, head of its judiciary, and twice, head of State: John Monash, Isaac Isaacs, Zelman Cowen. Not since the Diaspora has this happened in any other nation in the world.[10]

The Jewish population greatly increased after the Holocaust of World War II and with subsequent waves of immigration. Jew represent about 1% of the population of New South Wales. The Eastern suburbs and North Shore are the focus of the Jewish Community. New schools and synagogues were opened in both areas. The headquarters of most of the community organisations is the N.S.W. Jewish War Memorial Community Centre in Darlinghurst Road.

The Executive Council of Australian Jewry, the N.S.W. Jewish Board of Deputies, the Jewish Communal Appeal and the Australian Jewish Welfare Society are all centred there.

There are the offices of the Zionist Federation of Australia, the State Zionist Council, the United Israel Appeal, and other Israel-oriented organisations; as well, there is a small synagogue, a meeting and function hall, and a magnificent new Jewish museum.

Despite its official title, the building is colloquially called 'The Macc'. In its original, much smaller form, it was opened by Sir John Monash in 1923 with the name of Maccabean Hall, as a war memorial recalling the Maccabean virtues of courage and bravery and designed to bring the youth of the community together to develop their spirit of loyalty.

In the 'Macc' are the headquarters of the *Australian Jewish News*, published in English each Thursday. The *News* also distributes locally the Yiddish edition of the Melbourne Jewish Newspaper. (Many of the Synagogues and communal organisations publish their own bulletins, almost all in English.)[11]

From the Silver Bell to Kingfisher

In 1926 an earthquake on the Greek island of Castellorizo left Peter Manettas and his sister orphans. They wrote to uncles in

Australia and America, looking for a new home. Australia granted visas quickly and the two children arrived in Sydney in 1927. Peter was 13. Before long he had a job in the Silver Bell cafe opposite the Haymarket post office. He got £1 a week and every second Sunday off. By 21 he had gone into a prawn boat partnership working the Parramatta River. The catch was put into eight tins, each weighing 30 pounds, and suspended from shoulder poles. Peter then travelled from Rhodes via train, tram, ferry and bus to Narrabeen, where the catch was sold for 3d. a pound.

Eventually he was able to open his own Haymarket cafe, The Victory. It was well-patronised by members of the Trades Hall such as Jim Kelly, Albert Monk and John Ducker. By 1958 a company had been formed and freezers built at the old Sydney Fish Markets in Thomas Street. Four years later a chain of cold stores and restaurants were servicing 2,600 customers including airlines, hotels, clubs, shipping lines and government departments. The success of the Cyren restaurant at Broadway led to an explosion of fish restaurants. 'In Sydney now there are about 2,000 fish shops, restaurants and cafes but when I started the Victory there were very few,' says Peter Manettas.[12] He remains a family man and avoids the champagne, jet-set executive image. He carries his business papers in a black plastic briefcase, is active in the Greek Community and likes helping people.

Every Good Friday Peter Manettas arrives at the Blessed Sacrament Fathers Haymarket Church, bringing with him freshly cooked fish. He always rings beforehand, to check the numbers, and the Fathers are grateful, as Holy Week is a very busy time and the Chatswood formation community take up residence in the Haymarket as well to lend a hand.

In 1987 Manettas Limited was formed, and two years later N.P. Manettas replaced Peter Manettas, now retired, as chairman. In 1989 Felan's Fisheries were acquired at Rozelle. The company has a deep-sea fishing trawler, the *Megisti Star F*, and a fleet of 120 vehicles servicing 6,000 orders per week to government institutions (defence, hospitals, prisons) and the hotel industry. There were 362 employees at Sydney Fish Markets and other branches of the company at Newcastle, Brisbane, Sunshine Coast and a processing factory at Margate, Tasmania. According to Stock Exchange records, a profit of $791,000 had improved within 12 months to $2.06 million for the first six months of 1991/92, through reduced operating costs, such as labour costs, depreciation and interest.

Armenians Arrive

The Armenian people have experienced great hardship and persecution in their native homeland and many have come to Australian in search of freedom. Eventually Bishop Poladian arrived in 1957 and secured the former small Chinese Presbyterian church in Campbell Street, Surry Hills. This was consecrated as the Armenian Apostolic Church of the Holy Resurrection. When this church proved too small, a former Baptist church was bought and renovated for the Armenian community.[13]

GOVERNMENT

Inner-City Living

After the war young couples with families found it hard to get a house. Many of them crowded into single rooms in the inner-city slums. These wretched living conditions first gained wide public attention through Ruth Park's novel *The*

Harp in the South, which won the *Sydney Morning Herald*'s fiction prize of 1947 and was serialised in the same paper. The story was about everyday life in Surry Hills. Some people protested about the descriptions of the grim conditions. The *Sydney Morning Herald* surveyed the Surry Hills residents:

> One elderly widow said: 'I've got a pension of 32/6d. a week. The rent's 12/6 (two rooms and a kitchen). Grocer's bill is seven bob. No bugs since the house was repapered and had new floorings two years ago after a rat plague. There's gaslight down here—penny in the slot, I take a lamp upstairs. I've got no bath but I manage to wash all right. Quite a lot of places in the district have got baths, but there's not a bathroom in this street except for what some have made for themselves in their backyard.[14]

The Housing Commission built many high-rise flats in the 1950s and '60s. One such large project was the Sir John Northcott Housing Estate, a virtual city in itself in Surry Hills. In Redfern some of the housing towers were to reach 30 storeys. This high-rise policy has been reversed and for 1980s and '90s studies of the risks involved in inner-city living, see Chapter 7. However, the Richmond Report in the 1970s led to many people previously housed in mental institutions seeking Housing Department accommodation. This tinder-box situation eventually reached flashpoint in August 1990. At a public meeting in the Northcott Community Centre after the tragic Clisdell Street shootings, independent MP Ms Clover Moore said, 'The fact is there are more mentally ill people in this electorate than in any other'.

Marx House raid.

INDUSTRY AND TRANSPORT

Trade Union Reminiscences

Laurie Short was for many years secretary of the Federated Ironworkers of Australia.[15] His life is bound up with the inner-city region. Born in Rockhampton, he came to Sydney with his parents at the age of five and went to Crown Street Public School in Surry Hills. Later he went on to Camperdown Public School and then to Sydney Technical College in Ultimo. As a youth he visited the radical bookshop in the basement near the Great Southern Hotel. Not far away was Marx House, 695 George Street, the headquarters of the Communist Party after the

Pyrmont Bridge wheel house.

View of Darling Harbour (before renovation).

war. The police raided Marx House in 1949 during the national coal strike, which began on 27 July and lasted for seven weeks. Australia at the time was still very dependent on black coal: 'Not only was electricity in most states generated predominantly from it, but gas for domestic heating and cooking, the railways, and most industrial boilers also relied on it'.[16] The police raid was authorised by the Chifley Government.

The rank and file union membership began to lose faith in their union bosses, and Laurie Short was a leader of this revolt. On the night of 3 August he and four members of the Industrial Group were attacked by a dozen thugs outside the George Street building. The union elections took place in December, and the long incumbent 'red czar', secretary Ernie Thornton, finished with 9,280 votes to Laurie Short's 7,602. The ballot was challenged. Laurie Short recalls:

> A turning point in the case involving the national union elections of 1949 was the revelation in the court of the indentations on the ballot papers. The cross marked in the square was visible on the ballot paper next to it, which meant that one person had marked off a whole stack of ballot papers. It must be remembered that in any union election only half the members would vote, which means that there were thousands of votes that could be manipulated.

The 'forged ballot' case was one of the longest and most controversial in Australian industrial law. John Robert Kerr, later to become a controversial governor-general, was junior counsel to Short's solicitors. The inquiry commenced on 9 February 1950 and closed on 29 November 1951, with Judge Dunphy declaring Short elected national secretary.[17] The next day Short went to his office, where most of the staff were still Communists. After such a difficult beginning, Laurie Short proved an able union leader until his retirement after 30 years in office. His services to trade unionism were also recognised in such awards as the Order of the British Empire

(1971) and the Order of Australia (1980). In 1976 he was appointed an ABC commissioner, becoming vice-chairman the following year. The Wran Government appointed him to the Senate of the University of Sydney. At the time of my interview, Laurie Short was still on the Parole Board of the Corrective Services Department within the Roden Cutler Building. 'From the second highest level where we meet,' he said, 'I sometimes gaze down at the view towards the old Market and Darling Harbour area'.

The Ironworkers had their offices in the Old Trades Hall until they moved to 188 George Street. Now, however, they have moved back to the Trades Hall district, to a building on the corner of Day and Bathurst Streets. During World War II the heavily Communist-influenced union changed its policy after the invasion of Russia in 1941 (and less so after the bombing of Pearl Harbor).

Hire Purchase and Consumer Finance

There would be few Australians today untouched by the reforms or developments set in train by Ian Mathieson Jacoby. But how many would know his name at all? Born in Perth in 1901, Jacoby came from British and Polish grandparentage. His father was active in the fruit-growing industry and was speaker in parliament. However, the father developed a long incurable illness and Ian left school before he turned 14 to help support the family. He began as a shipping clerk and quickly learnt the bookkeeping trade. The demand for motor cars after the war was great, but Perth had no finance companies and the banks were not enthusiastic to issue loans. In 1927 a visiting representative of the American finance company, Industrial Acceptance Corporation, learnt of Jacoby's enthusiasm for instalment credit and offered him a job in Sydney. By 1946 Jacoby had become managing director of IAC. More was to come. In 1953 he formed, in an old paint shop in Buckland Street, Chippendale, the Custom Credit Corporation. There was a staff of three. The National Bank was 40 per cent shareholder. This nexus of Custom Credit and the National Bank caused a stampede among the other banks to set up similar lending bodies. Jacoby retired in 1963 and returned to Perth, where he died in 1973.

Walkley Awards for Downtown

The print media have annual nationwide awards for excellence in a variety of categories such as best news story, best feature and so on. Downtown features in the best news picture of 1956. Photographer Maurice Wilmott of the *Daily Mirror* was asked to provide something unusual for Anzac Day. As he saw a war widow planting the small white crosses in the lawn outside St Andrew's Cathedral, he wanted a wounded ex-soldier to complete the picture. He found a one-legged man drinking, and offered him a few pound notes if he would pose for a picture. The man agreed provided his face would not be seen. Wilmott asked the man afterwards whether he had lost his leg in the First or Second World War. The man casually replied it was in neither, but in a tram accident in George Street.[18]

Ron Iredale of the *Daily Mirror* was in the right place at the right time too, as he was going home when he came across a building on fire in Surry Hills. A fireman on an extension ladder was about to rescue a man standing at an open window with jets of water playing on the fire. Iredale won the Walkley best news photo of 1959 with his picture.[19]

RELIGION

Dutch Protestants

In 1953, the Dutch Protestant community resisted the prevalent and official government policy of assimilation. The community first assembled at St Stephen's (Macquarie Street), moved to Stanmore and finally took over and restored a run-down church in Ultimo.[20]

This was a Presbyterian church, the third established by Scottish Presbyterians in Ultimo, the first chapel being built by the fiery Dr John Dunmore Lang in 1842. George Harris had bequeathed money to the 'Presbyterian and Protestant poor of Ultimo' and the Quarry Street church was built in 1883. In April 1960 the Dutch Presbyterians took over the manse and the church. The Rev. C. Ulidam was assistant pastor and gave over 20 years service. In 1972 the manse became the Harris Centre, from which a cooperative sought to have the former Buckland Estate, within the area bounded by Harris, Fig, Bulwara and Quarry Streets, given over for low-cost housing. The attempt failed.

Later Eucharistic Traditions

The traditional Catholic practice of regular Diurnal Exposition of the Blessed Sacrament would appear to have been begun in Sydney in 1880 by the Marist Fathers at St Patrick's, Church Hill. A most beautiful altar and reredos was imported from France. It was made of solid brass and still stands in the rear of the apse of the church. Because of its antiquity, St Patrick's is classified by the National Trust.

The Blessed Sacrament tradition associated with Fr Jeremiah O'Flynn was so enduring 'that it impressed Pope Pius XI to authorise the holding of the XXIVth International Eucharistic Congress in Sydney in 1928'.[21] It was as a consequence of this congress that the Blessed

Sacrament Fathers accepted the invitation to make their first foundation in Australia. Dr Mannix welcomed a group of French-Canadian priests and brothers to the historic Melbourne city church of St Francis. In 1953 the Blessed Sacrament Fathers came to Sydney, where they were graciously welcomed by Cardinal Gilroy. A small Blessed Sacrament chapel was opened in a converted furniture store adjacent the Haymarket post office. The religious somehow lived as a community in ramshackle old wooden rooms alongside.

Right from the outset, perpetual exposition and adoration took place. The cost and hardship of this one-hour prayer at the prie-dieu every eight hours was high in such poor, noisy and 'unholy' surroundings. Yet the band of four priests and eight brothers saw the foundation progress and flourish. A special appeal was held to gain the spiritual and financial support of Sydney's Catholics. The parish priest of the Haymarket, Monsignor Freeman, came to the primitive foundation and preached the special appeal sermon in 1953. Eventually, on 17 March, 1964, St Patrick's Day, Cardinal Gilroy blessed the new church of St Peter Julian and the new monastery alongside. The church would seem to have been the first one dedicated to the recently canonised founder of the Blessed Sacrament Fathers. Pope John XXIII declared Peter Julian Eymard a saint on 9 December 1962, at the end of the first session of the Second Vatican Council. At the silver jubilee of the eucharistic foundation, Monsignor Freeman returned as Cardinal Archbishop for a solemn concelebrated Mass of thanksgiving. The work of the Fathers in providing Mass, confessions, prayer and counselling had come to be widely known and appreciated, not only within Sydney but by visitors as well.

Tales Told by Workers

When the Haymarket was flourishing as the Growers and Producers Markets, Ted Sullivan was a seed merchant at 7 Ultimo Road. He dislocated his spine and was laid off work. One day there was a knock on Ted's front door. His wife took a peek and saw three rather scruffy men outside. She said to Ted, 'I don't like the look of them'. The men turned out to be brothers from the Blessed Sacrament Church, enjoying a well-earned day off, who had gone fishing. There was such amusement when the truth came out. Ted's wife could be pardoned for the error of judgment as the usual dress for the brothers in those days was a black suit and hat with a half-clerical collar.

'To Pray and Not to Prey'

One day an irate man approached one of the brothers serving at St Peter Julian's. 'Brother,' he said, 'you'll never believe what has just happened to me. I have actually been propositioned in the church!' The brother found that a little 17-year-old girl had been flown over from New Zealand by a man and had to work for him in a Haymarket brothel. When she arrived by taxi she always called in first at the church. So brother kindly but firmly pointed out some churchly do's and don'ts. 'You come into a church to pray, but not to prey! Got that?' 'Yes, brother,' was the meek reply. And she was true to her word until she went home again.

Greek Orthodox Archdiocese

In 1954 the census revealed that immigrants of Greek birth in Australia numbered 25,862. Greek immigrants have preferred to settle in cities. Indeed the first Greek Orthodox church in Australia is marked by the laying of a foundation stone on 29 May 1898 on a site in Surry Hills. In 1927 Sancta Sophia was consecrated as Orthodox Cathedral for Australasia. On 1 September 1959 the metropolis of Australia and New Zealand became an archdiocese. In 1970 New

Zealand was separated. The present head is Archbishop Stylanos Harkianakis, and the headquarters of the Greek Orthodox Church is at Cleveland Street, Redfern. The Church numbers one archbishop, two bishops, 100 priests, 105 churches, 120 communities and four monasteries. The 1982 census listed 250,000 Greek Orthodox Christians in Australia.[22]

PERSONS AND EVENTS

Downtown's Firebrand

Eddie Ward was born in Darlington on 21 March 1899, one of five children. At five years he attended St Francis School, and later, public schools in Cleveland and Crown Streets. His father worked as a fettler in the Tramways Department and his mother was Irish and Catholic. Times were hard for the Ward family and at 14 Eddie left school. A year earlier he had begun taking violin lessons at Sacred Heart School, practising late at night in his room. This continued for several years until he could no longer pay the tuition fees. In 1915 he joined the Surry Hills Branch of the Australian Labor Party through the influence of an elderly lodger in the family home, Miss Mary Beddie, who was a prominent member of the ALP women's organising committee.

Ward opposed the conscription campaign of Prime Minister Hughes, but at 18 he was liable for home military service under Hughes' War Precautions Act. Ward failed to attend the necessary parades and spent seven days in a military discipline camp at Middle Head. He was also involved in the railway strike of 1917. The union objected to Premier Holman's card system, on which each railway employee's daily work was noted. After the war and penniless, Ward was courting Edith Bishop, his future wife. After visiting her and her parents at Parramatta, Eddie, unbeknown to them, walked the 25 kilometres back to Surry Hills. To assist in his search for a job he obtained a character reference in 1922 from William McKell, the State MP:

> This is to certify I have known Mr Edward Ward of 518 Cleveland Street, Surry Hills, for a considerable number of years and have always found him to be a trustworthy and deserving young man in every respect. I can confidently recommend Mr Ward to anybody requiring his services, and I will always be pleased to do anything in my power to advance his interests.[23]

The friendship continued for many years until McKell, as governor-general, granted the Menzies Government a double dissolution in 1951. Ward found this an unforgivable act against the Labor Party.

Ward openly admired Jack Lang, the more so when in 1925 Lang honoured an election promise to restore seniority to the 1917 railway strikers. Ward assisted Jack Beasley, president of the Electrical Trades Union, obtain preselection for West Sydney. On one occasion Ward was part of a picket line at Pyrmont during a timber workers' strike. He got involved in a punch-up, was arrested and charged with using indecent language. This was ironic as he was not a man to swear. He defended himself successfully in court. Ward, a non-drinker, non-smoker and vegetarian, ran with the Redfern and later the Botany Harriers. He liked to box, was good at it and enjoyed going to the Stadium. Edith Ward says her husband read the Bible every night, and other reference books.

In 1930, for the fifth time, Ward found himself unemployed. He had been elected alderman of the Sydney City Council after having had to resign his job on the tramways, since no public servant could contest an election. He formed a relief committee which received donations of fruit and vegetables from sympathetic stall holders at the City Markets. The food was distributed to needy families. The same year Ward started a bakery in Bourke Street, Surry Hills. The bakery sold two loaves for 7½d. when the ruling price was 5d. per loaf. The master bakers saw to it that Ward's supplies of flour were cut off, so his cheap bakery had to be sold.

Ward entered Federal politics when elected member of East Sydney at a by-election in the shadow of the Lang plan. His arrival in Canberra as a member of the Lang Labor faction spelled the doom of the Scullin Government. Ward lost his seat at the ensuing election. However, the newly elected member John Clasby died a month after the election and Ward scraped in at the by-election by 173 votes. It had taken him three elections in 18 months to secure the seat. From then on his majorities ranged from 5,000 to 20,000.

He soon carved out a unique niche for himself in parliament, for though a Catholic and a non-Communist he was regarded as extreme left-wing. He didn't break with his humble origins or cut himself off from people. His electorate idolised him and Eddie always made himself available to see people in an office set up in the family home in Heeley Street, Paddington. Ward was suspended for the last time (no-one else has been called to order, named and suspended as often in parliament) on 23 May, 1963, after interjecting during William McMahon's reply to a question concerning a U.S. naval communication station in north-west Australia. He was never to enter parliament again, collapsing with a heart attack at home and dying at St Vincent's

Hospital shortly after admission on 31 July 1963.

After Solemn Requiem Mass at St Mary's Cathedral Eddie Ward was buried in the Catholic Section of Randwick cemetery. The Council of the City of Sydney named a reserve in his memory, while his spirited advocacy and affection for the people of Surry Hills earned him the title of 'Firebrand of East Sydney'.

The Youngest Lord Mayor

Patrick Darcy Hills was born on 1 December 1917 in his parents' house in Belmore Street, Surry Hills. He served as an altar boy at St Francis', Albion Street. His leadership qualities were already in evidence, as he was prefect of the servers. The Eucharistic Congress of 1928 entailed many extra church services. Sacred concerts were held at St Francis' and also at the Showgrounds nearby. Pat's early schooling was at the De La Salle Brothers school at Surry Hills. The priest at St Peters, Fr Foley, was affectionately remembered by the local boys as they would be ferried, 14 at a time, on a powerful Indian motorcycle and side-car to the Domain baths. Later schooling was at the Marist Brothers High School in Darlinghurst. Two other Lord Mayors of Sydney, Harry Jensen and John Armstrong, also attended the school.

Pat Hills then became an apprentice fitter and toolmaker. He went into partnership with Gallagher & Murray, so the toolmaking business in Belmore Street was called GHM—not to be confused with a firm of similar initials! Pat's father was president of the Belmore/City Labor branch, so young Pat became involved in politics at an early age. In 1950 he was chairman of the County Council and the following year, at 34, he became the youngest ever lord mayor of Sydney. By this time the Hills family included five children aged from 10 months to 10 years. Danceroom balls were the popular form of evening entertainment in the early '50s. In one week the lord mayor and his wife attended six balls. The lord-mayoralty was a no-frills job. There was no salary, only an allowance for receptions and clothes. As the Council met during the day, the youthful lord mayor had to work in his engineering business at night to make up for lost time.

One of the programs introduced by Pat Hills was Meals on Wheels. He and the Deputy Town Clerk, Ted Adams, went to Adelaide to check out a service there and a decision was made to institute a similar one in Sydney. A kitchen was built in the basement of the Lower Town Hall. Although support came from Monsignor McCosker, the RSL, the Anglican Church and other church bodies, obtaining volunteers was always a difficulty.

> When my wife was short of drivers she would ring me and ask me to drive a car. One day we were over at Glebe and because she had to call on me we were a bit late on the run because a regular driver did not turn up. The soup was a bit cold when we took it to this dear old soul up in a two-storied building. We served the soup up and when we came downstairs she tipped the soup over us.

Summing up his public life, Pat Hills said: 'I am grateful to the people of Surry Hills. I am not saying this for the sake of saying it, but for their giving me the opportunity to represent them—lord mayor, member of parliament, member of the cabinet, deputy premier.'[24] Amongst the many achievements would be the two pools for which Pat Hills was responsible—one at Prince Alfred Park and the other at Victoria Park.

Pat Hills retired from politics in 1988 and became chairman of the Sydney Cricket Ground and Sports Ground Trust. His name was removed from a stand that he built and replaced by that of the former Test spin bowler Bill O'Reilly. Hills died on 22 April 1992 after a long illness. The State President of the ALP, Terry Sheahan, praised him during the funeral held at St Mary's Cathedral, at which Premier Greiner was sitting next to Prime Minister Keating.

Dan Minogue

As the *Beltania* docked in Melbourne on Easter Sunday, 23 March 1913, Dr Mannix was met by his new and excited flock. Another fellow Irish passenger, Daniel Minogue, made his way to Sydney soon afterwards. After working as a shunter in Darling Harbour rail yards and other odd jobs, Dan bought the White Horse Hotel in Surry Hills. One of his customers was a Galway ballad singer, Paddy Collins.

> One day Paddy got locked up while trying to sell his ballads at a park near Central Railway Station. Next day, Paddy and others came before the Court, all charged with being drunk and disorderly. The Magistrate, Mr Smithers, fined each of them £2 or two days in gaol. Paddy stood up in the Court and said—'Mr Smiters, if you please, make it hours instead of days, and if you do I humbly pray, you may live for many long days'. Mr Smithers removed his glasses and asked the Prosecuting Officer—'Are you sure Mr Collins was offensive, or was he there to make a living?' 'I am a married man with wife and children,' Paddy said. 'I was never in a Court before.' Mr Smithers discharged Paddy, and advised the Police to be more careful in future.[25]

Dan entered local politics and became a member of the Sydney City Council. In 1949 he won the Federal seat of West Sydney (which included half of Surry Hills—Eddie Ward had the other half in the seat of East Sydney). This election made Dan the third Irishman, after Hugh Mahon and Dan Mulcahy, to be a Federal MP.

Dan was instrumental in obtaining the land now occupied by the Irish National Association Club in Devonshire Street. It is the site where the Irish chieftain, Michael Dwyer, and his wife are buried. On the centenary of the 1798 uprising their remains were removed to a vault in the Waverley cemetery. The spectacular procession of a gold-plated casket drawn by six horses, each attended by a page, was watched by 200,000.

During World War II Mother Mary Saint Justin and four Irish Sisters came to Surry Hills to take charge of an old convict building. It was located at 51 Buckingham Street. Minogue recalled that:

> The place when I first visited it was named St Magdalen's Retreat and the dungeons are still to be seen where the women convicts were housed at night. The walls and floors are of stone with slits in the walls to serve as windows. In the old days the convicts were compelled to work in the laundry for their keep.[26]

A committee formed to convert the building into a refuge included Dan, Pat Hills (State Labor leader) and Tom Shannon, MLA. The new name of the building was henceforth Our Lady of Consolation Home for the Aged and Infirm. Seventy old people could be accommodated. The Sisters eventually moved to Rooty Hill, where there are extensive grounds for 300 guests.

Dan's political office was in the Commonwealth Bank Building in Martin Place. It irked him that the GPO clock, erected in 1874 and dismantled in 1942, had still not been restored. 'That clock had marked the passing of time for many of our elderly citizens. I should see no reason why it should be rusting away out at Malabar.'[27] Eventually his campaign succeeded and Prime Minister Menzies in 1962, at a cost of £194,000, had 10 tons of chimes and eight tons of bells returned to the Post Office Tower.

Ever the champion of the underdog, Minogue pleaded in Federal parliament for an equitable redistribution of the electorates in Northern Ireland. This speech was made in March 1969, after two years of warfare in the streets of Ulster. Another time a man came to his office for help. Dan listened to his story and approached his Queen's Counsel colleagues in the Labor Party. The unfortunate man worked at Tattersalls in Elizabeth Street and in an accident, while moving a sofa, lost first one testicle and then the other. The lawyers laughed. But

Dan did not give in. The man's wife had been to a solicitor who said she could win compensation on the grounds of being entitled to conjugal rights. Dan finally won in the parliament, under the Commonwealth Employees' Compensation Act, November, 1968: 'Provision will be made for lump sum compensation for the loss of power of speech, for facial disfigurement and for the loss of genital organs or complete and permanent loss of sexual function'.[28]

Dan was a strong supporter of state aid to non-government schools. In a caucus debate,

> I said that in West Sydney we had Blackfriars Correspondence School, the largest of its kind in the world with 7,000 pupils and the teachers had many problems with old-fashioned school accommodation but these conditions were still better than the position of children attending denominational schools whose parents got no aid of any kind from the Commonwealth Government.[29]

Even in his retiring speech in Canberra in 1969, Minogue returned to the same issue. Having left school at 13, he was very conscious that first-rate education should be available free for all children. 'It is silly and sinful to deprive young children, irrespective of religion and colour, be they black, white or brindle, of the opportunity to be educated. They should not be kicked about at election time.'[30]

Wild Men of Sydney

In 1958 a new Defamation Bill was rushed through the N.S.W. parliament. The *Daily Telegraph* claimed that the government had rushed it through to stop the sale of Cyril Pearl's *Wild Men of Sydney* and told its readers to buy the *Sunday Telegraph*. However, when the paper appeared it contained a small notice which said that, on legal advice, the previously announced serialisation of the book would not proceed. The substance of the new bill was that a living person could sue an author or publisher for defamation of a deceased member of his or her family. The attorney-general, Mr Downing, was asked in the Legislative Council whether Mr Ezra Norton, the managing director of Truth and Sportsman Ltd, had instigated the bill. In the event, the bill was passed, but the book was still published in London and no action was taken against Cyril Pearl. Soon afterwards, Ezra Norton sold his interest in the *Daily Mirror.*

The chief character in Pearl's book is undoubtedly John Norton. Norton was brought up by his Anglican step-father, the Rev. Benjamin Herring, who held that birch whippings and solitary confinement were necessary corrections.[31]

Through *Truth*, Norton mercilessly attacked his political opponents, one of whom was George Black, MLC for West Sydney who earlier had been 'a lecturer at the Cyclorama on the horrors of Gettysburg'.[32] Black retaliated through the *Australian Workman*, the Trades and Labour Council paper he edited. Richard Dennis Meagher was another politician Norton tried to force out of parliament. Exasperated beyond endurance, Meagher bought a heavy greenhide whip in the saddlery department of Anthony Hordern's. The headlines of the *Evening News* of 1898 tell what happened next:

A CITY SENSATION
Fracas in Pitt St
An Editor Horsewhipped
Meagher attacks Norton
Exciting Encounter
Norton Uses a Revolver.[33]

Meagher was fined £5 in Central Police Court. However, the incident does not seem to have damaged his career, as he became speaker in parliament, president of the Labor Party and first Labor lord mayor of Sydney.

Pearl describes Norton's alcoholism in great detail. The motivation behind the enthusiastic demolition would seem to consist in the rhetorical question asked on page 244.

How then did this power-drunk megalomaniac, rejected by the Labour movement, exposed and self-exposed countless times as an enemy of Labour, a hater of democracy, an anarchist with the soul of a dictator, bemuse so many Australians into believing he was their tribune, champion—even martyr?

Pearl harks back to Norton's obsession with Napoleon and advances Jung's description of Hitler as Norton's epitaph: 'An irresponsible, ranting psychopath cursed with the keen intuition of a rat or a guttersnipe'.

Mr Eternity

For 37 years a little man would bend down and write with a crayon on the footpaths of Sydney city in an elegant copperplate script—'Eternity'. This one-word sermon was written more than half a million times. For over 10 years there was speculation about the author, who clearly disliked publicity, even though he clearly had a serious mission from his Maker.

Arthur Stace was born in a Balmain slum in 1884. His parents, brothers and sisters were all drunks. His sisters ran a brothel in Surry Hills. Stace earned his keep as a 'cockatoo' at gambling dens or with break-in gangs and he ferried liquor to brothels in the district. He served with the First AIF in France and returned to Surry Hills after being gassed and half-blinded in one eye. He turned to drink. There followed many court appearances. A magistrate in Central Court lectured the offender in ringing biblical phrases, 'Don't you know that I have the *power* to put you in Long Bay gaol or the *power* to set you free?' The word 'power' lingered on. How could the power be got to give up the drink? A search in the streets began,

from Regent Street Police Station to St Barnabas' Broadway until in the Burton Street Baptist Church, Darlinghurst, he heard the preacher shouting 'I wish I could shout eternity through the streets of Sydney'. 'Suddenly I began crying and I felt a powerful call from the Lord to write ETERNITY. I had a piece of chalk in my pocket and I bent down there and

Memorial to Arthur Stace.

wrote it. The funny thing is that before I wrote I could hardly write my own name. I had no schooling and I couldn't have spelled ETERNITY for a hundred quid. But it came out smoothly in a beautiful copperplate script. I couldn't understand it and I still can't.'[34]

Stace and his wife Pearl lived in Bulwarra Road, Pyrmont. He rose at 4.00 a.m., prayed for an hour, and after breakfast set out from home. He would begin writing his message down at dawn every 100 yards or so, wherever it could be seen best. By mid-morning he was home again. On Saturday nights he led a gospel meeting on the corner of George and Bathurst Streets. Arthur Stace died in a nursing home at the age of 83 on 30 July 1967. He left his body to the University of Sydney—the remains were buried more than two years later at Botany cemetery. After much debate about a public plaque or statue of Stace, the architect of Sydney Square set a message plaque cast in aluminium near the square's waterfall. The architect as a boy heard Stace preach on the George Street corner nearby and the plaque bears the famous copperplate message —'Eternity'.

Bea Miles

There was, perhaps, nothing blessed about Beatrice Miles except her name and the spirit and humour which never left her in the vale of tears, the streets, lanes and vehicles of Sydney where she spent her life. Father Tom McNevin, SSS, remembers Bea Miles as a brilliant university student and in later years she always gave her name as 'Bea Miles, student, NFPA'. When asked to explain what NFPA meant she would say, 'No Fixed Place of Abode, of course'. This was very true, as Bea was the scourge of tram, bus and taxi drivers, cinema managers and city churches, any one of whose appliances or buildings she might choose to regard as her temporary abode. She totally ignored conventions of every kind. She would ride a pushbike in full evening dress whilst blowing a policeman's whistle and once rode to Newcastle on the front bumper of a motor car. In 1923, when 21, she was committed to a mental asylum for three years. She believed that all public transport should be free and acted accordingly. Some treated her kindly for the character she was, but others got tough or threatened to take her to the police. Bea's special gift was in breaking car doors. She would flop into a taxi cab without expecting to have to pay. Once, when a driver got abusive at Bea's refusal to pay she just bent back the taxi cab door until its hinges snapped.

Such behaviour landed her at Central Police Court quite frequently, where she always conducted her own defence. The Police Prosecutor once said 'Have you any bruises to show where this driver kicked, and punched on this occasion?' 'Yes, I have. I've got them on my bottom—' and with a curl on her lips—'but you're not going to see them.' That resulted in a fine and costs of £24 10s. 0d. On another occasion she was discovered dripping wet, sitting in a taxi outside the police station in Central Lane. As the crowds gathered round, she sobbed, 'He's thrown three buckets of water over me, but I'm not leaving'.

When in court she would give a little hand-out to the press reporters.

The police have victimized me for 23 years for six reasons: 1. They can't make me leave the city 2. They can't get me on a criminal charge 3. Nor on a vice charge 4. Nor on a drunk ditto 5. They can't vag me 6. They can't get an honest doctor to declare me insane.[35]

On one occasion Bea announced she was going to Perth to collect wildflowers for the Sydney Herbarium. Naturally, she went by taxi cab. As the cost of the fare was a shilling a mile, every hundred miles she would fish out of her purse a five-pound note and hand it to the driver. The trip cost her nearly £700. This did not include hotel fees, as Bea had the two drivers sleeping out in the open.[36]

Another time she yelled at her taxi driver to stop, made him turn back to pick up an Aborigine, and drive 15 kilometres in the opposite direction. 'Bea went in, met the family, and gave them a ten-shilling note. The Aboriginal said: "God bless you missus—you're a real fine lady. How would you like a drink of plonk?" Bea declined gracefully.'[37]

Eventually sleeping in Belmore Park (Bandstand), cinemas or city churches became too much for Bea, and when 62 she was both diabetic and arthritic. The aggressive atheist found no home for the aged would take her in, except the Little Sisters of the Poor at Randwick. One taxi driver, John Beynon, did remain her friend for 22 years. He would pick her up from the Little Sisters of the Poor on Thursdays and take her to the Public Library. Bea was a voracious reader and a competent Shakespearean orator.

Then she would go to the city, buy cases of oranges and ask Beynon to drive around so that she could distribute them to the poor people. Shortly before her death she did receive baptism as a Catholic. She died on 2 December, 1973, aged 71. She had some interesting ideas even at the end. She wanted a band to play 'Advance Australia Fair', 'Waltzing Matilda' and 'Tie Me Kangaroo Down Sport' at her funeral. She also wanted a ribbon draped over her coffin with the words 'One who loved Australia' written on it. All this was done.[38]

ENTERTAINMENT

Entertainment Mandarins

The Wong family played an important part in the entertainment industry of postwar Sydney. Brothers Denis and Keith Wong were involved in a number of nightclubs, ranging from the Mandarin Club and Chequers to the Whiskey Au Go-Go. The Mandarin Club is a popular nightspot with dining facilities, etc. in elaborate Chinese decor. A nephew of Keith Wong was secretary for many years. The Wong family and a number of business associates started the club in 1964 in 'aid of fellowship and service in the Chinese community and to improve relations between the Australian Government and the Chinese Republic'. Also in 1964 the Wong brothers teamed up with greyhound bookmaker, John Harrigan, in the Whiskey Au Go-Go at Kings Cross. Harrigan's family had been running nightclubs in Sydney since the 1920s and Harrigan, like the Wongs, had spent his early childhood in Shanghai in the 1940s. Not long after the Wongs arrived in Sydney they opened, in 1959, the Cathay Chinese restaurant and Chequer's Night Club. Chequers provided glamour and excitement as international stars like Shirley Bassey, Sammy Davis, Jnr, and Lisa Minelli, as well as local political show business and media personalities, liked to go there. The Wongs also ran Australia's biggest toy wholesale importing business, Trans World Agency, and an associated company, Trans World Travel, from premises at Ultimo. Trans World Agency collapsed in 1982 with debts of $37 million.

Sir Nicholas Shehadie

Nick Shehadie was the son of an Orthodox Lebanese clergyman and pharmacist whose shop once stood in Broadway before Tooth's Brewery extensions. His grandfather founded the first Antioch Orthodox Church in Australia in Redfern, on the corner of Walker and Redfern Streets. The Shehadie house was nearby and Nick went to school at Cleveland Street Public School. After several jobs, he settled in with Wormald's, eventually becoming personnel manager. With a 6 foot 2 inch and 17 stone frame he was to become a second-rower or prop Rugby union player. He gained Test selection in 1947 and played in 30 Tests. He started his own floor-tiling business in an old £1 per week shop in Redfern, on the corner of Walker and Cooper Streets. Nick Shehadie served on the Sydney City Council for 14 years, had three terms as deputy lord mayor, and was elected lord mayor in 1973.

CRIME

Ultimo's Gunman

Mr Justice McClemens read out John Hayes' criminal record after Hayes had been found guilty of murder on 28 May 1952. Ninety convictions over a period of 20 years were listed. Hayes was sentenced to death, but as Labor was in office the sentence was commuted a few months later to life imprisonment. The story behind the murder goes back to 'Chow' Hayes' life as a standover man in the twilight world of illegal gambling places, prostitution and sly-grog houses. Chow Hayes' house in Mary Ann Street, Ultimo, had been staked out and his nephew killed by rival gunmen. Hayes discovered the killer, an ex-boxer Bobby Lee, and shot him several times, fatally, in the Sydney Ziegfield nightclub.

Hayes' whole life was lived in Downtown. His family came from the Coonabarabran district, settling in Shepherd Street, Chippendale, and Hayes went to school at St Benedict's nearby. It was after a victorious fist fight with a rival over selling newspapers that his fallen foe screamed out, 'You Chow bastard'. The name stuck. Hayes was sent to Guilford Truant School at 11 for skipping local classes. This was the start of his life of stints in state institutions. His father had gone to the war when Hayes was three and returned six years later with shellshock in 1921, dying from his injuries in 1924. Hayes' mother married again after 18 months, and 'permanently abandoned her children'.[39] Hayes had a brother and younger sister.

He began his life of crime by thieving. There were plenty of pawnbrokers in the area. However, Hayes found it more profitable to have a gun and demand money from the illegal gambling operators who were only too glad to pay the 'protection' money. He was on the payroll for Thommo's two-up school in Surry Hills. In all, Hayes spent 45 of his adult 67 years in prison. He was a violent man, either shooting, bashing, battering or hacking any who dared stand against him. Hayes himself was shot only once, in the abdomen, by 'Knocker' McGarry after a dispute over a woman.

ARTS

Ruth Park's Novels

Ruth Park came to Sydney from her native New Zealand in 1942, staying at the YWCA on her arrival and marrying the writer D'Arcy Niland in the same year. Niland had come to Sydney from the bush to get a job as a copy boy for the Sydney *Sun*, but lost his job during the Depression and went bush again. The Nilands wrote a joint autobiography, *The Drums Go Bang!* (1956), in which they describe the first years of their marriage when they lived in Surry Hills and began to earn their living from writing. Ruth Park won the *Sydney Morning Herald*'s novel competition of 1946 with her *The Harp in the South*, published in 1948. The sequel, *Poor Man's Orange*, was published in 1949. Both of these works were made into television serials during the 1980s. They give a good feel of life in Surry Hills at the time of the war's end. There are cameo descriptions of the streets, markets, churches, flophouses, ham'n'beef shop, the prostitutes, the rats, and the housing demolition. A small sampling from her two novels dealing with life in Surry Hills is here offered:

New Year in Surry Hills:

> Where Coronation Street met Plymouth Street there was a rough rectangle striped silver with tramlines. Every year it was the custom to build a bonfire there, just out of reach of the trams, which rushed past in a fleeting crimson glow from the flames. The authorities always forbade it, and nobody ever took any notice of what they said, but went on lighting New Year bonfires just the same.[40]

Saturday Afternoons in Surry Hills:

> Saturday afternoon was the great afternoon of the week in Plymouth Street. The factory girls washed their hair and did it up in perforated aluminium curlers, put on old print dresses with sagging necklines and torn pockets, and sat on the peeling, cocoa-coloured balconies of the tenements, beating off the flies and saying: 'Gawd, ain't it hot!' Downstairs, on the pockmarked steps of the old houses and the drab boarded-up shops, old men sat, legs wide, their stomachs bulging open the top buttons of their pants, hats pulled down over their grey frowsy faces, and talked politics, racing, or lang syne.
>
> Down into the mean canyon of the street the sunshine poured, like yellow wine, and under its magic there was a gleam and a glimmer over everything, so that shadows seemed furry and mysterious, and the iron lace around the balconies Moorish and exotic.[41]

Surry Hills Dialect:

> The harsh chirpiness of the Surry Hills girls, the raucous laughter, and the slurred, twanging vowels of that district's argot.[42]

Good and Evil:

> Then the walls of the houses would seem transparent to her eyes, and she would see other Kilroys beating their wives and their daughters; mean, dirty women blowing their noses on their aprons, and letting their children play round garbage tins heaving with maggots; women who suckled their children to three years old in an effort to prevent another conception, oblivious to the ill-nourished and imbecilic look of the child; fathers who violated one daughter after another as they grew to the age of twelve or thirteen years, and mothers who stood by and allowed it; grimy-fingered old hags up dark alleys who would abort you with a crochet hook for ten shillings— all the commonality of sin was laid before her in the streets. She saw the reverse of the tapestry, hidden, unfinished, grotesque, thinking it was peculiar to Surry Hills, and not knowing that the whole world was the same, if you wanted to look for those things. In these bad times she did not see any of the good and heroic things that were going on about her, the tubercular mother fighting to feed her children, the kindness and generosity of the poor to the poorer, the old man tending his blind and crippled

friend on the park bench, the returned soldier with no legs, sitting in the window whittling wooden toys, as un-bitter as a bird. She did not see that for every sin in Surry Hills there were a thousand heart-warming words and deeds.[43]

Both Ruth Park and D'Arcy Niland went on to write many other works. Niland's six novels, *The Shiralee* (1955), *Call Me When the Cross Turns Over* (1957) and *Dead Men Running* (1969) were made into films and television mini-series. His novel *The Big Smoke* (1959) is set in inner Sydney among the boxing fraternity.

Come In Spinner

'Come in spinner' is a term from the gambling game of two-up. It is also the title of a novel about wartime Sydney co-authored by Dymphna Cusack and Florence James, and published in 1951. It was not Cusack's first venture at collaboration. She and Miles Franklin had written a satirical novel about the sesquicentenary celebrations of 1938 called *Pioneers on Parade*. Amongst their other tasks, both Cusack and James helped out at the Children's Court in Surry Hills, the former in school counselling and the latter in voluntary public relations. The overriding theme of the novel is women's experience during October 1944, amidst a background of rackets, greed and ugliness. The novel was awarded first prize in the 1948 *Daily Telegraph* Australian novel competition. When the novel was published in 1951 it was heavily abridged, and not published in its entirety until 1988. It was made into a television series in 1990. One wonders now what all the fuss was about. In fact what really happened at the time is considerably worse when the criminal milieu of Chow Hayes, which covers the same time and place, is placed alongside that of *Spinner*. The authors centre their novel around several women working in a beauty salon of a well-to-do Sydney hotel. Scenes of wartime Sydney are woven into the novel. Downtown spots include the Anzac Memorial, Central Station, the Glaciarium, a Sydney Town Hall concert where Marjorie Lawrence sings, of all things, Wagner's 'Liebestod', the 'Coconut Grove' club in George Street (near Goulburn Street), and above all, the Children's Court. The scenes in the Albion Street Children's Court are amongst the more powerful social comments in the novel. These scenes occurred when one of the principal characters, Peg 'Guinea' Malone, seeks out her sister who has been arrested after running away from home to escape working under the Manpower regulations in a factory but has ended up drunk in a brothel.

A Memory of Raymond Longford

The Brickfield Hill region of George Street is established as the centre of Sydney's and Australia's movie world. In 1983 the Australian Film Institute awards were presented in most lavish Hollywood style at the Entertainment Centre. There were spectacular dance routines. Short clips from films competing for the awards were shown on a giant screen behind the stage. Most of the awards were taken out by the film *Careful He Might Hear You*, set around Balmain and Sydney Harbour.

It is ironic to reflect that Raymond Longford, regarded as one of the founders of Australian cinema, had to find employment at the end of his life as a night patrolman on the wharves of nearby Pyrmont. The director who filmed the great Australian silent classics *The Sentimental Bloke* (1919) and *On Our Selection* (1920) died in obscurity in 1959 at the age of 81.[44]

In both films Longford deals with the 'battler' myth—in the bush *(On Our Selection)* and in the city *(The Sentimental Bloke)*. Longford took the C.J. Dennis story and filmed it in Woolloomooloo. After the film's success it was said young men were scouring the back lanes of Surry Hills and Chippendale looking for their 'Doreen'. Lottie Lyell, who played Doreen, became Australia's first film star. She figured in another Longford film, *The Dinkum Bloke*, in which a family struggles to send their son to a private school. She also co-directed with Longford, but her career was cut short by tuberculosis. She died in 1925, aged 24, and was buried in Northern Suburbs cemetery. Raymond Longford was buried beside her.

Charles Blackman

Born in Sydney in 1928, Charles Blackman was the only boy in a family of six. His father left when he was four and his mother remarried when he was nine. Early days were at Kings Cross and Redfern, before the family moved into Mrs Blackman's mother's home at Harbord. He left school at 14, had a job as a subeditor's copy boy with the Sydney *Sun* till he was 18 and then went to Brisbane, where he met the poet and child psychology graduate Barbara Patterson, whom he was to marry. 'I didn't really start painting until Barbara came to Sydney and we lived together'.[45] Barbara's eyesight was already rapidly failing.

Blackman's first noteworthy paintings of the 1950s portray the emotionally vulnerable world of childhood. In the late 1950s, when his wife borrowed *Alice in Wonderland* from the Talking Book Library for the blind, Blackman went on to project his wife as Alice into a world of topsy-turvey objects, dimensions and happenings. He had discovered the way to release his full artistic imagination in the service of his disoriented heroine. Blackman's blind-girl paintings were well received in Paris and London. 'Is it fanciful to see in this painting not only a new and original talent but a sign that Australian painting is at last moving away from its obsession with the outback?' asked *The Observer*.[46] Blackman's painting has appealed to many writers, critics and poets. The imagery works through grief, loss, guilt, persecution and tenderness.

The Artist as Battler

In the Antipodean Exhibition (seven painters and one academic who felt obliged to defend figurative art—'Today that loyalty requires, beyond all else, the defence of the image'), Robert Dickerson's *Wynyard Station* was singled out for special mention along with the work of Charles Blackman. Art critic Robert Hughes provides a perceptive introduction to Robert Dickerson: 'In Sydney where tragedy had little place in the painting vocabulary, Dickerson's work had been there to remind us that the Australian sun has its dark side'.[47]

Like Blackman, Dickerson is a self-taught painter. Born in Sydney in 1924, the son of a tinsmith, he attended Bourke Street Public School in Surry Hills. Leaving school at 14, he became a professional boxer at 16. He bottled gas for the Blue Ray Gas Company at Annandale for eight years. 'It wasn't much fun, in near freezing weather I had to put two pairs of socks on my hands and ride a bike to the factory at 5 a.m.' It was there he painted one of his best paintings, *KO'd by Griffo*, in the men's toilets.

Dickerson's paintings contain no luxuries. They reveal people, trapped in city streets. Their faces are grim and melancholic. The titles of the paintings themselves reveal a poet of the inner city at work: *Man Asleep on the Steps, The Tired Man, Boy in the Street, The Escalator, Woman at the TAB, Smoko, Redfern Park*. He has noted:

> I abhor the idea of prettiness and could not paint pretty pictures. Beauty I believe is something individuals give to what they see and feel. I find beauty in the working people, especially children and old people. Their eyes say something and I like to get this into my work. That is why it says something to people who see it and perhaps why it moves them. I try to paint something that will be different from all the escape rubbish around everywhere. My work is a protest against this if you like. I am not trying to prove something. I just paint what I feel like painting.[48]

7 Wealth, Crime and Redevelopment (1962–1990s)

POPULATION

Coming of the Whirlwind

Mum Shirl recalls meeting Charlie Perkins, the senior Aboriginal public servant, for the first time in a hotel commonly called the 'Bunches' which was in Sussex Street and had a very bad name.[1] In the seventies the Foundation for Aboriginal Affairs, in George Street near Christ Church, was another meeting place for young Aborigines. It was the time of the Aboriginal Tent Embassy in Canberra and many black radicals had come to Sydney and Canberra. It was on the night of 26 January 1972—Australia Day—that the 'Aboriginal Embassy' sign was first displayed in Canberra, outside Parliament House.

Political activism and protest was becoming the norm. There was trouble in Chippendale when homeless and alcoholic Aborigines occupied old deserted houses. These had been earmarked for purchase by the Whitlam Government for the future Aboriginal Housing Company. Priests and nuns were joining militant young Blacks to prevent evictions by the police. Mum Shirl recollects how Sister Ignatius Jenkins, alone in full religious habit, and despite being in her seventies, helped greatly in defusing a dangerous situation.[2]

Black Health Care

Mum Shirl has had the cross of epilepsy from an early age. It thwarted her schooling: 'I can't read or write now'.[3] On the missions and reserves the staple diet was flour, sugar and bully beef. When the Aboriginal Medical Service was established at Redfern, Mum Shirl discovered through the doctors the importance of vitamins and nutrition. She now saw that some food was good and some bad. So she began to go with Sister Mary Oliver, very early in the morning, down to Paddy's Market to buy the freshest fruit and vegetables for those families who had nothing. She relates:

> I guess we looked like a strange pair to be out buying at a time when mostly only greengrocers were getting their stock for their shops for the day. Sister Mary Oliver could drive a hard bargain and many of the men and women who run the markets were Italian, Catholics who respected the nun's habit when they saw it.[4]

Eventually the Aboriginal Medical Services turned it into a major program with a truck funded from Freedom From Hunger. A Breakfast for Children was started about the same time by Mum Shirl's nephew, Paul, who was also instrumental in starting a preschool centre which is now run by Aboriginal women. The preschool was originally at 72 Shepherd Street, Chippendale.

The Paradoxes Continue

One year Mum Shirl was actually arrested and charged by two policemen. The

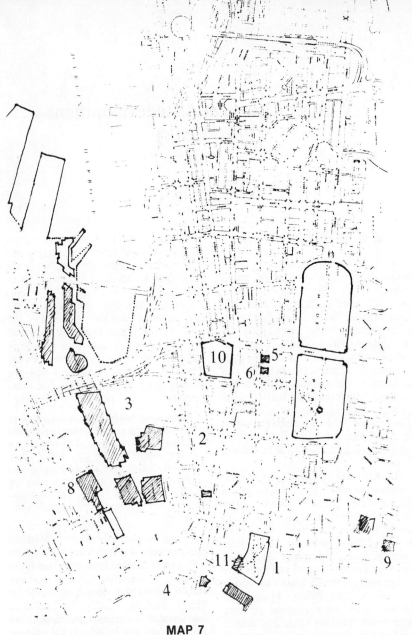

MAP 7
1962 – 1990s

1 BELMORE PARK
2 CHINATOWN ARCH
3 DARLING HARBOUR
   REDEVELOPMENT
4 HER MAJESTY'S THEATRE
5 PITT ST UNITING CHURCH
6 POLDING HOUSE–PITT ST
7 POLICE STATION–SURRY HILLS

8 POWERHOUSE MUSEUM
9 SHELTERS–EDWARD EAGER/
   FOSTER HOUSE/CAMPBELL HOUSE
10 "ETERNITY PLAQUE",ST ANDREW'S SQUARE
11 "OUR LADY OF THE SNOWS" SHELTER–
    RAILWAY SQUARE

charges were false and unjust as it turned out. But she was in hospital at the time she received news she had won the 'Parent of the Year' award.

> I went from my hospital bed, along with a young Black woman who had come to collect me for the occasion, down town to collect the award. I feel I am going to end up with so many medals and pieces of paper. They must be worth something in the end, mustn't they?[5]

On Australia Day 1984 the official civic presentations were made by the governor-general, Sir Ninian Stephen, at the Sydney Entertainment Centre. The ceremonies were televised live throughout Australia. As might be expected in an Olympic Games year, the accent was on sport and Robert de Castella justly deserved the Australian of the Year Award for his marathon wins against world-class competition. A young blind man, Michael Waldock, came forward with his labrador dog Robbie to receive his Young Australian of the Year Award. Despite his blindness he had operated a radio station at Bermagui on the South Coast, picked up many distress signals and had been instrumental in saving the lives of more than 30 people in the previous year. Among this select group of Australians who had devoted themselves to the betterment and service of their fellows, whether by cancer research or social work was one woman, a black woman. It was Mum Shirl.

The New Chinatown

When the Growers' Markets shifted from the Haymarket to Flemington during the 1970s, efforts were made to revitalise nearby areas. The most immediate and effective success was in Dixon Street, where large ceremonial arches were constructed to serve as gateways to Chinatown. The beautification of Dixon Street was a joint project of the City Council and the Dixon Street Chinese Community, Stanley Wong being president and King Fong, secretary.

The Chinatown arch.

Eating out in Chinatown had become one of Sydney's favourite pastimes. But on 20 April 1983 one restaurateur had every reason to be smiling more broadly than usual. For Stanley Wong was having the premier of China, Zhao Ziyang, as his guest at the Tai Yuen Palace in Sussex Street. There were 300 paying guests for the 90-minute lunch and another 70 non-paying guests. Tickets were reputedly $17 each. New South Wales Police Special Branch provided a food taster who must have enjoyed his duties among the 11 cooks. Applause and an enthusiastic toasting of friendship between the Chinese and Australian people marked the banquet's ending. 'Few, however, appeared ready to take up the premier's invitation "to go back to China and see the great changes that have taken place in your home towns".'[6]

A few years later Stanley Wong, his wife and a maid were viciously attacked in their home. Only Mrs Wong survived. Her life was saved by Dr Victor Chang, who had only a few months earlier performed a heart bypass operation on Stanley Wong. Two young Chinese men were arrested and gaoled. They had 14K triad insignia on their key rings. The triads are Hong-Kong-based organised crime gangs.

One Survivor of the Boat People

After the defeat of South Vietnam by the Communists in 1975, there followed a period of restrictions on individual freedom. Many Vietnamese fled their own country by boat. By 1979 nearly 300,000 boat people had reached other countries; however, almost as many perished at sea. Ethnic Chinese living in Vietnam were forced out of business or out of traditional fishing or farming work, and they too sought to escape. There resulted a massive, disorderly exodus in which half of those who perished were children. One family that sought to flee was the Tran family, Cantonese-speaking and Buddhist in religious belief.

Plans for the escape went wrong when the family became separated. The riverboat set out for Malaysia, 400 kilometres away, without the captain and without the engineer. There were 50 people on board, including Hue Hue (pronounced Hway-Hway) and her brother Trung, their Aunt Binh and Uncle Ba. A serious navigation error led to a course away from their escape route to Malaysia and instead straight out into the South China Sea. After a voyage of 760 kilometres the boat was wrecked on Ladd Reef. Ships passed nearby but did not see the desperate survivors. Death was a permanent danger, through malnutrition and dysentery or pirates. The black escape boat was abandoned for another wreck, a white Korean fishing vessel where the survivors died one by one. Every night Hue Hue prayed with others on the deck.

When only five were left, Hue Hue as the only one who still prayed 'Send us a ship, please, or let us die quickly'. A small miracle occurred when flocks of seagulls came to visit the wreck. With difficulty they were caught and provided vital food. Her last companion was the boy Quan, who had collected his father's bones and kept them beside him. Now she was alone after four months on the wreck, pitifully thin and weak, full of head lice, clothes reduced to rags. The seagulls that she caught every day gave her life. Night after night she dreamt of her family and the people she loved.

After two further weeks of solitude she woke up to see a boat 50 metres away. She waved a shirt 'Cun toi voi, cun toi voi!' (Help me, help me). Two strange young men came on board. Hue Hue was terrified they might kill her. The boat was a Muslim Filipino fishing vessel. The men could barely cope with the stench and the skeletal remains. But with her realisation of deliverance, Hue Hue's first action was to release the seagull she had caught the previous night. Before she could untie a cloth strip, the gull flew off, trailing it behind. During her first meal, Hue prayed silently, 'Thank you God for listening to me'.

Her father and mother had fled to Malaysia and were living there in a refugee camp when they received news that their daughter was alive. They could scarcely believe it. Uncle Ly The was in Sydney and became the sponsor for the family's reunification. On 31 May 1979 Hue Hue flew to Sydney, facing a media barrage at Kingsford Smith airport, and with her uncle went to a refugee hostel at East Hills. On 25 October her parents and brother Quang arrived. On 16 November, Hue Hue's mother gave birth to a son in Crown Street Women's Hospital. Hue Hue worked as a waitress in Chinatown as she continued her education.[7]

The Lebanese: Maronites and Melkites

The Lebanese presence in Australia goes back to last century. Father Silwanus Mansour was ordained in 1880 in his native land and arrived in Australia in 1891 in answer to requests from the Melkites resident in Sydney. Two years later, with help from Cardinal Moran, he was able to lay the foundation of old St Michael's Church in Waterloo. In 1895 Cardinal Moran consecrated the church.

In 1966 Monsignor Aftimos Haddad became the church's fourth pastor. One of his first tasks was to renovate old St Michael's Church in Waterloo. The great increase in the Melkite Community on account of emigration from Lebanon, Egypt, Syria and Jordan and other parts of the Middle East occurred in the 1960s and early '70s. There was no meeting hall or parking facilities. The trustees approached Cardinal Freeman and in 1977 St Kieran's Church and School in Darlington (Golden Grove) became St Michael's Melkite Church. The foundation stone was laid by Cardinal Freeman in 1979. The marble iconostas altar and baptismal font from the old St Michael's were relocated in the enlarged Darlington church. The baptismal font had been blessed in 1902 by the Very Rev. Silwanus Mansour, PP. Baptism in the Melkite rite is by immersion so the babies need plenty of water, which is supplied by pipeline. The Scarf, Herro, Malouf, David, Mousally and Baz families formed the trustees during this time of relocation. The new church was consecrated and blessed by His Beatitude Maximos V. Hakim, Patriarch of Antioch, All the Orient, Alexandria and Jerusalem, on a special visit to Sydney on 4 January 1981.[8]

The number of Lebanese-born persons in Australia increased from 3,861 in 1954 to 10,668 in 1966. As a result of the conflict in the Middle East during the 1970s as many as 12,000 arrived in the year 1976–77. The number of Muslims is increasing. Within the total Lebanese population, apart from the Maronites and the Melkites are included the Antiochian Orthodox, the Lebanese Muslim Association and the Lebanese Druze.[9]

Those now called Lebanese were regarded as Syrians at the time of World War I and 'classified as Turkish subjects by the Australian government. Consequently, they had to register themselves as enemy aliens at their local police station at regular intervals during the war.'[10] The greater majority of Lebanese who came to Sydney between 1880 and 1920 were Christians. Often they cited religious persecution and lack of religious freedom as the reason for emigrating. During World War I control of Lebanese territory passed from Turkish to British sovereignty and eventually it became a French mandate.

After World War II the Lebanese were classed as 'southern Europeans' rather than as Asians, but they were not given the status of assisted migrants. While this entailed greater hardship at the outset, it also meant greater freedom. The new settlers chose to live in close proximity, in fact within walking distance of each other. This has resulted in neighbourhood clusters. The greatest concentration of Lebanese people is in Sydney, which contains 72 per cent of the national Lebanese population in Australia.[11] Original settlement was at Redfern, and now whole areas of Punchbowl, Hornsby and Lakemba are settled by Lebanese. Those who fled from the civil war in Lebanon during the 1970s were not given refugee status or benefits by the Australian government.[12] Perhaps this is a partial reason for the extraordinary unemployment rate among Lebanese in Australia, rising from 21.5 per cent in 1980 to 30.8 per cent in 1982, and up to 36.8 per cent in 1992. The national unemployment rate rose from 5 to 9.1 per cent and to 11.2 per cent over the same period.[13] Christians now number 59 per cent of Lebanese in Australia and Muslims are 31 per cent.[14] In 1981 there were 10 Arabic newspapers in Australia, each identified with one of the warring factions in Lebanon,[15] but by the beginning of the 1990s the number of Arabic papers was down to six.[16]

GOVERNMENT

The Homeless

In 1973 the 'Report to the Minister of Social Security' estimated that Australia's homeless male population was over 10,000. The numbers have increased since then, with the economic downturn and the growing unemployment, and Sydney has its fair share of the homeless. Traditionally, Central Railway Station has acted as a major focus for unattached males arriving in Sydney on the lookout for seasonal work. Nearby were the 'labour exchanges': the wharves, the markets, the breweries and the Redfern Mail Exchange. There gradually emerged an entire hobo-dependent cluster of buildings, institutions and businesses such as the liquor shops, pawnshops, snooker parlours, cheap cafes, second-hand clothing shops, disposal stores, boarding houses and cheap hotels.

The churches run a number of downtown missions whose aim is to provide hostel accommodation for homeless and unemployed men. These hostels are: Campbell House Men's Rehabilitation Centre, Campbell Street, Surry Hills (Anglican)[17]; Edward Eagar Lodge, 348 Bourke Street, Darlinghurst (Uniting Church—under the aegis of Wesley Central Mission); Foster House, 64 Foster Street, Surry Hills (Salvation Army, see previous chapter); Matthew Talbot Hostel, 22 Talbot Place, Woolloomooloo (Catholic); and Scholastica House (Women), 84 Albion Street, Surry Hills (Catholic). On sunny days, Hyde Park and Belmore Park are pleasant places for the hoboes. On cold and rainy days, the public libraries are a haven.

In recent years the city environment for the hobo has changed dramatically. The relocation of the markets and the disappearance of the market-related pubs has perilously narrowed the gap between the central business district and the townhouse-style revival of the old inner-city working-class suburbs. This process has been called 'gentrification'. Another new feature of the urban homeless is the increasing number of younger men and boys. The older tattoo shops and pinball parlours have now been joined by newer video game palours.

The hoboes are pretty tolerant people. They will not mind if unofficial brothels, sex shops and porn shows proliferate in their neighbourhood. Such things would not be tolerated in suburban or residential areas, yet it would be the population from these areas who set them up and provide the clientele. A *Sydney Morning Herald* investigator found that the sex shops were run in the style of supermarket chains by a few owners, many of whom lived in exclusive suburbs such as Vaucluse. The powerful impose their will on the powerless!

The hobo does not work, nor does he have a desire to work. He is therefore a misfit, an outsider, a parasite to 'normal' society. He is treated either benevolently as 'undersocialised', 'alcoholic' and 'endowed with poor personality', or, more likely, vindictively as a 'dole bludger', a 'no-hoper' and a 'bum'. Yet the hobo does work of a kind, which increases his pension cheque. He will fossick through the city's garbage. He will lift an apple from the city's fruit barrows. He will ask for money, and he knows exactly the right person to ask—say a clergyman or a young swain out with his girlfriend. He will be able to spin a good yarn and provide opportunities for those approached to alleviate their guilt feelings. He will also be skilled in conning church and social agencies for a handout.

Homeless women are fewer in number, but they do exist. Society is harder in judgment on drunken, dirty women than drunken and dirty men. In New South Wales a survey of such temporary accommodation found that, in October 1973: 'there appear to be only four hostels for destitute women, and together these can accommodate approximately 73 women and 75 children, whereas for

Edward Eagar Lodge.

destitute males there are seven hostels providing accommodation for approximately 1,379 men.'[18]

Inner-City Education

Government primary
Chippendale:
Blackfrairs Infant and Nursery School, Buckland Street
Darlington Public School, Golden Grove Street
Redfern:
Primary, George Street
Surry Hills:
Bourke Street, infants and primary
Crown Street
Ultimo:
Quarry Street
Government secondary
Surry Hills:
Sydney Boys' High School, Moore Park
Sydney Girls' High School, Moore Park
Cleveland Street High
Technical and Further Education
Redfern:
External Studies College, 199 Regent Street
Sydney:
Head Office, 323 Castlereagh Street
Ultimo:
Sydney TAFE College, Mary Ann Street
Tertiary
Broadway:
University of Technology
Sydney:
Post-Graduate Veterinary Science, University of Sydney, 280 Pitt Street
Workers' Educational Association, 72 Bathurst Street
Teachers
Independent Teachers' Association, 176 Day Street
Independent Teachers' Federation, 176 Day Street
Teachers' Club, 72 Bathurst Street
Teachers' Federation, 300 Sussex Street
Government departments
State:
Department of School Education, 55 Market Street

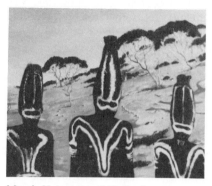

Mural, University of Technology.

Performing Arts Studies, Blackfriars Street, Chippendale
Sports Council, 175 Liverpool Street
Church schools in downtown Sydney
Sydney:
St Andrew's Cathedral College
Bedford College (Baptist premises—Girls' Business School)
Redfern:
St Maroun's School (Catholic Lebanese), Elizabeth Street

Parents seeking a Catholic education for their children in downtown Sydney no longer have the schools they did in 1883. However, there are schools nearby at Church Hill (now closed), St Mary's Cathedral (boys' primary and secondary), Potts Point (girls' primary and secondary), Darlinghurst (primary), Forest Lodge (primary), and Glebe Point (girls' primary and secondary).

Preparing for the Worst

Despite the Sydney City Council's curb-side shields which once prominently displayed the slogan, 'This is a nuclear-free zone', the State Emergency Services (SES) are prepared to consider the unthinkable. SES scientific adviser, Dr Des Posener, estimates that in the event of a limited nuclear attack on Sydney, four in five will survive, if adequate planning and preparation are undertaken.[19] However, most of the SES emphasis on counter-disaster planning is on natural disasters.

In 1955, at the height of the Cold War, Premier Joe Cahill recommended the formation of a civil defence unit. Prime Minister Menzies ignored the request. Premier Wran at the twenty-fifth anniversary of the SES pledged support but only specified the natural-disaster aspect of the SES operations.

The SES director is the commissioner of police, who will operate from the Emergency Operations Centre in Surry Hills. Jim Falk, the former convenor of MAUM (Movement Against Uranium Mining), envisages a scenario of the total destruction of Sydney. In 1983 the chief planning officer of the SES, Robert Maul, said that Sydney had been surveyed for radiation shelters to be used in the event of a nuclear attack: 'We have published certain pamphlets which would be issued to people en masse. They are available now to people who are interested.'[20]

Child Welfare

In 1980 the New South Wales Supreme Court made an historic decision in the McGuire v. Tull case. The court ruled that the welfare of a child had precedence over the claim of the natural mother to have the child returned to her. So the child remained with its foster parents. An appeal against the decision was later dismissed. The Department of Youth and Community Welfare, which was involved in these proceedings, is housed in a building at the end of Castlereagh Street in the Haymarket.

The Bourke Street Reserve

For such a tiny park, this reserve has done very well for itself, boasting no fewer than three plaques. The site was originally called Wimbo Park in the 1910s and was a place of recreation. A mural in the reserve depicts some of the activities which took place in those days: men playing marbles, a carnival with a carousel, a razzle-dazzle, Blondin the

tightrope walker and Captain Penfold taking off in his hot-air balloon. As the area became developed this site was used as a stonemason's workshop by the Sydney City Council from 1955 to 1981. Now the reserve is once again used for recreation.

The mural is dedicated to the long-term residents of Surry Hills, and was made by them with the coordination of community artist Peter Day and the sponsorship of the Sydney City Council.

The Year of the Tree

The City Council has tried to participate in such international events as the Year of the Tree—1982. A tree-planting exercise was carried out in a small section of Moore Park, ambitiously called an 'urban forest'. Let's hope it comes true!

Downtown Education Developments

In 1979 the State Department of Education opened a brand new high school at Blackwattle Bay. Such a move represents a marked change as no *new* schools had been opened in the region for most of the century. The school is not far from the historic Lyndhurst College, which was run originally by the Church of England before Archbishop Polding turned it into a Benedictine College.

In 1980 the Commonwealth Higher Education Board formed the Sydney College of Advanced Education. This meant that the independent Guild Teachers' College in Ultimo was amalgamated with the Nursery School Teachers' Association (Newtown), Sydney Kindergarten Teachers' College (Waverley), Alexander Mackie CAE (Oatley and Surry Hills) and Sydney Teachers College (Camperdown, Newtown and Ultimo). Meanwhile the Catholic Education Office, located in the former St Benedict's School, Broadway, had adopted an archdiocesan plan of regionalisation. The regional Catholic education offices were now based at Concord (Inner West), Hurstville (South), Marayong (Outer West) and Randwick (East).

The major change to the education scene in downtown Sydney since then has been the upgrading of the Institute of Technology to the University of Technology. There have been private education initiatives. One was the International Grammar School in Riley Street, Surry Hills. The school has been there since November 1984, after a false start in Randwick earlier in the year. This experimental multilingual school is the brainchild of Reg St Leon, formerly associate professor of German at the University of Sydney. Despite initial lack of government registration the school has survived because of the loyalty of the children's parents. Another private venture for teaching English to Asian students in Chippendale, International House English College at 55 Regent Street, had to close down because of financial difficulties. The managing director, Max Suzuki, owed $3.5 million in loans. Thirteen ELICOS (English Language Intensive Courses for Overseas Students) colleges closed in 1990–91.

A Number of Dubious Firsts

After a seven-year research project by a team of behavioral scientists and sociologists the fairly obvious common wisdom is scientifically confirmed—high-risk areas produce high-risk families and children.

First 25 social factors were fed into a computer—things like each suburb's divorce rate, criminal activity, accidents, court appearances and child protection orders. The computer then 'drew' a risk profile of 72 suburbs which formed the basis of the second stage of the research—to fit the human faces to the statistics and find out if the families and children who lived in the high-risk areas really had been affected by the depressing slums and factories, the noise and

dangerous neighbours. Part of the problem for Sydney people is that many of the inner city areas of high risk are also the most trendy—the high real estate prices defying all the dangers.[21]

Locality	Risk Score	Rank
Sydney	4.90154	1
South Sydney	3.03626	2
Leichhardt	2.44038	3
Marrickville	1.94696	4
Liverpool	1.35963	5
North Sydney	0.01920	28
Randwick	−0.0053	29
Lane Cove	−1.28935	71
Ku-ring-gai	−1.88503	72

The researchers were Dr Ailsa Burns, a developmental psychologist, and Mr Ross Homel, a senior lecturer in Behavioural Science at Macquarie University.

An earlier study had come up with much the same conclusion: 'Inner-Sydney ranked first in the State on five of the six health indices (perinatal mortality, pedestrian casualties, mental hospital admissions, suicides and mortality ratio)'.[22]

This conception of physical and mental health problems within Sydney Municipality poses a unique challenge to health and welfare planners. The State government cut back severely on inner-city hospitals in the early 1980s. The Albion Street Clinic provides free outpatient services for those suffering from AIDS and other sexually transmitted diseases.

In the 1990s the grim scenario for Downtown has not changed much, as perusal of the pertinent data of *A Social Atlas of Australia* makes clear. This two-volume study, based on data from the Australian Bureau of Statistics, provides maps, charts and tables and links health and wealth of the whole country by local government areas. Six tables were provided in a review of the *Atlas* published in July 1992.[23] Each table featured one local government area per state. The tables provided indices of relative social disadvantage, incidence of female deaths (aged 15–64), incidence of male deaths (aged 15–64), incidence of childhood respiratory disease, incidence of deaths of children under one year and hospital admissions due to accidents, poisonings and violence. Five of the six tables featured gave the Sydney City statistics. The areas were social advantage (Sydney City least advantaged, Ku-ring-gai most advantaged), female deaths (Sydney City nationally highest, Baulkham Hills lowest), male deaths (Sydney City nationally third-highest, Kur-ring-gai lowest), deaths of children under one year (Sydney City highest, Concord lowest), and hospital admissions due to accidents, poisonings and violence (Sydney City highest, Baulkham Hills lowest). *A Social Atlas of Australia* is backed up with a computer-disk package, HealthWIZ, containing all the statistics information, and HEAPS, a database of health education and promotion programs.

Those with the HIV/AIDS virus are at risk from infections of all kinds and require a lot of help. Dr Julian Gold is the director of the Albion Street clinic which has extended its work from testing for the AIDS virus to day care services involving opthalmologists, dentists, psychiatrists and dermatologists. About 3,000 people with HIV have attended the clinic. In 1992 as many as seven or eight patients have died each week. As no cure has yet been found for the virus, the stress and pressure on staff and patients is considerable.[24]

Darling Harbour Redevelopment

In the centre of the goods yards at Darling Harbour stood from the 1870s a curved woolshed stretching more than 300 metres. This building, supported by 36 pairs of cast-iron columns, followed the curve of the then existing waterfront. The old wharf nearby was buried when the bay was reclaimed during the 1920s. Rockfill from the excavations for the city underground railway was used. Wool from all over New South Wales came to this shed during the great wool boom of the 1890s. From Murray Street, Pyrmont, ran a huge two-tier goods shed. Railway lines ran at an upper and a lower level. When the shed was constructed in 1914 it was the most up-to-date of its kind in the Southern Hemisphere.[25]

The National Trust favoured retention of the two-tier shed, the curved shed and the signal box with its interlocking chain mechanism to raise the gates at the level crossing, the State government chose to redevelop the whole site as a bicentennial project. The plans included exhibition buildings, gardens, a maritime museum and commercial housing and office blocks, and were carried out with the exception of the housing and offices. The minister for public works, Mr Laurie Brereton, and the Darling Harbour Authority, a seven-member body, were put in charge of the redevelopment and given

Tourists, Darling Harbour.

The monorail.

special powers to expedite the work. This created many problems, as plans included a monorail, a gift from TNT, which aroused much opposition as it was planned to run not only around Darling Harbour but through the streets of Sydney as well. Part of the route is alongside such venerable structures as the Queen Victoria Building and over the Pyrmont Bridge.

For most of the nineteenth century Darling Harbour was chock-a-block with sailing ships. Now it houses the Maritime Museum. Perhaps signs of things to come occurred on 24 November 1983 when, inside the new Entertainment Centre, the now famous 12-metre racing yacht with its secret winged keel had to be lowered through an opening in the roof so as to leave the 90-foot mast intact. This was *Australia II* which, skipped by John Bertrand on behalf of Royal Perth Yacht Club and the syndicate headed by Alan Bond, won the America's Cup held by the New York Yacht Club for 132 years.

A favourite section of the Darling Harbour development is the beautiful Chinese gardens and tea-house, near the Haymarket. This is a quiet and restful spot in the heart of the city, complete with lake, waterfalls and peaceful walks and seats.

Sadly, the magnificent Australian Mercantile Land and Finance building is one that can no longer be seen in the area or included in the City West Urban Strategy for the 1990s. The property had been earmarked by Essington Pty Ltd for interior rebuilding as office space, a project costing $200 million, before the company was liquidated in February 1992. The seven-storey AMLF wool store had been built in 1909 and heritage listed in 1979, but on 6 July 1992 Sydney's biggest fire for 25 years totally destroyed the building. Twenty cars were crushed when one wall collapsed into Harris Street.

Sydney City Council is Sacked

The State government dismissed the Sydney city council from office on 26 March 1987. Control of the council's operation and 2,500 employees was entrusted to a three-member commission. Premier Barrie Unsworth said the dismissal removed council obstruction to the redevelopment of the Anthony Hordern site and the building of five hotels. The secretary of the Municipal Employees Union said the government had done Sydney a service by clearing away the problems caused by 'unruly' independents. The council had vigorously opposed the building of the monorail and Darling Harbour projects.[26] This has not been the first time that the Sydney city council has been dismissed and replaced by a three-member commission. It also occurred in the periods 1854–6, 1928–30 and 1967–9.

Judge Goran recommended the formation of a Central Sydney Commission and the State government adopted this proposal. The commission split the council into two, one covering Sydney and the other South Sydney. A crossover agreement was made whereby servicing could be carried out by one council in the area of the other council. The new Sydney city council came into being after 1 January 1989, with Jeremy Bingham as mayor and Ross Bonthorne as deputy. At the next elections in September 1991, Frank Sartor was elected mayor and Henry Tsang as deputy.

TRADE AND INDUSTRY

Redfern Mail Exchange

The old Sydney Mail Branch was among the first in the world in 1930 to use electrical and mechanical sorting and handling means. In 1962 the postmaster-general set the foundation stone for a brand new Sydney Mail Exchange at Redfern on the corner of Chalmers and Cleveland Streets. The construction was completed in 1964 and the mail-sorting equipment installed in mid-1965, but it was another two years before its operation was perfected. Mails at Redfern were phased out at the end of the 1970s in favour of regional centres. The Redfern exchange was troubled by considerable industrial disputes. In a visitors' brochure of 11 February 1972 the centre was stated to process 3.5 million articles per day with a staff of 3,800 personnel rostered 24 hours a day, every day of the year, and that in the pre-Christmas period about 8 million articles were handled each day by 5,000 staff. The initial building and equipment installation contract price came to $10 million. The exchange was demolished in 1987 to make way for the new New South Wales administrative headquarters of Australia Post.

New Technology

It has become commonplace to contrast traditional values as embodied within the family and the churches with the unbelief or secular attitudes of critically minded men and women. Possibly the focal areas are transport and communications. The public transport system continues to pass through the Haymarket corridor—trains via the city underground rail and buses above ground. Private cars congest the streets and many carparks provide off-street parking. The communications system includes the traditional press with the press barons John Fairfax (no longer family-owned), Murdoch and Packer operating large business complexes near the Haymarket region. A Chinese-language newspaper can now be printed from a computer-controlled typesetting machine in the former Trades Hall Hotel, on the corner of Goulburn and Sussex Streets, that is linked to Hong Kong and other Asian centres. The last licensee of the Trades Hall Hotel was Mrs Eleanor

Grassby, wife of the then commissioner of race relations, Mr Al Grassby. Radio Stations 2GB and 2KY (located within the Labour Council building) are also located in the district.

Another arrival in the entertainment market is the electronic video games machine. Linked to a computer with an input program based on speed of eye and hand coordination, and pitched at a mix of aggression, flight and fantasy, the Space Invaders generation now haunts downtown Sydney in the numerous new video parlours from morning to midnight. However, the focal point of technologies old and new, colonial or space-age, is the Powerhouse Museum, incorporating the former Powerhouse which generated electricity for Sydney's tram network. This spectacular project was part of the Wran Government's vast redevelopment of Darling Harbour, described earlier in this chapter.

Downtown Dynasty

In the streets of Sydney during the 1980s a battle to the death was in progress. Morning and evening the war chariots emerged from the fortresses of two newspaper groups. Down Broadway roared the golden chariots crested with the red sun representing the Fairfax motto 'Fer Fax Lucem' (O Torch, Bear Light!) and the dark blue chariots of Rupert Murdoch. The battle was not so much for the hearts and minds of Sydney burghers as for their dollars and cents, and from the spoils emerged king and pretender. The royal mantle and crown were worn in the early 1980s by the House of Murdoch, thanks to Lotto, Page 3 pics and held-back price increases.

The dynastic aspects of this titanic contest are revealed in such details as the amazing association of the Fairfax family with the *Sydney Morning Herald* and its even more amazing demise: 'As far as was known, no other newspaper in the world had been in the control or influence of a single family for as long'.[27] At News

Limited Rupert Murdoch followed in the footsteps of his father, Sir Keith Murdoch, who was a press baron of the 1940s and '50s. Rupert Murdoch is actually a cousin of Ranald MacDonald, one-time managing director of *The Age* and a descendent of David Syme, the founder of *The Age*.

For the first 124 years the *Sydney Morning Herald* was located in the far end of town, in Hunter Street. Though claiming independence from the outset, the paper was essentially conservative. 'It believed as firmly in twentieth-century free enterprise as John Fairfax had believed in the voluntaryism of the Congregational Church and the *laissez-faire* political economy of Adam Smith. It upheld Christianity, monarchy, law and order, and middle-class values.'[28] With the takeover of the chariot of Phoebus-Apollo driving his seven horses straight out of the rising sun (*Sun* and *Sunday Sun*) between 1953 and 1956, new and larger premises were required. After hypothetical plans for the Haymarket were mooted, the present Broadway site was secured and made operational.

For the *Sydney Morning Herald*, a paper that had Protestant clergymen as five of its first six editors, a shock was in store for its readers in the late 1950s with the appointment of Colin Bingham, a Catholic of Irish parents who ran the North Star Hotel near the outer northern railhead at Richmond. A conscriptionist, his anti-Mannix stance led him to leave the Church as a youth, and he was opposed to State Aid. The 'credit-squeeze' resulted in severe criticism of the Menzies Government by the Fairfax publications and an economic policy wherein the Labor Opposition suddenly discovered a new ally. Arthur Calwell had been the *Sydney Morning Herald*'s great antagonist during the war years, but there was a reconciliation at Broadway with Rupert Henderson, the managing director. Henderson became in effect Calwell's campaign manager, assisted by senior executives Lou Leck and Maxwell Newton who wrote his speeches. In the 1961 election Menzies scraped back in with a

Herald mural by Salvatore Zofrea.

majority of two and in his first speech he vigorously attacked the *Sydney Morning Herald*. This inspired Colin Bingham to counter-attack with one of his best editorials, 'A Mockery of National Leadership':

> The brazen front which the Prime Minister presented, and the juvenile gibes of a lower-deck jester in which he indulged, accorded ill with the situation to which he was supposed to be addressing himself. During the greater part of his speech he attempted to pour scorn upon the *Sydney Morning Herald* and its support of the Federal Labor Party in the recent election. His resentment of the fact that this newspaper's attitude was confirmed by the votes of more than two and a half million electors benumbed his better judgment, limited though it has proved to be in the later years of his regime. The result was a speech, directed not at illuminating the vital national issues raised by Labor's censure motion, but vainly at discrediting a single newspaper in a single city of the Commonwealth.[29]

Nonetheless, since Federation, Australia has had 13 Labor Federal ministries and 28 Labor N.S.W. ministries. Only at the Federal election of 1961 did the *Sydney Morning Herald* support Labor.

While Rupert Murdoch had 13 editors

in 15 years for his *Australian*, Fairfax had only 12 editors in its entire history up to 1983. Before accepting his second term Pringle asked for, and obtained, full editorial powers, something the *Sydney Morning Herald* had not seen since the editorship of T.W. Henry (1903–18). Doubts about the Vietnam War, about Gorton's nationalism (republicanism?), film censorship and a humanistic leader article for Easter 1970 led to chairman Sir Warwick Fairfax's increasing displeasure. After writing an Anzac Day leader on 24 April 1970, Pringle departed Broadway without any formal farewell, overtly on leave, but in fact for good.[30]

The 'Granny' image of the *Sydney Morning Herald*, stemming in part from Column 8 (once 10), was becoming less predictable and one quite progressive position adopted by the *Sydney Morning Herald* came in 1979, when it commended a proposed Treaty of Peace and Friendship between Aboriginal Australians and the Commonwealth:

> The treaty, proposed by a committee of Australian historians, anthropologists and others, was intended to guarantee the protection of Aboriginal identity, languages, law and culture; the recognition and restoration of land rights by applying throughout Australian the recommendations of the 1974 Woodward Commission; conditions governing mining and exploitation of other natural resources on Aboriginal land; compensation to Australian Aborigines for the loss of traditional land; and the right of Aboriginal Australians to control their own affairs.[31]

There were seventeen editors of the *Sydney Morning Herald* while it remained within Fairfax control. In 1991 James Fairfax published his account of growing up in the Fairfax family, *My Regards to Broadway: A Memoir.* The chapters which describe the 1987–90 family company take-over by his half-brother Warwick—which led to the family losing control of the company—are revealingly called 'Cuckoo in the Nest' and 'The Butchering of Broadway'. Various offers were made for the Fairfax group, the bidders including Sir James Leslie, Qantas chairman and head of Australian Newspapers Industries; Irishman Dr Tony O'Reilly, the chief executive of H.J. Heinz; and the eventual successful bidder, Tourang, headed by the Canadian media mogul Conrad Black. However, the Tourang bid had a subplot all of its own. It originally involved two of media magnate Kerry Packer's associates, Malcolm Turnbull and Trevor Kennedy, both of whom severed their ties with Packer's Consolidated Press empire. With long-standing friendships thus broken, the Australian Broadcasting Tribunal still queried Packer's involvement. Finally John Singleton emerged to lobby successfully on behalf of the then isolated bidder Conrad Black. The background to this whole drama was the leadership crisis in the Federal ALP as Prime Minister Hawke sought to remain in power and dismissed Treasurer John Kerin, whose last act was virtually to insist on no more than 15 per cent foreign ownership, which turned out to be the amount of Conrad Black's stake.

RELIGION

Recent Church Development

The Cook Bicentenary of 1970 included a Papal visit, during which Pope Paul VI joined in an ecumenical service in Sydney Town Hall. The growth of ecumenism has been a notable achievement in the years since the Second Vatican Council, and St Peter Julian's Church has held a number of ecumenical services over the years and striven to contribute to the Ministers' Fraternal of the City of Sydney. The official photographers covering the Pope's entire visit were Studio Commercial, operating from premises near Central Railway.

Cardinal Gilroy missed by a whisker to qualify for the legacy of Dr Polding's episcopal ring. Archbishop Simmonds just preceded him by becoming the first Australian-born Archbishop. Dr Polding's name lives on in the day-to-day life of the Church through the building which houses the administrative offices of various church works such as adult education, confraternity of Christian doctrine, family care and counselling, marriage tribunal. The building is centrally located in Pitt Street, halfway between St Mary's Cathedral and the former Pitt Street South Centre where Dr Polding founded the Good Samaritan Order. The building was blessed and opened in 1977, on the centenary of Dr Polding's death, by his fifth successor, Cardinal Freeman.

In 1970 the National Council of Priests was formed. The executive of the NCP has often met at St Peter Julian's, Haymarket, because of its centrality, the hospitality of the local community, the priests and brothers of the Blessed Sacrament Fathers, and the truly cosmopolitan character of the surrounds.

St Vincent de Paul Night Patrol

A Haymarket branch (conference) of the St Vincent de Paul Society was inaugurated in 1970. The basic work was visitation of the poor and destitute who either lived in cheap city hotels and boarding houses or who came to St Peter Julian's for help. Some idea of the harsh grinding life of poverty may be gained from John de Hoog's *Skid Row Dossier*, written from the viewpoint of the derelict, and Ruth Park's *The Harp in the South*. Another part of the work was with the Children's Court in Albion Street. The conference consisted of highly educated laymen who worked in the city while living in the suburbs. In the mid-'70s

women too became part of the conference. The closure of the city markets, the increasing redevelopment and the centralisation of the City Conference at Young Street, Circular Quay, resulted in the closure of the conference by 1976. However, the Maternal Heart Conference —the 'Night Patrol' whereby a van is driven by night around the lanes and alleys of the city and inner city to provide help, support and shelter, if need be, to the derelicts and homeless—had its first base at St Peter Julian's. The work was begun by a young man who had recently left St Patrick's College, Strathfield. Aided by his former school mates, and using his own vehicle, Brian McCheane began the night patrol on his own initiative and at his own expense. The approach was eventually accepted by the St Vincent de Paul Society as integral to its mission.

The Nocturnal Phantom Raider

In the mid-'70s a mysterious drama was unfolding in the Church of St Peter Julian's. The altar was always most beautifully decorated with flowers, as befitted a church of special devotion and meditation, but suddenly some very strange things began to happen. Early one morning the new Sacristan was amazed to find his magnificent floral display was now minus all blooms, a pitiful sight of spiky stalks. Brother Sacristan bought more fresh carnations and the same thing happened. Rumour and suspicion were rife, as the vandalism had taken place when the Church was closed and locked for the night. Torches were fitted with new batteries; a roster of vigils was arranged and doors were sealed with tape, but come morning the blooms were tattered and scattered again. It all made for lively discussion around the breakfast table each morning. Whodunnit—jealous insider, malicious outsider, tradesman … animal? Eventually, talcum powder sprinkled near the altar at night revealed tiny footprints. The market rats had found a new home!

Chinese Christians

The Chinese Catholic Mission went through several stages. Fathers Leonard Hsu and Paschal Chang began the apostolate in 1954 after their arrival. Many overseas Asian students came to Australia and Sydney with the introduction of the Colombo Plan. A centre for this work was established at Ashfield. However, in the '70s previous restrictive immigration policies were relaxed. As well many refugees, the boat people, arrived and increased the welfare load of the chaplaincy. The Business Migration Programme and the Family Reunion Policy resulted in a greatly expanded Asian and Chinese Catholic community. Religious activities were centred at St Peter Julian's Church, thanks to the hospitality and generosity of the Blessed Sacrament Community. Three religious sisters and two priests serve the needs of the old and the young. Two Sunday masses are attended by up to 800 people. There are Bible classes, student groups and music ministry. As well there are six catechism classes. Adult baptisms take place at Easter and in August. There are usually about 160 adults baptised on these two occasions. Child baptisms take place three times a year, about 120 to 130 on each occasion.

A Unique Statement

Since 1973, Social Justice Sunday and an accompanying Social Justice Statement have been observed in the Catholic Church on the last Sunday of September. The statements have been prepared by a national body, the Catholic Commission for Justice and Peace. The issues that have been taken up include: social sin, the position of women, of migrants, of Aborigines, of the unemployed and the homeless. A permanent secretariat operated first in the old Anthony Hordern Emporium and subsequently in offices in Elizabeth Street opposite the Mark Foy Building. (There has been another move to Surry Hills.) In 1983 the commission's statement was the culmination of four years of exchanges with parallel commissions from the Uniting Church, the Anglican Church and the Australian Council of Churches. The joint consultation resulted in a common Social Justice Statement, entitled *Changing Australia*, outlining questions to be addressed in establishing conditions for a just Australia: (1) What is Australia as it is?; (2) What does the Good News offer Australia?; (3) What could Australia be?; and (4) How can we change Australia?

A discussion guide for use in small groups was set out after each section. Christians concerned for social justice in Australia have set an ecumenical initiative in motion comparable to the Action for World Development program 10 years earlier. The media were shocked by the statement. What are these 'soft-minded believers' doing in the 'real world' of power, investment, taxation, public honesty and other pressing social questions?

The statement was indeed a new Christian utterance for Australian society for a number of reasons. It was a joint statement of the Christian community, and a very effective example of practical ecumenism. While church leaders approved the statement, it was more the work of the laity and this was certainly a decisively new utterance instead of the expected 'clerical' voice. The focus was not churchly self-concern, but the wider horizon of God's redeeming word in the world. A voice was given to the powerless and underprivileged. A stance of change was adopted, as the statement: 'locates itself in the process of change, even revolutionary change. Far from being a conservative voice in a forward-looking world, it is a disconcertingly progressive summons to all who have settled so easily for the way things are.'[32]

Churches in Downtown

The Jehovah's Witnesses, the Mormon Church and the Seventh-day Adventist Church have no Downtown presence.

Area	1892	1992
Broadway	St Barnabas (Anglican) St Benedict's	St Barnabas (Anglican) St Benedict's
Golden Grove	St Kieran's	St Kieran's/St Michael's Cathedral
Haymarket	St Francis in Castlereagh Street	Demolished (1909) St Francis, Albion Street St Peter Julian's
Pyrmont	St Bartholomew's (Anglican) St Bede's	Demolished (1971) St Bede's
Railway Square	Christ Church (Anglican)	Christ Church St Laurence
Redfern	St Paul's, Cleveland Street (Anglican) St Vincent's	Greek Orthodox of Annunciation St Paul's, 45 Pitt Street St Vincent's St Maron's St George Antioch Orthodox, Walker Street
Surry Hills	Welsh Church in Chalmers Street St Michael's (Anglican) 196 Albion Street St Peter's, Devonshire Street Christian Israelite Congregational Church in Bourke Street Congregational Church, Pitt Street Salvation Congregational Hall	Welsh Church St Michael's St Peter's Chinese Presbyterian Christian Israelite Greek Orthodox, in Bourke Street Uniting Church, Pitt Street Salvation Army Congress Hall
Sydney	Central Baptist Church in Bathurst Street Presbyterian Church in Bathurst Street Presbyterian Church in Hay Street Presbyterian Church in Liverpool Street St George's Presbyterian Church in Castlereagh Street	Central Baptist Church in George Street Demolished Demolished Demolished Demolished
Ultimo	St Francis Xavier	St Francis Xavier

Anglicans in Surry Hills

At the end of the nineteenth century there were three Anglican churches in Surry Hills: St David's, St Michael's and Ss Simon and Jude. The last-mentioned originally stood in Foster Street but was rebuilt at 112 Campbell Street (on the site of the recently built Police Centre). In 1923 St Simon's was closed down. The occasion was recorded as follows:

The old church is now closed. After 45 years of useful work it ceases to exist as far as we are concerned. On Sunday, the 12th August, the final service was held. The Rector took for his text, 'I have finished my course, I have kept the faith'. There was a large congregation consisting of many of St David's people who went down in a feeling of sympathy with their neighbouring parishioners. Also there were present many of the old friends of St Simon's, who had moved away and

Area	Religious Orders	1992
Broadway	St Benedict's 1875—Marist Brothers	Closed
	1885—Good Samaritans	Closed
	(Business College) 1937—Good Samaritans	Closed
Golden Grove	St Kieran's Primary 1899 ?	Lebanese Melkites
Haymarket	St Francis Primary 1867	Demolished
	Hay Street—Marist Brothers	Demolished
	Albion Street 1901—Good Samaritans	Closed
	Pitt Street South 1862—Good Samaritans	Demolished, but relocated in
	St Scholastica's—Good Samaritans	Glebe Point
Pyrmont	St Bede's Primary 1870 ?—Good Samaritans	Asian Partners (closed)
Redfern	St Vincent's Primary 1893—Mercy Sisters	Aboriginal Medical Service (now 36 Turner Street)
	St Maroun's School	Lebanese Community Hall
Surry Hills	School 1847—P.M. Ryan, Teacher	Replaced by Darlinghurst
	St Kilda Boys 1879—Jesuit Fathers	Relocated as St Aloysius
	St Peter's Primary 1889—Mercy Sisters	Primary School
	Boys 1906—De La Salle Brothers	Portuguese Community
Sydney	St John's Poor School (Kent Street)	First Matthew Talbot Hostel, now Genesian Theatre
Ultimo	St Francis Xavier's School 1900 Good Samaritan Sisters	St Vincent de Paul Store and Josephite Sisters

came back to see the last of the dear old place. They remembered when the locality was a real bright happy place, full of all that goes to make life worthwhile. The Rector gave some extracts from the early business books of the Church, showing the struggle our fore-runners had to pay for the land and the building. Also it was noticed that the people of St David's had their share in the establishment of the church. The church is gone, *but the work goes on.*[33]

Even St David's was not destined to survive. Located in Arthur Street, between Bourke and Crown Streets, the parish had been established in 1874, but constant suburbanisation and immigration led to the decision to close the church. However, its place in history is assured by a special event. The church hall was the location of the first telecast by Channel 9 in New South Wales. Who would have guessed that the powerful and omnipresent television industry in Australia had such a humble beginning? The first telecast was made on the evening of 16 September, 1956, according to Channel 9 operations manager, Mr Peter Cox.[34] The *Australian Encyclopaedia* records that,

On Sunday, 16th September, in Sydney, TCN 9 (operated by a company in which Frank Packer, the newspaper and magazine publisher, had a major interest) launched Australia's first regular television service. This was followed at short intervals by national and other commercial stations in both Sydney and Melbourne.[35]

St Michael's, a fine Blacket church, still stands and functions at the corner of Flinders and Albion Streets. During the 1980s it obtained government assistance for maintenance works.

Catholic Schools Serving as Social Welfare Centres

The above list suggests the enormous changes that have occurred in the inner city—especially the dwindling population—that have led to the religious orders and the Church closing the schools and sending their personnel into other areas or apostolates. However, new and powerful forms of presence have emerged and, with them, new forms of religious life. Some religious are attempting to live out a 'preferential option for the poor'. A bird's eye view of inner Sydney would reveal a network of houses, with one or two permanent residents, where people living on the fringes of society find a human support system on which they can rely. What has developed here is not a 'network of communities' so much as a 'network community'.

As one who has visited some of these houses, I can vouch for the good done by these new works. Brother Mark Brereton is the core person of the De Porres Family, which began in Chippendale in October 1976. Good Samaritan Sister Pauline Fitzwalter is the key person behind a community development now known as the St Francis Houses. This work began in Surry Hills in 1978 and now numbers eight St Francis Houses which provide community and healing for the homeless. Sister Fitzwalter was joined by Sister Diana Law in reaching out to marginalised, unwanted and damaged people. This work began in Surry Hills in 1978. The needs of homeless people in the inner city were pressed upon Sister Pauline by a number of experiences, including her encounter with the talented but mentally disturbed poet Francis Webb.

The Good Samaritan sisters have been joined by lay people who are little sisters and brothers of St Francis, a growing movement in establishing parish-based houses of hospitality. There are now four main areas of communities: Sydney (Surry Hills, Hurstville, Leura), Gympie–Brisbane, Guyra and Termeil–Bateman's Bay.[36]

Pitt Street Uniting Church

After a memorial service marking 150 years of Pitt Street Uniting (formerly Congregational) Church, the governor of New South Wales, Sir James Rowland, unveiled a small plaque in the foyer which acknowledged 'the timely action by the Builders' Labourers' Federation and concerned citizens of Sydney' in preserving the building. In the official party was Communist union leader Jack Mundey, whose BLF 'green ban' had 'saved' the church. The present church, known then as the Independent Chapel, was built in the 1840s and described by the *Sydney Gazette* as 'the handsomest building of its kind in Sydney'.[37] The manager of the building committee and later secretary of the church was newly arrived immigrant John Fairfax, who founded the newspaper dynasty. Another prominent member of the dissenting, non-conformist congregation was David Jones.

The church had the largest seating capacity in the city—2,000—but by the 1960s the congregation had dwindled alarmingly. In 1970 Reverend John Bryant announced a $5.5 million redevelopment project. The existing church would be demolished, and replaced by a 26-storey office block incorporating a church for 300 and a meditation chapel on the top floor. The project was approved by the Sydney city council and by the minister for local government, but not by the BLF. In June 1974 a shop-front chapel across from the church was closed and the existing church was re-opened. After the formation of the Uniting Church in 1977, the adjacent church offices were cleaned up and rented to new tenants—amongst them Amnesty International, Community Aid Abroad, N.S.W. Aboriginal Land Rights Support Group, various Uniting Church agencies and two Catholic organisations, the ecumenical magazine *National Outlook* and the Catholic Tertiary Federation. The current and twenty-first minister is Dorothy McMahon, the first woman to superintend a Sydney City church.[38]

Mission Bell to Coober Pedy

How did the bell of the Chinese Presbyterian Church in Surry Hills find its way to Coober Pedy? It all began when

Michael Costello was visiting Coober Pedy and noticed cardboard boxes in the bank, post office, hotel and main store: 'Collection Money for Memorial Bell for Father Cresp'. The hard-drinking, gambling miners had a soft spot for their priest who had moved on to another parish. One wet Sunday during afternoon tea at St Joseph's College, Hunter's Hill, the school chaplain was innocently asked if by any chance he had a spare church bell for the boys in Coober Pedy? Monsignor Duffy, who was also cathedral archivist, said yes he had. There was only one catch. The bell was atop the Chinese Presbyterian Church in Campbell Street, Surry Hills. A letter

went off to the directors of the *Catholic Press*, owners of the church, who said yes. Another letter went off to the Lord Mayor of Sydney, Dr McDermott, asking for help. A letter came back granting the people of Coober Pedy the sum of £120, the amount necessary to get the bell to street level. Another letter went off to Sir Reginald Ansett, and in 1972 the 10-hundredweight Italian bell travelled freight free all the way to Coober Pedy. The bell was cleaned, revealing a date—15 August 1877. Now the bell hangs in a tower outside the Underground Church. It has a magnificent tone and has been used for announcing disasters and warnings.

PERSONS AND EVENTS

The Boxer

No-one seeing the stocky little man in the old gaberdine overcoat sitting quietly in St Peter Julian's could have guessed his background or identity. If you accidentally bumped him he would slip momentarily into a practised fighter's stance. Gerry Sullivan grew up in the inner city and went to school at St Vincent's, Redfern. He was far more than a tough street fighter. Once when he saw two nuns being jostled by a gang of louts he hopped off the tram and flattened their attackers. He trained at Les O'Donnell's Gym at Circular Quay and fought at Sydney Stadium. At 17 Gerry fought a visiting French champion and went the full distance with him. He was dapper and dressed well, a clean-living man who drank little and never swore but was not isolated from the world. Fighting in Flynn's Show Tent in the pre-Sharman era, he was a crowd pleaser with a big following. But when the Depression came, Gerry found himself with a family of young children to support and came out of retirement. He took on opponents in heavier divisions and the effort was too

much. Gerry sustained terrible punishment. Head injuries resulted in permanent brain damage. His friends dropped him. Yet Gerry could still think only of others. He remained a faithful member of the inner-city St Vincent de Paul Society and the author can only remember him as a quiet respectful man who would be the last to leave the Church each night.[39]

Foundation 41

In Surry Hills near the now long closed Crown Street Women's Hospital stood Foundation 41, a medical institute devoted to research into the first 41 weeks of human life. This institute came into being when Doctor William McBride won an award of $40,000 from the Institut de la Vie in Paris for his research into birth defects. This was his discovery of a possible link between the drug Thalidomide and the birth of malformed babies. This suspicion was sent to the *Lancet* in the form of a letter. McBride was subsequently made a Commander of the British Empire in 1969 and in 1977 received the Order of Australia. In 1982

Dr McBride published further findings on the drug Debendox and its effects on unborn children. After accusations from Dr Norman Swan of the ABC 'Science Show', Foundation 41 set up an inquiry which found that Dr McBride had published claims which were scientifically not proven. Since 1990 the New South Wales Medical Tribunal has been investigating the whole research career of Dr McBride, and has still not completed its task. Already the doctor who was once a hero may well become known for being at the centre of the longest hearing in medical history. The Foundation 41 building has been sold and the Institute closed.

The Royals of Belmore Park

When George Mezher and his sister Nola won nearly half a million dollars in Lotto they went on a spending spree, as most winners usually do. But there the similarity ends. For George and Nola are now spending the money on Sydney's down-and-outs. Every Sunday they provide a treat for the park-bench dwellers. Their loosely knit group is called by George The Underprivileged Peoples' Association. For Christmas 1983 in Belmore Park there were 200 turkeys, 20 kilos of sliced ham, 30 kilos of pork, 60 kilos of potatoes and 20 cabbages for coleslaw, 50 Christmas cakes and puddings and eight gallons of fruit juice to help it all down. 'No matter how wonderful a meal tastes, it is a dull affair if there is no one to share it with,' says Nola. This brother and sister team who came from Lebanon 37 years ago will surely never lack friends![40]

Ita Buttrose

There is a building in Downtown dedicated to Ita, and it is a church, near Wentworth Park. However there is also a living Ita who has been linked with Downtown in many ways. Ita Buttrose's first job was as a 15-year-old copy girl for the *Australian Women's Weekly*.[41] The magazine was produced in the Australian Consolidated Press building in Castlereagh Street. She remembers how her first chores were to have a senior staffer's shoes repaired, buy some bread rolls and make the morning tea. When newly appointed women's editor of the *Telegraph* she won a fashion show at Randwick racecourse Ladies' Day run by the rival *Sydney Morning Herald*. There were red faces on Broadway, the Fairfax headquarters, but Sir Frank Packer enjoyed it immensely—'Right Filly But Wrong Stable'. She was the founding editor of *Cleo* in 1972 and in 1975 Kerry Packer asked her to become editor of *Australian Women's Weekly*, in a venture to update a hitherto successful magazine. In 1979, and again in 1984, she topped the poll as the most admired woman in Australia. Her love of challenges led to her accepting an offer from Rupert Murdoch to become editor-in-chief of both his *Telegraphs*. The Holt Street offices were less congenial than the Packer suites at ACP.

At the end of 1984 she was asked by the Prime Minister to become chairperson of the National Advisory Committee on AIDS. In 1985 Ita Buttrose completed a remarkable circuit of Sydney's major newspapers by writing for Fairfax publications. However, by 1989 she sought to become powerful in her own right and launched her own magazine, *Ita*, aimed at women aged between 35 and 54. The new monthly magazine has survived its first three years and is published by Capricorn Publishing at 44 Buckingham Street, Surry Hills, not far away from her former executive suite at News Ltd, and close to Cleaveland House (see Chapter 1).

Anglican Press Fracas

Born in 1931, Rupert Murdoch, the son of Sir Keith Murdoch who had a life of distinguished service in Australian journalism and newspaper proprietorship, was educated at Geelong Grammar School and Oxford. This connection with the Anglican Church has some bearings on young Murdoch's struggle to be established in the tough Sydney newspaper scene.

Frank Packer and Rupert Henderson (Fairfax chief executive) were the established newspaper figures—Murdoch was the challenger. Clyde Packer had been appointed by Frank Packer and Rupert Henderson in a joint venture to protect their suburban newspaper interests against possible Murdoch competition. Clyde Packer wanted to prevent Murdoch from purchasing the Anglican Press (which was in receivership in 1960) and visited Francis James, who had founded Anglican Press. But James wanted to keep control of the printing house and warned Murdoch that the three-storey Anglican Press building in Queen Street Chippendale was to be sold to Packer.

Things began to happen rather quickly. One night, the *Anglican*'s receiver-manager rang James to tell him that he had been ejected by a group of men, including Clyde and Kerry Packer. James quickly rallied and so began the fracas of 7–8 June, 1960. The Anglican Press building had already been occupied, but James got together a gang of toughs. There were wild brawls involving monkey wrenches, mallets and a battering ram. Clyde Packer copped a black eye and had most of his ribs broken. Murdoch's *Daily Mirror* ran a scoop story on the following day:

> 'Knight's Son in City brawl' and a picture of Clyde Packer who was about twenty stone, dropping out of the front door holding, by the scruff of the neck, a one-legged Anglican clergyman.[42]

James retained control of the printery for a time thanks to £65,000 from Rupert Murdoch. As for Murdoch, as well as gaining control of the Anglican Press building for little financial return, he had also denied Packer a marketing base.

The story of Murdoch's business dealings is far too vast a subject for this study. However a short description of Murdoch's empire is given. From a marginally profitable newspaper in Australia in 1952, Rupert Murdoch has built a billion dollar empire on three continents encompassing print and electronic media, film-making, energy production and explorations and transport industries. The Murdoch stable of news media interests is located in Holt Street, Surry Hills.

As for Francis James, he died of cancer on 24 August 1992 aged 74. His rich and colourful life included being a fighter pilot shot down over France in World War II, an opponent of the Vietnam War, and a prisoner in China as a supposed Russian spy during the 1969 Cultural Revolution. He was always provocative and eccentric.

ENTERTAINMENT

Lake Northam

A small lake situated in Victoria Park, near the corner of Parramatta Road and King Street is named after Bill Northam, who made history when he took some time off his job as City of Sydney alderman to win Australia's first sailing gold medal at the 1964 Tokyo Olympics. Not bad for a 59-year-old, who skippered the 5.5-metre yacht *Barrenjoey*, assisted by his crew of Pod O'Donnell and Dick Sargeant. The lake also boasts a stylised sculpture of his history-making yacht.

Her Majesty's Theatre

On 31 July 1970 Her Majesty's Theatre in Quay Street was destroyed by fire. This building dated back to 1927, when it opened as the Empire, and was converted to a cinema in 1929. In 1953 the theatre was renamed Her Majesty's and staged the Australian premiere of the Rogers and Hammerstein musical *South Pacific*. However, after the 1970 fire a brand new theatre was erected on the site.

Popular shows including *Irene, Annie, A Chorus Line, Evita* and *Oklahoma!* were performed there but perhaps nothing matched the real life drama one night in September 1975. Marlene Dietrich had come to sing her old favourites—'I get a Kick Out of You', 'Falling in Love Again', 'When the World was Young', and the best remembered of World War II, 'Lili Marlene'. She would have been 72 when she fell and broke her leg during the evening performance. She left Australia in a wheelchair, and the accident virtually ended her regular live performing days.

Another famous person to grace the stage of Her Majesty's was Billy Hughes, who at the age of 17 carried a spear in front of the footlights in an 1887 production of *Henry V.* This happened in the old Her Majesty's.[43] Thirty-three years later, in 1920, the prime minister of Australia, the Rt Hon. William Morris Hughes, attended a gala performance by J.C. Williamson Limited at Her Majesty's Theatre, Sydney, in honour and in the distinguished presence of His Royal Highness, the Prince of Wales, during his visit to Australia.[44]

On Top of the World

An unassuming shop in Kent Street opposite the restored Judge's House is called Mountain Designs. The shop was the official supplier of equipment and expedition clothing manufacturing to the first Australian Mt Everest Expedition in 1984. Small in numbers and modest in back-up support for such a venture, there were only five climbers in a group of 12. The expedition received permission to approach Mount Everest from the north by way of China and Tibet. Without

oxygen apparatus, they pioneered a new route up the north face of the mountain and two members, Tim McCartney-Snape and Greg Mortimer, reached the summit of the world's highest peak at 8,848 metres on 3 October.

A few weeks later, on 24 October, the five Australian climbers faced a different kind of ordeal, that of the obvious admiration of a large assembly gathered at Sydney Town Hall. The lord mayor presented the rather shy climbers with the freedom of the city. 'Acting as a spokesman for the group, Mr McCartney-Snape, key in hand, told the gathering, that as a boy brought up in the bush, he had found Sydney as daunting as any mountain.'

Another unassuming shop in Sussex Street stands opposite the Teachers' Club. Australian Himalayan Expeditions manage a mountain and trekking equipment shop. Apart from organising treks to remote regions such as the Himalayas, they sponsor visits by famous climbers and adventurers. Prominent among these has been Reinhold Messner, who completed both the first ascent of Everest without oxygen in 1979 and, several years later, the first solo ascent. He visited Sydney in 1982.

The Bicentenary in Downtown

Events that occurred in the Bicentenary included the opening of the magnificent Powerhouse Museum Stage Two on the site of the refurbished Ultimo Power Station, and the spectacular Military Tattoo in August at the Sydney Entertainment Centre. However, the events that are most pertinent to this book were also quite essential to the successful staging of what many consider to be the highlight of the Bicentenary year, the arrival of the Tall Ships and the First Fleet Re-Enactment and their joint Parade of Sail on Australia Day, 26 January 1988. It is estimated that 2 million people gathered around the shores of Sydney Harbour in glittering sunshine. Via television, many million more Australians watched this magnificent spectacle.

The sailing ships were anchored at the newly constructed Darling Harbour berths. Darling Harbour itself had only been opened on 16 January and now found itself swarming with half a million visitors or more a day. The Polish training ship *Dar Mlodziezy* (The Gift of Youth) was a great favourite, a spectacular ship with masts 16 storeys high. Spain sent the *Juan Sebastian de Elcano*, Japan the *Nippon Maru*, Germany the *Gorch Fock*, and the United States the coastguard ship *Eagle*. The *Eagle* was formerly a German naval cadet training ship, built in 1936 with a steel hull and three masts of 90 metres each, which was acquired as reparation after World War II. The other noteworthy ship was the *Young Endeavour*, the Bicentennial gift of Britain to Australia and handed over by Prince Charles and Princess Diana at the Man-o'War Steps near the Opera House.

On the evening of Australia Day, huge crowds gathered outside the Entertainment Centre to catch a glimpse of the Royal couple who were guests at the N.S.W. Bicentennial Concert, compered by actor Jack Thompson. The concert opened with a spectacular pageant of choreographed history, followed by star international performers, including Cliff Richard, Olivia Newton-John, John Denver and Peter Allen. John English and Jackie Love recreated Lola Montez' visit to the Ballarat gold diggings. A history of Australian rock 'n roll music was featured, including many of the original artists, and 'Angry' Anderson brought the sequence to an end with a Johnny O'Keefe-styled rendition of 'Shout'. Rolf Harris was on hand with a little 'Ginger Meggs' in the person of young Brian Rooney. Comedienne Pamela Stephenson dressed in a dazzling golden wattle dress and Campbell McComas provided the lighter touch. Barry Crocker sang the praises of Don Bradman. Kingsford-Smith's trans-Pacific flight was feted in song and a replica aircraft descended from the vault. Debbie Byrne sang with great passion and intensity and led the rousing finale which featured hundreds of children in an action song. Brian May, Tommy Tycho and Don Burrows led the music.

However, it would be misleading to present only 'the celebration of the nation' theme. The Federal minister for education, John Dawkins, noted that the Bicentenary was also an occasion for white Australians to register the shame of their history in race relations. One expression of this sentiment came from the 67 members of the First Fleet Re-enactment who signed a paid *Sydney Morning Herald* advertisement:

> The way in which Aboriginal society has been disregarded and almost destroyed since the arrival of Captain Phillip's fleet must now be recognised. Their deeds must be acknowledged, their protests today must be heeded ... We are concerned for the welfare and future of all Australians, regardless of race ... We feel that only through education of all Australians on Aboriginal culture and history can the growing generation begin to understand and solve the problems which confront Aboriginal people today.[45]

A wreath was made up by a Sydney florist in the Aboriginal colours of black, red and yellow and dropped from the side of one of the First Fleet Re-Enactment ships, the *Tucker Thompson*, as it sailed past Mrs Macquarie's Chair where many Aborigines were camped in protest. Belmore Park, traditionally the resting place of the city's homeless, was a focal point for Aboriginal protest marchers and their white supporters. The Long March was the biggest gathering of Aboriginal people in their 40,000 year history.

Another irony regarding the Bicentenary is that the composer of the popularly successful tune 'Celebration of a Nation' and the New South Wales Bicentennial tune making the 'State Great' is an Australian-born Chinese, Les Gock. However, a 1988 poll found that 77 per cent of Australians believed there should be a slowing down of Asian immigration.[46]

CRIME

Australia's Master Criminal

To fraudulently appropriate more than $5 million in five years seems the stuff of Hollywood fantasy, but it happened right here in Sydney. At the Central Court of Petty Sessions in 1970 Peter Geoffrey Huxley pleaded guilty to 129 offences for which he was to be sent to the District Court for sentencing. Judge Head did not mince his words.

> Men in high office are generally so placed because they can be trusted, he warned. 'If any among them have a moral weakness of the kind displayed by this prisoner, they should know they give way to crime at their peril and that a heavy sentence will follow.' He described Huxley's crimes as being cunningly conceived and elaborately executed 'with the skill of a master criminal'. His victims, the judge went on, 'included friend, employer and charitable organizations, with heartless disregard of the consequences'.[47]

Huxley had been secretary of the New South Wales government-owned Rural Bank. Because of his position he was the automatic choice as honourary treasurer of several charities which had a high cash turnover. These included the United Nations Greeting Card Fund, the Art Gallery Society of New South Wales and the Australian Freedom from Hunger Campaign. The latter had its offices in Castlereagh Street, opposite the Mark Foy Building. The reason Huxley was manipulating these accounts was to finance his heavy betting. He would sometimes put $50,000 on a single horse and lost up to $300,000 in a day. He claimed he had lost $1.8 million in bets, most to one Sydney bookmaker. The Rural Bank actually made good any shortfall of funds but the damage had been done. The public were wary for some time of giving again to public charities. The judge imposed a sentence of 20 years, by far the heaviest sentence handed down in New South Wales for corporate crime. Huxley was released after nine years, a decision which caused widespread criticism at the time.

Other Unorthodox Creativity

The end of the 1970s saw two other endings. First, Harry M. Miller, the successful showbusiness entrepreneur of the rock musical *Hair*, was bringing to a close another rock musical, *Jesus Christ Superstar*. He had masterminded this latter show from his offices in George Street, across from the Capitol Theatre in the Haymarket. Those with memories will recall he was successful in restraining a religious sister from staging a school production of *Superstar* before his official version reached the footlights. However, he also found himself in court over charges involving his pre-booking Computicket business. Found guilty of aiding and abetting the fraudulent mis-appropriation of $728,000, he was sentenced to three years in gaol, though he served only 10 months. He was also legally restrained from holding a company directorship until 1988. In 1992 Harry M. Miller announced the revival of *Superstar*.

Second, the staid old Salvation Army Temple in Goulburn Street suddenly found itself in bright colours, renamed the Hippodrome—a name which had traditionally belonged to the Capitol Theatre, where elephants did perform—and showing 'blue' movies. This all came to a stop when it emerged that the Temple's new Chinese owner had been busy smuggling gold sovereigns out of the Museum.

Sergeant Beck's Hammer

As mortals and even gods quailed in fear at the wrath of the Norse god Thor and his mighty hammer, so quailed the nocturnal denizens of Sydney's underground gambling dens. Much sport was had by television journalists standing outside various 'clubs' and holding up gambling chips for close-ups while gleefully announcing the authorities' ignorance or inability to do anything about discovering, let alone closing, the illegal casinos. Bowing to public outcry, the authorities called Sergeant Mervyn Beck out of retirement in 1982 to deal specifically with the illegal casinos. Beck asked for, and received, permission to hand-pick his police squad. With his new force, soon to become known as 'Beck's Raiders', Sergeant Beck armed himself with a trusty sledgehammer, broke down the locked doors, the one-way mirrors and the gaming tables. In fact, despite threats against his life, Sergeant Beck, an honest, old-fashioned policeman, was dazzlingly successful. Perhaps he was too successful, as after only two months he was again retired. Who will now wield his mighty hammer? At any rate, the mysterious Goulburn Club, opposite old Anthony Horderns, is now a humble Chinese take-away.

Communist Newspaper

In 1923 the Communist Party of Australia launched a weekly newspaper from their offices at 2 Dixon Street. It was first called the *Workers' Weekly*, then the *Communist*, later the *Guardian* and then the *Tribune*. The offices were raided in 1940 and the paper went underground, printing on hidden presses when the Communist Party was declared illegal by the National Security Act. By 1942 the illegal press was reaching 50,000 people each week. In 1951 a *Tribune* journalist, W.E. Burns, was charged with sedition concerning articles published on the Korean War, convicted and sentenced to six months prison. The paper was banned in 1968 by the Warsaw Pact countries when it condemned the Russian invasion of Czechoslovakia. Aimed at radicals, activists and unionists, *Tribune* doubled its circulation after the Whitlam sacking,

coming out daily until the election. Circulation in the early 1980s was about 10,000, as it went nationwide and operated on an annual budget of $200,000. Perhaps the most unusual assistant at the *Tribune* in the early 1980s was Ann Stephen, the daughter of the then governor-general, Sir Ninian Stephen.[48] The collapse of Communism in Eastern Europe and the fall of the Berlin Wall in the late 1980s had a major impact on the party, which, under Brian Aarons' leadership, disbanded itself voluntarily in December 1990. *Tribune* continued to be published at 635 Harris Street, Ultimo, until 3 April 1991. True to form, right up to the end there was litigation with representatives of capitalism.

The Hilton Hotel and Other George Street Bombings

On Saturday, 14 September 1972, I heard two successive loud crashing noises. Perhaps a crane had dropped a container down at the docks? It did not occur to me that what I had heard was two bomb explosions in two Yugoslav travel agencies in George Street, either side of Goulburn Street, about 100 metres from each other. The first explosion, at the 'Adriatic Trade and Tourist Agency', injured 16 people. No arrests were ever made.

In February 1978, the Commonwealth Heads of Government Meeting (CHOGM) was held at the Hilton Hotel in George Street. Among those attending were Mrs Margaret Thatcher, prime minister of the United Kingdom, Mr Morarji Desai, prime minister of India and Mr Malcolm Fraser, prime minister of Australia. After the conference ended, an explosion occurred at 12.40 am on 13 February when a garbage can was being emptied into a council truck. Two council workers, Alec Carter and Arthur Favell, and a police constable, Paul Burmistriw, were killed.

On 16 June 1978 three members of the Ananda Marga movement, Ross Dunn, Timothy Anderson and Paul Alister were arrested and charged with the attempted murder of Robert Cameron, National Front leader. The Ananda Marga movement was a revolutionary movement originating in India, which seemed to countenance violence and terrorism in the pursuit of its ends. The male members of the sect were conspicuous by shoulder length hair and bright orange robes. The three were found guilty in June 1979 and sentenced to 16 years imprisonment. The Hilton Bombing Inquest on 13 October 1982 found a *prima facie* case of murder against Ross Dunn and Paul Alister. However, in 1985 they were unconditionally pardoned after a Supreme Court Inquiry by Justice Wood and released after having served seven of the allotted sixteen years.

Eventually Evan Pederick confessed to making and setting the bomb in place outside the Hilton Hotel. Pederick was found guilty and sentenced to 20 years gaol, but questions still remain unanswered about the whole affair. Pederick changed his evidence 52 times during the trial, on such occasions as being told by police that his 50 sticks of gelignite would not have fitted into the rubbish bin. The Sydney-based group, Academics for Justice, charge that Pederick constantly revised his testimony after learning the facts through tutoring by police investigators. Special Branch agent Richard Seary infiltrated the Marga movement after the bombing but his evidence was found to be untrustworthy.

The Academics pursue the need to clear up many unresolved issues: the failure of the security agencies to detect a bomb right in front of the hotel; the failure to call key security personnel to public account; apparent disinterest in pursuing evidence which might lead to the truth and concerted effort to deflect responsibility onto innocent individuals; the four-year delay of the inquest; the destruction in 1985 of evidence pertaining to explosives and a 11 February newspaper. This evidence had been found in a student locker and was ordered destroyed at the orders of a Special

Branch officer. The student who hired the locker, John Melton, committed suicide in 1989. The Academics allege the failure to disclose Melton's name at the inquest suggests a cover-up by the authorities. Former Senior Contable Terry Griffiths, badly injured in the bomb blast, has been pursuing his own enquiries. These suggest that it may have been ASIO and the N.S.W. Special Branch which planted the bomb. This seems bizarre, but the security forces did benefit 10 days after the bombing with extra budget funding. Mr Griffiths also found out that police received a warning phone call about the bomb a few minutes before it went off. The call is said to have come from a member of the Special Branch seen driving a red Torana around the hotel. A Mudgee farmer and former private investigator, Mr William Reeve-Parker, made a statutory declaration on 24 September 1982 that he received a phone call two days after the bombing from an anonymous caller who said he planted the bomb in 'a public relations exercise that went wrong'.

Meanwhile Tim Anderson had been found guilty of three counts of murder in 1990 for the Hilton bombing. But in an appeal in 1991, Anderson was found not guilty as charged and convicted, and released from prison. A hearing of the N.S.W. Independent Commission Against Corruption in November 1991 on the use of prison informants was marred by a confrontation between the notorious escapee Raymond Denning and Anderson. It had been on Denning's testimony that Anderson had been found guilty.

Further Hilton revelations came in a letter addressed to independent MHR Ted Mack from former Corporal Keith Burley of the military dog squad, who stated that his squad had been training intensively to detect letter and parcel bombs and that a stand-by decision was revoked by orders from the army's Eastern Command. N.S.W. Attorney-General Peter Collins claimed that there had been a cover-up of the Hilton bombing events by Federal officials and called for a joint Federal–State enquiry. Federal Attorney-General Michael Duffy dismissed the idea of a joint enquiry on the basis there was no new evidence. But former Commonwealth policeman Ian McDonald came forward to say that New South Wales Police had requested the use of the dog squad to check the hotel for explosives and the Commonwealth had turned down the request. 'NSW independent MP John Hatton and Mr Griffiths allege ASIO planned to uncover the bomb to show its effectiveness as a security organisation'.[49]

On Christmas Eve 1980, Brother Willie Bracken, SSS, had just returned from shopping at Woolworths Town Hall store, when he realised how fortunate he had been. A bomb had exploded shortly after he left. Shoppers were injured by flying glass and debris. It was part of a terror campaign against Woolworths Stores linked to extortion demands for $1 million. Eventually Gregory Norman McHardy and Larry Burton Danielson were arrested and found guilty of setting explosives and demanding payment. On 27 April 1982 they were sentenced to 20 years gaol.

German War Crimes Court

Located in the former Mark Foy Building, Court 13 of the Sydney Court of Petty Sessions went through a strange metamorphosis on Friday 1 July 1983. It became the Regional Court of Hanover. Four judges, two defence counsel and a public prosecutor had already heard evidence from witnesses in Poland, the United States of America, Canada, Israel and Germany. Now they heard the testimony of former Auschwitz prisoner No. 141,445, Joseph Pakula, a 75-year-old Polish Jew who became visibly upset as he recounted the punishments he and others received in the concentration camps, the floggings, the forced evacuation march and the shootings. Asked if he could have confused the accused, a Hanover locksmith, H. Niemeier, with someone else,

Mr Pakula shook his head and said: 'I don't think it is possible to mix Niemeier up with another man'.[50]

Pyrmont Counterfeiters

The name 'Pyrmont' seems to be derived from a German spa resort of the eighteenth and nineteenth centuries. A more unfortunate German connection happened on 12 September 1984 when nine people were arrested at a Pyrmont printing plant and fake 100 DM (Deutschmark) banknotes and printing plates were seized by police. The counterfeit notes, worth Australian $40 each, were of high quality and had been circulating since 1981. Investigating them had taken three years and involved the Federal Police, Interpol and the West German police. Those questioned had no links with West Germany or with the illicit drug trade. 'It was a cold business proposition,' said Detective Sergeant Brian Graham of the Federal Police Currency Squad.[51]

Prostitution Rackets

While Kings Cross has been the major area for prostitution, downtown Sydney is not altogether free from it. The area's centrality, cheap accommodation in the more dilapidated rooms and apartments put it in the firing line. While the markets have gone, tourism has now provided a new influx. And there have been some unsavoury developments.

In the 1980s it was discovered that young Asian girls were flown in to Sydney from Thailand on forged passports, kept in prison-like conditions to work in a brothel directly opposite the Central Baptist Church and threatened with death should they break their contracts. It is also hazardous for them to approach the State of Federal authorities as they are illegal immigrants. After their arrival at the airport their passports and visas are confiscated and they are taken to the inner-city and kept under tight security.

The fake passports cost up to $1,000 and the six-month visas cost a further $1,500.[52]

Nearby and also in George Street was a discreet sex shop which was a major distribution centre of child pornography and pederasty material. Thankfully this shop was closed down after protests to the Sydney City Council.

Chinatown Heist

The National Australia Bank in the Haymarket, which fronts both George and Sussex Streets, seems to have gained the dubious distinction of being the site of Australia's largest robbery. The exact time of the raid is difficult to determine because it took place in the basement of the bank and involved the safety deposit boxes. Eighty of these boxes were smashed open and rifled some time between 8 p.m. on 31 December 1987 and 11 p.m. on New Year's Day. A haul of $20 million has been suggested, but the exact amount will likely never be known. More than 90 per cent of the safety deposit boxes were rented by members of the Chinese business community. There was also speculation that the gang who carried out the robbery would have struck a bonus from Chinese underworld figures who were involved in money lending, illegal gambling and the drug trade. The thieves broke into a construction site alongside the bank, used ladders to climb into the bank's upper windows, used blowtorches and explosives to blast walls and cut grilles. The irony is that a guard heard the alarm go off but checked only the ground floor and did not proceed down to the basement where all the action was going on.[53]

Central Police Station

Until 1987 the major police station in Downtown was Number One Police Station located in tiny Central Street behind the Liverpool Street Court House, a fine classical building restored by the Public Works Department. Central police station is much harder to find. This hidden location is at variance with its busyness, as is indicated by a total staff of 199 (in 1985) who work in three shifts around the clock. Just to keep the station itself operating takes three shifts of 13 police officers. There is a charge desk near the holding cells for male and female offenders. The cell walls are massively thick and the ceilings on the ground floor are very high. The doors are made of steel and have small observation flaps. A shower, a toilet and a low sleeping bench are the only distinguishing features of the cells. The flooring is concrete. Nine thousand offenders are charged each year. Another two thousand are on drink charges. Detectives from the Criminal Investigation Branch, in the Remington Building, Liverpool Street, come to Central to lay formal charges. An inspector is in charge of the overall running of Central. In early 1985 there were also 15 women police working at Central. There is no rest for the police at Christmas, Easter, or public holidays. Instead they have four weeks leave per year plus 10 extra days for the public holidays that they work. A few patrol cars and wagons work out of Central and the powerful white motorcycles with their distinctive saddlebags and two-way radios mounted in the fairing are to be seen parked in the yard.

There is a room reserved for police use at the nearby Sydney Entertainment Centre, but it seems to be a dead duck, while plans for a Chinese-styled police station in the heart of Chinatown have not met with a favourable police response. Special attention has had to be given to the Redfern district. The potential for riots and other ugly incidents has been greatly reduced by recruiting of Aborigines into the police force.

The new Police Centre is now in Campbell Street, Surry Hills. Staff came from No. 1 Station (Central), No. 2 Station (Regent Street) and No. 4 Station (The Rocks). The new Sydney Police Centre, which was opened on 11 March 1987, covers a large area bounded by

Goulburn, Riley, Campbell and Brisbane Streets. This site was acquired by the City of Sydney council in 1923. The State government sought to purchase the land for £50,000 but shortage of funds made it impossible and the RAAF occupied the site towards the end of World War II. After the war the city engineer had plans for an expressway through the site. Finally the site was acquired in 1955 by the State government for £100,000. By 1975 it was reserved for the Police Department and building work began in 1980. Apart from receiving and holding offenders, there are specialised units including the Communications Branch, the Scientific Investigation Unit, the Computer Centre, the Disaster and Rescue Branch as well as Sydney Police Station. Office space, holding cells and vehicle parking are provided in a way that old Central could no longer match. The nearby Darlinghurst police station has closed down. The CIB is now decentralised and the South Sydney branch is located at the Sydney Police Centre.

Clisdell Street Massacre

On Thursday 30 August 1990, an unemployed young man, Anthony Paul Evers, was woken up, he claims, to the taunt of 'dole bludger'. He was a resident of the Housing Commission flats in Clisdell Street, close to the Northcott Community Centre in Surry Hills. Staying with him was his 21-year-old stepsister, on a visit from Holland. The police prosecutor at Central Local Court the following day alleged that Evers used his 12-gauge shotgun to shoot the man who had taunted him, then went back to his flat and shot his stepsister three times. After reloading he went out into the hall and shot an 80-year-old man. Then he went upstairs, forced his way into a flat and shot a woman aged 36 and a man ... the only victim not to die instantly. Evers then returned to his flat, left the shotgun there, and went to a shop nearby to buy some soft drink and cigarettes. On his return to the flat he was arrested by the police.

At a public meeting on the Saturday after the massacre, there was shock, fear, anger and confusion. Some stated there was a high ratio of mentally disturbed people in the Housing Commission flats. Concern was expressed at the gun laws of the State. Others objected to local residents being called social misfits or 'inner-city street rats', pointing out that this was a wrongful description of the people of Surry Hills. Anthony Paul Evers was found guilty of manslaughter in February 1992 and sentenced to 18 years prison.

The Old Bag Lady of Central Railway

Why should an old lady found slumped dead outside Central Railway Pharmacy on 15 September 1988 be mentioned in this history? Is it because she claimed Austrian-Hungarian royal kinship? Is it because a 14-year-old girl of no fixed address was charged over her death? Is it because police allege that this girl assaulted the elderly vagrant in an argument over who should sleep in an empty toilet at Central Railway Station? Or because the girl laughed in court and was rebuked by Magistrate Kevin Waller? Is it because Cardinal Freeman, once parish priest of Haymarket, came out of retirement at the age of 81 to perform her funeral service at St Francis de Sales Church? For all those reasons and because 'Madame' or 'The Queen', as she was known, is a symbol for the many homeless people of the inner city. No-one knew her by her real name, Elizabeth Gorm-Bayler. About 72 years old, she did not drink, her sole possessions were two small carry bags, and she would sit and watch people go by. Always maintaining her dignity, she had lived out at Rozelle Hospital and had contact with the St Vincent de Paul Scholastica Refuge in Surry Hills. There were TV cameras and photojournalists at the funeral, and large floral displays piled up on the coffin, but she was buried in a pauper's grave.

ARTS

Theatrical Encore

The Capitol Theatre, built in 1927–28 on the site of an old fruit and vegetable market and now in a sad state of repair, is to be restored as a major lyric theatre for large-scale productions. It is the only one of five such theatres around Australia that is still intact. The restoration will cost $40 million and is not expected to be completed until 1995. The Sydney City Council believes this project will provide the kind of theatre that Sydney has lacked since *Jesus Christ Superstar* was staged, at the Capitol, in the early 1970s.[54]

Haymarket Paintings

A painter who has used the Haymarket area for much of his work is Kevin Connor. The art critic James Gleeson remarked on Connor's first one-man show, 'a city street slips around a man's head like a strangler's noose'. Connor knows the urban landscape very well. He first featured the Haymarket in his paintings of 1962. What was depicted was no conventional landscape or pretty tourist views of downtown Sydney, if any such were to be had. A certain view of life emerges, of human life as fragile and vulnerable, subjected to evil and oppressed by forces, a victim figure. The art is not sentimental, nor indulging in pain. Certainly the style is expressionist in the tradition of Grünewald, Bosch, Breughel, Goya or Munch, Rouault and the German Expressionists. Such art does not amuse or entertain, but it does broaden horizons and deepen perception. The brush strokes of the early Haymarket paintings seem to be wild and at random, and convey a strong sense of life as transitory, passing, and frame-frozen. Fluency is a mark of Connor's art, as it is for Sidney Nolan, but Connor deals with a far from mythical world. Boldly outlined in black paint, his figures are bent double against the wind,

hauling loads of flowers and vegetables; old people sitting in the sun. Twenty and more years on Connor's new Haymarket paintings are richer in colour, forming a fluid skyline of buildings and buckled pavements. The speed and rush of city traffic is translated into a blurring and featureless streak. As Elwyn Lynn put it: 'Houses, bridges, roads and skies stagger in intoxicated delight ... Connor's is a celebratory expressionism free of gloom, despair and dire predictions'.[54]

In an interview with the author in 1984, Connor said:

'Expressionism' in art usually implies painting without too great an intellectual approach, but rather painting intuitively a reaction to a subject. This is the way I paint naturally, but I consider painting should consist of three elements: the artist, the subject and—most importantly—the work of art. It is this concept on which I have sought to base my work. So mine is an intentional, controlled expressionism. Occasionally it is uncontrolled. but anything creative has to have that element.

My father was a railwayman. He was sent as night officer to Wallendbeen, near Cootamundra, soon after I was born and we lived there until 1939, when I was seven. So my earliest memories of Sydney were of visits to the city during that time. We would arrive at Central Station where, outside the vast, busy concourse, trams would be waiting on the ramp. On one visit, I remember, we stayed overnight at the People's Palace, a hotel nearby, run by the Salvation Army. Central Railway Station was the gateway to the city for country people.

It was a part of the city I came to know well after beginning work in 1947, at the age of 15. For a while I attended Joe Holloway's sketch club opposite the Capitol Theatre in Parker Street. There was an art community in that area which later moved to lower George Street, to Kings Cross and thence to Paddington.

I painted the first Haymarket series

in 1963 and a second series between 1974 and 1975. Then it was Skid Row. The Haymarket seemed to me to reflect the truth of a city, its life, its poetry and the continuous change it undergoes, decaying and being reborn. For me the markets were one of the happiest places in the world: fresh fruit and vegetables, singing and laughter, and sustenance for the people of the district. In fact, Chinatown grew up because of its proximity to the markets.

I visited Cairo in 1954 and have returned several times since. It seemed to me that Cairo bears some resemblance to Sydney in the '40s and '50s. It has the same feel. The architecture is, in some ways, similar because of the British influence. I also lived in New York for nearly two years in the '60s, and found there the 'Haymarket' that exists in all cities; that honesty is found in poorer areas and in the lives of those who inhabit them.

People sometimes find a grimness or gloominess in my paintings of the Haymarket, but that is not the way I see it. I see it as a beautiful place. The earlier paintings depict what you might call 'Haymarket people', particularly people who lived on the streets. That is not necessarily tragic. It is a way of living one's life. I don't believe you can clean up a city, or plan how it will be (as in Darling Harbour, or Canberra, for instance). Derelicts are perhaps people who have looked at themselves, and their abode is not such a terrible place. I am talking from a poetic point of view. The 'Haymarket wino'—perhaps more likely to be found nowadays somewhere up near Taylor Square—seems to me to have an honest, poetic approach to life. My painting *Haymarket Prayer* possibly has a poor title, but the work says what I have been trying to put into words. It is not a picture of a derelict; it is a portrait of life.

Kevin Connor won the Archibald Prize twice: in 1975 for his portrait of Sir Frank Kitto and in 1977 for his portrait of Robert Klippel.

THE FUTURE

Strategy for the 1990s

In 1989 the State government launched the City West Urban Strategy. This project will have a major impact on Pyrmont–Ultimo, Glebe Island–White Bay–Rozelle Bay, Central Railway and Eveleigh. Over 300 hectares of land are involved in this mammoth and complex re-development proposal. Up to 10 kilometres of harbour foreshore is to be returned to public use. Residential suburbs are to be created in Pyrmont, Glebe Island and White Bay districts. A rail service using the existing goods line from Pyrmont to Central is to be introduced. Networks of paths, cycleways, squares and open spaces are to be created. Heritage sites of significance are to be retained.

CONCLUSION

Sesquicentenary Celebrations

A great birthday party took place on the shores of Darling Harbour on Sunday 19 July 1992 to mark the 150th anniversary of the City of Sydney. More than 250,000 gathered. There were mountains of free lamingtons to eat and a splendid

*Aerial view of Sydney. (Photo by Sharrin Rees
is from the Dept of Planning's publication
'City West Urban Strategy', 1990.)*

display of fireworks provided by Sydney's Chinese sister city Guangzhou. At 3 p.m. the Lord Mayor, Alderman Frank Sartor, cut open the giant 5.2-metre high birthday cake which contained the lamingtons and Sydney City's town crier Mr Graham Keating decreed the recession was over. The day before, about 80 floats and 2,500 people took part in a grand parade, the Sydney's biggest ever, through the streets to Darling Harbour. The official birthday actually fell on Monday 20 July and was marked by a special meeting of the Sydney City Council, attended by the governor, with an ecumenical prayer by Cardinal Edward Clancy. Visiting dignitaries included the lord mayors of Sydney's five sister cities, Nagoya (Japan), San Francisco (U.S.), Portsmouth (Britain), Wellington (New Zealand), and Guangzhou (China). Church bells rang throughout the city from St Mary's Cathedral, St Andrew's Cathedral, St Benedict's, St Philip's Church Hill and Christ Church St Laurence.

Notes

Chapter 1

[1]K.G. McIntyre, *The Secret Discovery of Australia: Portuguese Ventures 250 years before Captain Cook*, Souvenir Press, 1977 (revised and abridged, Pan Books, Sydney 1987).
[2]E.P.Walsh, *Australian Dictionary of Biography*, Vol. 1, Melbourne University Press, Melbourne 1966, p.306.
[3]*Ibid.*, p.58.
[4]*Sydney Gazette*, 21 December 1806.
[5]*Sydney Gazette*, 14 August 1823.
[6]Jack Pollard, *The Formative Years of Australian Cricket, 1803–93*, Macmillan, Melbourne 1987, p.8.

Chapter 2

[1]*South-East Asian Register*, Sydney, December 1828, p.326.
[2]*Sydney Gazette*, 17 August 1835.
[3]C. Wilkes, *Narrative of the United States Exploring Expedition during the years 1838, 1839, 1840, 1841, 1842*, London, Vol. I, p.210.
[4]W.S. Jevons, 'A Social Survey of Sydney in 1858', *Sydney Morning Herald*, 6 November 1929.
[5]*Sydney Gazette*, 5 March 1828.
[6]Pollard, *The Formative Years of Australian Cricket, 1803–93*, p.8.
[7]Angus Cameron and Belinda Henwood, eds, *The Australian Almanac, 1988*, Angust and Robertson, Sydney, 1987, p.98.
[8]Alan Sharpe, *Crimes That Shocked Australia*, Currawong, Milsons Point 1982, pp.9–13.

Chapter 3

[1]G.C. Mundy, *Our Antipodes: or, Residence and Rambles in the Australian Colonies, with a Glimpse of the Gold Fields*, London 1852, Vol. 3, pp.306–07.
[2]*125th Anniversary of Railways in New South Wales, 26 September 1855–1980*, An Abridged Chronological History.
[3]J.F. Watson, *The History of the Sydney Hospital from 1811 to 1911*, W.A. Gullich Government Printer, Sydney, 1911, p.130.
[4]Alan Hunt, 'Outline of the History of St Benedict's', unpublished paper for the Australian Catholic Historical Society, July 1982.
[5]Archives of the Sisters of Charity, Potts Point, Sydney, EAR/595.
[6]Pollard, *The Formative Years of Australian Cricket, 1803–93*, p.8.
[7]*Ibid.*, p.225.
[8]Jack Egan, *The Story of Cricket in Australia*, Macmillan, Melbourne 1987, p.70.
[9]*Ibid.*, p.223.
[10]Sharpe, *Crimes That Shocked Australia*, pp.60–64.

Chapter 4

[1]C.F. Young, *The New Gold Mountain*, Raphael Arts, S.A., 1977, p.5.
[2]*Ibid.*, pp.222–23.
[3]*Ibid.*, p.101.
[4]Robert Travers, *Australian Mandarin: The Life and Times of Quong Tart*, Kangaroo Press, Kenthurst 1981, p.186.
[5]*Tagebuch meiner Reise um die Erde 1892–1893*, Vol. 2, Vienna 1896, pp.63*ff*.
[6]*Sydney Morning Herald*, 18 January 1897.
[7]Graeme Davison, 'Sydney and the Bush: An Urban Context for the Australian Legend', in *The Australian Legend Re-Visited*, Melbourne University Press (Historical Studies, October 1978), pp.191–209.

[8]Quoted in *ibid.*, p.39.

[9]*Sydney and the Bush*, New South Wales Department of Education, Sydney 1980, p.103.

[10]*Ibid.*, p.107.

[11]Michael Easson, *110th Anniversary of the Labour Council of N.S.W.*, J.D. Moore, Melbourne 1981, p.17.

[12]*A History of Dentistry in New South Wales, 1788–1945*, original manuscript of R.W. Halliday, arranged and edited by A.O. Watson, Australian Dental Association, 1977, p.56.

[13]*Ibid.*, p.139.

[14]Extract from a letter by 'Humanitas', *Sydney Morning Herald*, 27 July 1910; quoted in *ibid.*, p.231.

[15]*Sydney Morning Herald*, 24 January 1911, quoted in *ibid.*, p.232.

[16]Frank Clune, *Saga of Sydney*, Halstead Press, Sydney 1961, p.213.

[17]*Ibid.*, p.215.

[18]G.P. Walsh, *Australian Dictionary of Biography*, Vol. 8, Melbourne University Press, Melbourne 1983, pp.507–71.

[19]The author interviewed a descendant of Mark Foy in the picturesque Megalong Valley on 16 January 1985, and has further material on the business and the family, e.g. the Mark Foy balloon that draped itself around the Anthony Hordern tower, the Mark Foy Annual Picnic Programme of 1 October 1900, the 'What is Love' essay competition of 1910, and the publicity stunt of a suit made from the wool of a shorn sheep on 23 October 1931: '1 Hr. 51 Min. – From Sheep's back to Man's Back'.

[20]*Sydney Morning Herald*, 20 July 1914.

[21]R.J. Murphy, SJ, *The Transactions of the Medical Guild of St Luke*, 1943, p.54.

[22]C.M.H. Clark, *A History of Australia*, Vol. 5, Melbourne University Press, Melbourne 1981, p.359.

[23]St Vincent de Paul Society, *Annual Report*, 1980–81, Sydney, p.9.

[24]Br B.F. Purcell (President of St Francis' Conference, Sydney), 'Is the Institute of Night Refuges a Work for St. Vincent de Paul Society?' (September 1906), reprinted in *St Vincent de Paul Centenary*, p.12.

[25]H.G. Hepburn, *2nd Australasian Catholic Congress, 1904*. Saint Patrick's College, Melbourne 1905, p.374.

[26]Ian Howie-Willis, *A Century for Australia*, Priory of the Order of St John in Australia, Canberra 1983, pp.382–83.

[27]*Ibid.*, p.160.

[28]*Ibid.*, p.356.

[29]Barbara Bolton, *Booth's Drum*, 1983, p.128.

[30]Canon M.C. Newth, *Serving a Great Cause*, Ambassador Press, Granville 1980, p.340.

[31]*Ibid.*, p.37.

[32]L.C. Rodd, 'Notes on History of Christ Church St Laurence', p.1.

[33]John Spooner, 'The People of Christ Church St Laurence: The Changing Profile of an Inner-City Parish of Sydney, 1838–1981'. MA thesis, History Department, University of Sydney, 1981, pp.8, 11.

[34]L.C. Rodd, *John Hope of Christ Church St Laurence*, Alpha Books, Sydney 1972. pp.60, 79, 204.

[35]*Ibid.*, p.101.

[36]*Ibid.*, p.125.

[37]Spooner, 'People of Christ Church St Laurence', p.36.

[38]*Ibid.*, p.37.

[39]*Ibid.*, p.45.

[40]*Ibid.*, pp.51, 53.

[41]*Ibid.*, p.55.

[42]*Ibid.*, p.65.

[43]*Ibid.*, p.69.

[44]*Ibid.*, p.73.

[45]*Ibid.*, p.77.

[46]*Ibid.*, p.78.

[47]C.M.H. Clark, *A History of Australia*, Vol. 5, Melbourne University Press, Melbourne 1981, p.394.

[48]Axel Clark, *Christopher Brennan: A Critical Biography*, Melbourne University Press, Melbourne 1980, p.226.

[49]*Ibid.*, p.293.

[50]Bede Nairn, *Australian Dictionary of Biography*, Vol. 3, Melbourne University Press, Melbourne 1969, pp.224–27.

[51]Frank Clune, *Try Nothing Twice*, Angus and Robertson, Sydney 1946, pp.5–6, 16, 17, 28.

[52]J.T. Lang, *I Remember*, Invincible Press, Sydney 1956, p.217.

[53]J.T. Lang, *The Turbulent Years*, Alpha Books, Sydney 1970, pp.3, 4.
[54]From *Henry Lawson*, edited by Brian Kiernan, University of Queensland Press, St Lucia 1976, pp.50, 54, 55.
[55]Geoffrey Dutton, *The Australian Heroes*, Angus and Robertson, Sydney 1981, p.67.
[56]Lang, *I Remember*, p.8.
[57]Brian Dickey, *No Charity There: A Short History of Social Welfare in Australia*, Nelson, Melbourne p.110.
[58]Heather Radi's entry on Ardill in *Australian Dictionary of Biography*, Vol. 7, Melbourne University Press, Melbourne 1979, pp.90*ff.*
[59]*The Australian Encyclopaedia*, Grolier Society of Australia, Sydney, 1973 edition, Vol. 4, p.365.
[60]Max Kelly, *A Certain Sydney*, Doak Press, Paddington 1977.
[61]*Ibid.*
[62]The Chief Medical Officer of the Government, J. Ashburton Thompson, to the Premier of New South Wales, Sir William Lyne.
[63]*Ibid.*
[64]Bertha McNamara, *Workingmen's Houses in Commercialism and Distribution of the Nineteenth Century*, Sydney 1894, p.11.
[65]Private Papers of Dr R.M. McCredie, Sydney, 1983.
[66]L.C. Rodd, *A Gentle Shipwreck*, Nelson, Melbourne 1975.
[67]Clune, *Saga of Sydney*, p.312.
[68]Jack Pollard, *Australian Cricket*, Hodder & Stoughton, Sydney 1982, p.1010.
[69]*Ibid.*, p.1009.
[70]Jack Fingleton, *The Immortal Victor Trumper*, Collins, London 1978, p.93.
[71]*Ibid.*, p.39.
[72]Ray Robinson, *On Top Down Under*, Cassell, Sydney 1975, p.91.
[73]*Ibid.*, p.92.
[74]*Ibid.*, p.94.
[75]*Ibid.*, p.98.
[76]Pollard, *Australian Cricket*, p.764.
[77]*Ibid.*, p.650.
[78]*Ibid.*, p.682.
[79]*Ibid.*, p.683.
[80]*Ibid.*
[81]Christopher Baker, *Depressions: 1890s,*
1930s, Oxford University Press, Melbourne 1982, pp.24, 25.
[82]Sharpe, *Crimes That Shocked Australia*, pp.87-95.
[83]*Ibid.*, pp.109, 111.

Chapter 5

[1]*Wise's N.S.W. Post Office Commercial Directory*, H. Wise & Co., Sydney 1937.
[2]H.J. Goth and B.B. Thümling, *100 Jahre Concordia*, New Life Printers, Marrickville 1983.
[3]Ian Turner, *Sydney's Burning*, Alpha, Sydney 1967, p.211.
[4]*Ibid.*, p.231.
[5]J.T. Lang, *I Remember*, Invincible Press, Sydney 1956, p.163.
[6]Turner, *Sydney's Burning*, p.241.
[7]*Ibid.*, p.250.
[8]*Ibid.*, p.254.
[9]Peter Grabosky, *Sydney in Ferment*, Australian National University Press, Canberra 1977, p.108.
[10]*Ibid.*, p.141.
[11]Lang, *I Remember*, pp.155-56.
[12]*A.N.Z.A.C. War Memorial* (brochure), Hyde Park South, City of Sydney, 1984.
[13]*Sydney and the Bush*, New South Wales Department of Education, Sydney 1980, p.195.
[14]*Sydney Morning Herald*, 23 July 1931.
[15]G. Souter, *A Company of Heralds*, Melbourne University Press, Melbourne 1981, pp.138-39.
[16]Humphrey McQueen, *Social Sketches of Australia: 1888-1975*, Penguin, Ringwood 1978, p.162.
[17]*Ibid.*, p.170.
[18]Clune, *Saga of Sydney,* p.438.
[19]*Ibid.*, p.439.
[20]*Ibid.*
[21]*Time*, 21 November 1983, p.93.
[22]*Fifty Years of Government Bus Services* (brochure), Urban Transport Authority of New South Wales, 1982.
[23]K.S. Inglis, *This is the ABC*, Melbourne University Press, Melbourne 1986, p.27.
[24]*Ibid.*, p.95.
[25]*Ibid.*, p.97.
[26]*Ibid.*, p.98.

[27]Archival papers on St Benedict's, St Mary's Cathedral Archives, Sydney.

[28]Letter, 22 January 1940, J.J. Norris to Most Rev. N.T. Gilroy, DD, St Mary's Cathedral Archives, Sydney.

[29]Michael McKernan, *Australian Churches at War*, Southwood Press, Marrickville 1980, p.164.

[30]*Ibid.*, p.162.

[31]*Ibid.*, p.124.

[32]Br Redmond Adrian Fulton, FMS, *Blue and Blue Magazine*, 1968, pp.5-20.

[33]Patrick O'Farrell, *The Catholic Church and Community: An Australian History*, New South Wales University Press, Kensington 1985, p.380.

[34]*Souvenir History*, Published on the Occasion of the Opening and Dedication of the Lutheran Church Centre and Trinity Church, Valentine Street, Sydney, Sunday, 24 July 1960, pp.1-4.

[35]Alan C. Prior, *Some Fell on Good Ground*, Baptist Union of New South Wales, Sydney 1966, p.254.

[36]*Ibid.*, p.255.

[37]Donald Horne, *In Search of Billy Hughes*, Macmillan, Melbourne 1979, pp.58-59.

[38]Lysbeth Cohen, *The First Fifty Years*, Rachel Forster Hospital, 1972, p.7.

[39]*Ibid.*, p.8.

[40]Chris Cuneen, *Australian Dictionary of Biography*, Vol. 8, Melbourne University Press, Melbourne 1981, p.553.

[41]The *Times*, 13 April 1962.

[42]Cohen, *First Fifty Years*, p.26.

[43]*Ibid.*, p.39.

[44]*He Lived to Care*, Dr Barnardo's in Australia, 7 Wilmot Street, Sydney, 1966, p.8.

[45]*Ibid.*, p.8.

[46]*Ibid.*, p.29.

[47]Lang, *I Remember*, p.187.

[48]Bruce Stannard, *The Face on the Bar Room Wall*, Angus and Robertson, Sydney 1982, pp.27, 31, 67, 123.

[49]M. Easson, 'Sir William McKell: A Biographical Sketch', in *110th Anniversary of the Labour Council of New South Wales*, 1981.

[50]Vince Kelly, *A Man of the People*, Alpha, Sydney 1971, p.24.

[51]*Ibid.*, pp.81, 82, 93.

[52]*Ibid.*, pp.151*ff*, 158, 165-66.

[53]*Ibid.*, p.90.

[54]Easson, 'Sir William McKell'.

[55]*Journal of the Retail Traders' Association of N.S.W.*, Sydney, 1924, pp.40*ff*.

[56]Lionel Bibby, *Mick Simmons Specialist Gun Catalogue*, p.3.

[57]Jack Pollard, *Australian Cricket*, Hodder & Stoughton, Sydney 1982, p.191.

[58]*Ibid.*, pp.653-54.

[59]*Ibid.*, pp.772*ff*.

[60]F.C. Green, *Servant of the House*, Heinemann, Melbourne 1969, p.63.

[61]Recollections of Jean Andersen, Devonshire Street, Surry Hills, 1983.

[62]*Sun*, 16 April 1971.

[63]Eric Bell-Smith, *Sun*, 6 February 1964.

[64]*Daily Mirror*, 7 February 1964.

[65]Quoted in Douglas Stewart, *A Man of Sydney: An Appreciation of Kenneth Slessor*, Nelson, Melbourne 1977, p.60.

Chapter 6

[1]Bobbi Sykes, *Mum Shirl*, Heinemann, Melbourne 1977, p.19.

[2]*Ibid.*, p.21.

[3]*Ibid.*, p.23.

[4]*Ibid.*

[5]*Ibid.*, pp.38-41.

[6]*Ibid.*, pp.54-55.

[7]*Ibid.*, p.59.

[8]Kevin Gilbert, *Living Black*, Penguin, Ringwood 1977, p.251.

[9]Sykes, *Mum Shirl*, p.14.

[10]Raymond Apple, *The Jews*, Nelson, Melbourne 1981, p.52.

[11]*Ibid.*, pp.56-57 (amendments to text by Rabbi Apple, 1992).

[12]Peter Waterman, *Australian Financial Review*, 7 October 1988.

[13]Fr Aramais Mirzaian, *Armenians: A Pilgrim People in Tierra Australia*, published by the author, Sydney 1976, p.21.

[14]Souter, *A Company of Heralds*, p.181.

[15]Laurie Short, interview with author, 27 November 1984.

[16]Robert Murray and Kate White, *The Ironworkers*, Hale and Iremonger, Sydney 1982, p.189.

[17]Commonwealth of Australia, *Arbitration Records*, Vol. 73, 1951-52, pp.27-81.

[18] John Hurst, *The Walkley Awards: Australia's Best Journalists in Action*, John Kerr, Richmond 1988, p.174.
[19] *Ibid.*, p.176.
[20] James Bell, *The Dutch*, Nelson, Melbourne 1981, pp.85–86.
[21] Patrick O'Farrell, *The Catholic Church and Community: An Australian History*, University of New South Wales Press, Kensington 1985, p.15.
[22] 'Greek Orthodox Church', *The Australian Encyclopaedia* (5th edn), Australian Geographic Society, Terry Hills 1988, p.1459.
[23] Elwyn Spratt, *Eddie Ward, Firebrand of East Sydney*, Rigby, Adelaide 1965, p.19.
[24] P.D. Hills, interview with author, 16 February 1984.
[25] D. Minogue, *A Rambler from Clare*, Cresta Printing Co., Sydney 1972, p.14.
[26] *Ibid.*, p.64.
[27] *Ibid.*, p.53.
[28] *Ibid.*, p.36.
[29] *Ibid.*, p.37.
[30] *Ibid.*, p.38.
[31] C. Pearl, *Wild Men of Sydney*, Cheshire Lansdowne, Melbourne 1965, p.21.
[32] *Ibid.*, p.63.
[33] *Ibid.*, p.130.
[34] Keith Dunstan, *Ratbags*, Golden Press, Sydney 1979, p.181.
[35] *Truth*, 11 February 1951.
[36] *Truth*, 23 January 1953.
[37] Dunstan, *Ratbags*, p.10.
[38] *Ibid.*, p.12.
[39] David Hickie, *Chow Hayes, Gunman*, Angus and Robertson, Sydney 1990, p.349.
[40] Ruth Park, *The Harp in the South*, Angus and Robertson, Sydney 1948, p.86.
[41] *Ibid.*, p.106.
[42] *Ibid.*, p.138.
[43] *Ibid.*, pp.210–11.
[44] *The Australian Encyclopaedia*, Grolier Society, Sydney 1983, Vol. 6, p.141.
[45] Thomas Shapcott, *Focus on Charles Blackman*, University of Queensland Press, St Lucia 1967, p.13.
[46] *Observer* (London), 4 June 1961.
[47] *Nation*, 2 July 1960, p.17.

Chapter 7

[1] Sykes, *Mum Shirl*, p.71.
[2] *Ibid.*, pp.83–84.
[3] *Ibid.*, p.12.
[4] *Ibid.*, p.90.
[5] *Ibid.*, p.115.
[6] *Sydney Morning Herald*, 21 April 1983.
[7] Peter Townsend, *The Girl in the White Ship*, Collins, London 1981.
[8] Raymond G. Hallit, *History and Souvenir of the Blessing and Consecration of the new St Michael's Melkite Church;*, Kentley Printing, Carlton 1981.
[9] 'Lebanese in Australia', *Australian Encyclopaedia*, The Grolier Society, Sydney 1983, Vol. 6, p.76.
[10] Andrew and Trevor Batrouney, *The Lebanese in Australia*, Australasian Echuca, Melbourne 1985, p.27.
[11] *Ibid.*, p.126.
[12] *Ibid.*, p.101.
[13] *The Labour Force in Australia*, Australian Bureau of Statistics, Canberra, January 1992, pp.20, 7.
[14] Batrouney, *Lebanese*, p.97.
[15] *Ibid.*, p.92.
[16] *A Guide to Ethnic Media in Australia*, Ad-Vic and the Victorian Ethnic Affairs Commission, Melbourne 1990, pp.13–14.
[17] 'The [Sydney City] Mission has now found a way to encourage the chronically unemployed to work at Campbell House in Sydney, where the homeless men, classified as chronic alcoholics, work in a sheltered workshop complete with bundy clock.' Margaret Conley, 'The "Undeserving" Poor: Welfare and Labour Policy', *Australian Welfare History*, edited by Richard Kennedy, Macmillan, Melbourne 1982, p.291. Scottish Congregational minister George Campbell of Redfern (1881–1910) was founder of the Sydney City Mission: Malcolm D. Prentis, *The Scottish in Australia*, Sydney University Press, Sydney 1983, p.148.
[18] Anne Summers, *Damned Whores and God's Police*, Penguin, Ringwood 1975, p.132.
[19] Barrie Watts, 'The Day They Drop the Bomb on Martin Place', *Sydney City Monthly*, September 1980, p.28.